Improve Your Own Boat

Improve Your
Own Boat

IAN NICOLSON

W · W · NORTON & COMPANY
New York   London

Copyright © 1985 Ian Nicolson

All rights reserved. For information address
W. W. Norton & Company Inc., 500 Fifth Avenue,
New York, New York 10110

First published in Gt. Britain by
George Allen & Unwin Ltd. in 1985

Published simultaneously in Canada by Penguin Books Canada Ltd.
2801 John Street, Markham, Ontario L3R 1B4

Printed in the United States of America

First American Edition, 1986

Library of Congress Cataloging in Publication Data

Nicolson, Ian, 1928–
Improve your own boat.
1. Boatbuilding.   2. Boats and boating—Maintenance
and repair.   I. Title.
VM321.N524   1986   623.8′223   85–15320

ISBN 0-393-03310-4

W. W. Norton & Company, Inc., 500 Fifth Avenue, New York,
N.Y. 10110

W. W. Norton & Company Ltd., 37 Great Russell Street,
London WC1B 3NU

1 2 3 4 5 6 7 8 9 0

To Elsa Barkway and David Ryder-Turner

Contents

List of Drawings

1 *A better boat*

We race our 28 foot cruiser a few times every year. With our teenage children and one or two friends we get a lot of fun from our attempts to win the occasional cup. When the excitement runs high we know the hours spent fitting out, anti-fouling and doing the other less exciting jobs have been well worth while. There was a marvellous race in the Firth of Lorne when the wind howled in the rigging and we watched with glee as lesser boats gave up, one by one, and sometimes two or three together.

We were down to two deep reefs and the working jib and even then it was sweat-making work on the sheet winches. As we beat to the weather mark which was regularly obscured by high white spray, I started to worry about the turn.

'We must come to the buoy on starboard tack to have right of way,' I repeated three times, just to be sure that my youngest son at the tiller would hear through his concentration and the crashing thumps as we pounded through the breaking seas. With three classes all racing round the same turning point there was a good chance of meeting a bunch of boats, and this was no weather for collisions.

'We can lay the mark,' my daughter yelled, and so we swung round in a quick tack, with that delicious whirling rattle from the sheet winch working hard and the tense crackle of juddering sails.

Our boat lay far over to port, speeded up and we began to wonder about making the mark with the foul tide sweeping us to leeward. Not so far away off to port the big class were coming for the same mark. Four of them, all on port tack, were so close to each other a man could have jumped from deck to deck. As each wave swept towards them all four pitched up together, then plunged into the following trough. The spray from one whirled to leeward across the deck of the next two. They made a perfect line with the leeward boats just a few feet further ahead so that there was no serious blanketing and all the while none of the four went ahead or dropped back.

No one on the leeward boat of the four looked under the sails to see we were coming dangerously towards them. The crew of the next three boats could not see us because of that leeward boat. And we had right of way.

'We'll have to call for water early and VERY loud,' I said. So as soon as we thought we could make ourselves heard above the sea and wind noises, everyone except the helmsman on our boat slid down to leeward, looked at those four big, fast, powerful boats getting closer and yelled

'STARRRRRRRRRRR-BOAAAAAAAARD!!!!'

It had no effect at all. Twice more we tried and it was obvious that the situation was going to be hazardous in a matter of seconds.

'We'll try once more. If they don't hear we'll have to tack. We can protest later.' So we yelled again and a startled face appeared round the front of the leeward boat's genoa, then disappeared instantly and we saw that boat start to turn off round our stern. The next boat followed after a few frightening seconds. Just in time, faces appeared round the sails of the remaining two big yachts and they flung round on the other tack. This was taking them away from the finish, and they would turn again soon, but for the moment we had to ignore them.

Meanwhile the first two were tearing round our stern inches away and we were almost up to the buoy.

'Steer for the middle of the buoy and luff hard as we reach it,' I said to my son, who just nodded and sailed the boat nonchalantly. Of the two boats which went behind us the first could not tack till the one close by her did. They both came round together in a noisy uproar of thrashing sails, yelling crews and shurring sheet winches. We had two big boats astern and to windward of us, coming up fast. The other two had tacked back towards us so they were blocking any chance we had of slipping to leeward of the buoy if the tide set us down-wind of it. Because we were pinching, we were slowing all the time. Our deck was heeled so much it made it difficult to keep track of the crowd round us. The two boats coming in on port thought they could slither round our stern and get between us and the two coming in on starboard. It was impossible, but when the blood runs fast and the excitement pounds madly, helmsmen take wild risks.

We watched as the first and then the second boat on port swung inches away from us, while we crawled the last few feet towards the buoy.

Our helmsman moved down to leeward to watch the closing gap between us and the buoy. All round there was a crescendo of uproar as the four big boats crowded in towards the mark.

'I can't see to windward. Are we clear?' the helmsman called. One of the big ones was coming in hard, but we had space . . . just.

'Yes! Luff NOW!' we shouted, and our little cruiser started to come up. A heavier squall blasted down on us . . . exactly what we wanted. Ignoring the frantic crackling of sails and the terse shouts, my son luffed our boat neatly round the buoy with inches to spare.

When I should have been freeing off the lee sheet the nearby big boat plunged right at us. A wave erupted under her bow and she reared up. Her gleaming metal stem-head fitting thrust forward right between our backstay and mainsail. I had to leave my job on the winch and jump to fend off. The big boat fell clear, but by the time I'd got back to the cockpit someone had taken my place and the whole area was a whirl of flaying arms, shrieking winches and scrabbling feet. I looked at the frantic energy . . . it did seem slightly chaotic but it was really a good team racing hard. One person was wrenching the main sheet traveller across, someone else was plunging a sheet winch into its socket, nothing was jamming or snarling, nothing looked over-stressed or likely to break. With so many big bullying boats scarcely under control right round us, this was no time for gear failure.

As peace returned to our boat we had time to look astern. Only one of the big four was under control and going the right way. Spontaneously we all started to laugh.

'It's great when you have right of way.'

'And when all the gear works well.'

At first and even third glance our sloop looks just like many other modern boats. It is only when going onto her that the details show she is special. We climb aboard right aft, pulling ourselves up on the aft pulpit which has four strong feet each secured down with bolts through large wooden pads under the deck. So if two or three of us all scramble out of the dinghy together, there is no risk that a stanchion or two will be uprooted. The dinghy, incidentally, has our name stencilled all over it, as have the oars; if our gear goes adrift there is a good chance it will be returned to us and if it is stolen, the thieves will have a lot of work getting rid of the identification.

The cockpit has no sharp edges to bruise the crew or tear clothes, because the engine controls are inside a locker and the locker lid handles are fully bevelled. Though the bilge pump is inside a locker, its portable handle is fitted through a watertight seal so we can pump out without opening the locker lid and letting water below in rough conditions. At the fore end of the cockpit there is a Nicolson-Hughes handle bag, an improvement on the usual type of winch handle container in that its contents will stay inside even if the boat turns over, yet there is no cover or closure or other obstruction to prevent the quick grabbing of a winch handle.

To go below, the main hatch is unlocked. A mortice lock looks neat but it is vulnerable to thieves and hard to replace when it goes wrong, so there is a hasp and padlock instead. The hasp is set right to one side where it will virtually never cause injury or catch on clothing as one on the centreline will. Each weather board has a small jam cleat to take the lashing which prevents the boards tumbling out if the boat rolls over too far.

There are teak steps down into the cabin. It's true teak is heavy and very costly but there is nothing like it for standing up to conditions afloat, and it does not blacken or soften if it is wet for long periods. The sides of the steps are slotted because this reduces the weight, makes them look attractive and gives a handy grip when the steps have to be lifted aside to remove the engine casing.

When the boat is sailing hard on the wind, it is easy to put a foot wrong when going below and tread not on the top step, but onto a galley fiddle. On plenty of yachts this mis-footing results in a splintering crunch because the fiddles are dainty and delicate. Our fiddles are high and thick and rugged, so they withstand the careless foot and also make useful hand-holds in severe conditions. Close by are the galley lockers and when we first built these they

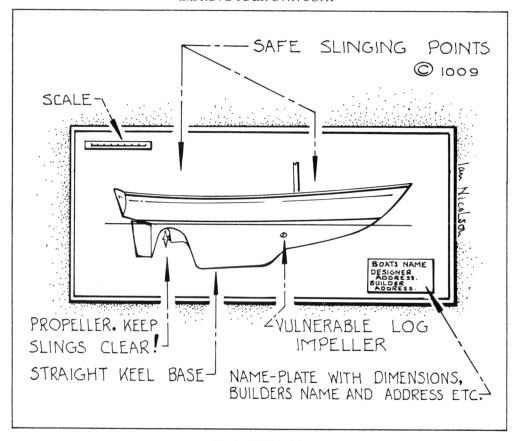

Fig. 1 Half model

For a boat which is cruising in waters remote from its home port, a half model on the bulkhead can be extremely useful. If the yacht runs aground or has to be hauled up, an exact knowledge of her underwater body can be vital. For slinging or any underwater work, a knowledge of where the vulnerable equipment is eliminates risk of causing damage to items like the log impeller, the propeller, rudder, and so on. Almost as important, the half model should have the name and address of the builder and designer so that they can be contacted easily for technical information. The back board should have a scale on it and the mast should be located so that the positions of things like the log impeller are known in relation to the mast. Inside any cruiser there is no better decoration than a half model, quite apart from its usefulness.

had 3 inch (75 mm) high fiddles which we knew would retain cups and pans safely. We were mistaken. On an old-fashioned boat with lots of weight and a fairly steady motion this height of fiddle is enough, but a modern boat is so light it jumps about with a quick jerky motion which throws gear about. So now the crockery lockers have doors as well as high fiddles along each shelf front.

Amidships there is a special locker for life-jackets. If the boat has to be abandoned through the main or fore hatch, the locker is accessible for the crew whichever way they are departing. Opposite is the main fire extinguisher because it has to be well clear of the cooker and engine, the two probable sources of fire. The extinguisher has a trigger which gives us a chance to do some intelligent fire-fighting by squirting off several blasts in the right direction. Most of the cheap extinguishers totally discharge in one long swooooooosh which does not last as long as the early surge of panic in the crew.

Our extinguisher is also non-toxic because I was once driven out of a boat's cabin by one of those toys which discharge lethal gases. It went off accidentally and, as the nearest land was two weeks away, I thought I was going to have to camp out in the cockpit till I reached home. Getting rid of the gas taught me some useful things about ventilation. Our present boat has a special closable vent at the aft end of the recessed anchor locker on deck right forward. When we want to take our sailboard on our cruiser we can put the board's mast in the cabin by sliding the top end of the mast through the vent hole and into the anchor locker. Admittedly, the board's mast is obtrusive as it extends through the middle of the saloon and fore cabin, but it makes a grand grab-rail when the weather cuts up rough.

In the cockpit we have a pair of self-tailing winches at the forward end of the coamings and two-speed ordinary winches aft. This means that we can use the self-tailers for cruising, and the two-speeds are grand for racing. When racing we can handle both genoa and spinnaker sheets at once, or the headsail on the main outer forestay at the same time as the sail on the portable inner forestay.

This flexibility makes for easy handling and forms part of the varied convenience and safety arrangements. It makes for peace of mind to have everything that matters on board simple, duplicated where possible, easy to repair and reliable.

=2 Working inside the hull=

A main reason why boatbuilders, amateur and professional, are so clever and resourceful is because they have to work under such difficult conditions. The lack of space and daylight inside any hull would baffle an ordinary wood-worker or engineer, or electrician or plumber. The absence of neat right-angles in the structure, the varying curves, the tiny size of the crannies and access holes baffles anyone less adaptable than that cunning fellow, the average boatbuilder.

Light

However, only a particularly stupid builder puts up with bad conditions because there are plenty of ways of making life inboard easier. Light is the first requirement. For even the smallest job, two lights are needed so it is best to have a single electric lead brought on board with a multi-socket box on the end. Even one man working on his own in a small boat needs four sockets: two for lights, one for the main drill and one for the secondary drill or counter-sink. If there has to be a heater, then a five-socket box is needed. It is far better to have the lights and drills on short leads, led to the multi-socket box, rather than each electric item on its own long lead led to sockets outside the boat, because this results in miles of electric cables getting in everyone's way.

Whether one or a dozen wires are led on board, they should be kept clear of the hatchways. Sometimes the vents can be used as access points for the cables; sometimes a window is deliberately left out till the boat is complete, not least because it is also a useful exit for rubbish and an inlet for fresh air.

Temperature

If the boat is cold inside, the unglazed window may have a piece of canvas or an old blanket draped over it to keep in the warmth. A single 1 kilowatt heater is no good for raising the temperature usefully; a 2 kilowatt unit is fine for a boat about 32 feet (10 metres) long, but on craft much bigger than this a separate heater for each cabin will be needed, at least at the beginning of the day, if people are working in each compartment. Once the boat has been fully warmed through, fewer heaters are needed. When working in really chilly conditions, for instance in Northern Europe or the regions within a few hundred miles of the Canadian border during the colder months, an automatic time switch is needed so that the heaters come on well before the workers arrive. If this is not done, hands will be too cold to do fine work until half the morning has passed. Of course the boat may be in a heated shed, but it is more economical to heat the confined space inside a boat rather than the whole of the shed in which she lies.

For hot conditions, cooling arrangements are important. Fans arranged to push or pull a draught through the boat work well, provided they are fully protected. Where fibreglassing is being carried out, fume extraction by fans is needed, but too much draught can cause problems, so the aim here is a gentle but clearly detectable movement of air, not a small hurricane. If the boat's specification includes fan-assisted ventilators, it is worth fitting these early on, even if they are only temporarily wired up at first.

Protecting the work

Before going aboard a boat street shoes are taken off and soft-soled shoes put on. The latter are kept clean and never used off the boat, so that they do not scratch the deck or cabin sole. I have seen careful shipwrights work in socks (complete with large holes with protruding toes) and I think this is an excellent idea because it ensures that no metal tools, fastenings or components are left lying about where they may cause damage to finely finished surfaces.

A hat to protect the head from bumps in confined spaces and to retain heat is traditionally worn by boatbuilders. It used to be common to see those boatbuilders who were paid hands on yachts at the weekends wearing last year's yachting cap, much the worse for hard usage, when working aboard. The peak keeps the glare from overhead light out of the eyes and the crown has enough thickness and padding to soften the blow when meeting a low beam. Nowadays one sees amateur boatbuilders wearing wool skiing caps with small peaks to get the same degree of protection. This explains those paint-streaked caps seen hurtling down the ski slopes.

No one can work well if the 'walking area' is not level and stable. However, some boat plans show the lower furniture built in before the cabin sole. This means that all the time the furniture is being fitted the wretched people on the job have to perch on the sloping side of the ship, or balance on top of keel bolts. The choice here is to change the assembly procedure and put the sole in first, or put in a temporary sole. This second option has a lot to recommend it, as it can be used right up to the day of commissioning, so that the proper sole never gets worn or scratched. If the main sole is put in at an early stage it must be sheathed in old sails, or covered with carpet strips well taped on, or otherwise protected. Newspaper sellotaped down is not effective for more than a few days because it cannot stand up to the hurly-burly of energetic work aboard.

All fine work, once completed, has to be protected. Different locations require different treatment. Corrugated cardboard can be taped round pillars and onto bulkheads, but pieces of cloth tend to be better since they stand up to wear and tear so much better. At door sills and on the toerail where everyone comes aboard, the protection must be resilient and semi-permanent. Wood battens screwed or bolted down, or made into rebated capping pieces held by clamps, or heavy-duty rubber matting tied down firmly is what professionals use. Pieces of new carpeting (never gritty old pieces) are useful in a dozen places. They can be held down with staples or screws with washers under the heads, or tied in position.

Work benches

For almost every sort of job on board some form of work bench is an asset and often essential. Portable work benches designed for the Do-It-Yourself man (but much appreciated by professionals) are fine, especially as they fold up so they can be eased through a main hatch. However, they do tend to slide about when the work gets hectic, so they need clamping or bolting down. An alternative is to build in a temporary work bench. For the professional a little bench (complete with a vice) which can be moved from boat to boat is a most useful tool. Many riggers use a sawing horse with a vice on one end, but this is not suitable for wood or metal working. The rigger sits on the horse to steady it when forcing wires into sleeves, or splicing, but the wood-worker needs to be able to get at his work-piece from different angles, so he does not want to have to sit or stand on his bench to hold it still.

If necessary, the cabin sole can be lifted and the temporary work bench bolted to the sole bearers. Four bolts are needed, two in each of two bearers, to give a good spread. Ideally, adjacent bearers are not used, so that the work bench is rigid by virtue of the wide spacing of the fastenings. Where bolting down is not possible it is worth considering whether the work bench feet can be temporarily glassed onto the inside of the hull in a place which will not show later because it will be covered by furniture or lining. When the time comes to remove the work bench it is not a big job to cut or grind off the glassing-in.

A few boats have built-in work benches and these should be completed early on in the construction so that they can be used during the rest of the building time. The only trouble with this is that by the time the boat is launched the work bench will be scarred. To overcome this problem the bench top may be

---

Fig. 2   Semi-portable work bench   ▷

By undoing the bolts through the bulkhead, and the bolts along the outer edge this work bench can be taken out of the boat when she is racing, or for cleaning or painting. A bench which is not rigid and firm is hard to use, so there are two stiffeners along the underside. The inboard one is not too thick, otherwise G-clamps will not be able to clasp the bench and anything being worked on. The central stiffener is made rugged to give the bracket onto the bulkhead a good base.

When this bench is not being used, the cot berth can be folded down over it, but cots sag in the middle when anyone is sleeping in them, and this means the cot frame has to be about 6 inches (150 mm) clear above the bench. The tools stowed round the bench need moisture proofing otherwise they will soon rust even if the boat seems dry inside.

made over-thick and used while the boat is being built. When the boat is due to go into the water, the bench top is unbolted and put through the planer after careful cleaning. It is hand-finished to bring it up to a new condition before being re-bolted home.

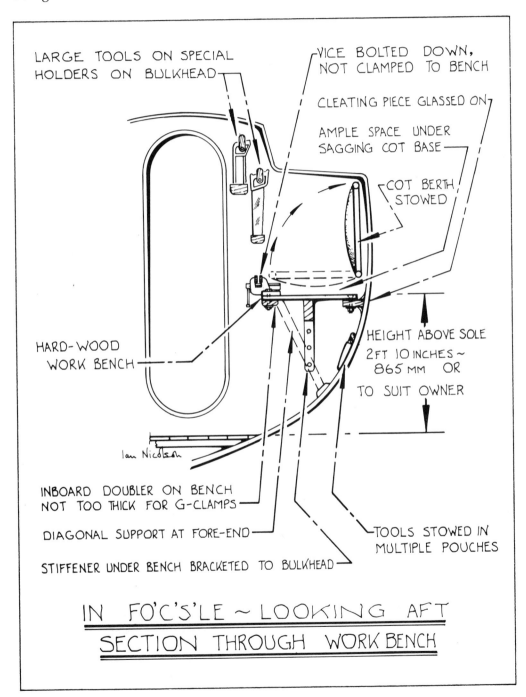

LARGE TOOLS ON SPECIAL HOLDERS ON BULKHEAD

VICE BOLTED DOWN, NOT CLAMPED TO BENCH

CLEATING PIECE GLASSED ON

AMPLE SPACE UNDER SAGGING COT BASE

COT BERTH STOWED

HARD-WOOD WORK BENCH

HEIGHT ABOVE SOLE 2FT 10 INCHES ~ 865 MM OR TO SUIT OWNER

Ian Nicolson

INBOARD DOUBLER ON BENCH NOT TOO THICK FOR G-CLAMPS

DIAGONAL SUPPORT AT FORE-END

TOOLS STOWED IN MULTIPLE POUCHES

STIFFENER UNDER BENCH BRACKETED TO BULKHEAD

IN FO'C'S'LE ~ LOOKING AFT
SECTION THROUGH WORK BENCH

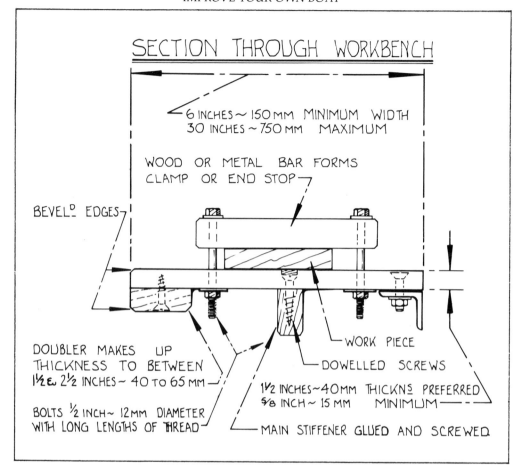

SECTION THROUGH WORKBENCH

6 INCHES ~ 150 mm MINIMUM WIDTH
30 INCHES ~ 750 mm MAXIMUM

WOOD OR METAL BAR FORMS
CLAMP OR END STOP

BEVEL^D EDGES

WORK PIECE

DOUBLER MAKES UP
THICKNESS TO BETWEEN
1½ & 2½ INCHES ~ 40 TO 65 mm

DOWELLED SCREWS

1½ INCHES ~ 40 mm THICKN^S PREFERRED
⅝ INCH ~ 15 mm MINIMUM

BOLTS ½ INCH ~ 12 mm DIAMETER
WITH LONG LENGTHS OF THREAD

MAIN STIFFENER GLUED AND SCREWED

Fig. 3 On-board work bench

This type of work bench is easy to make, need not take up much room, and can be used for woodwork, rigging repairs, for mending engine parts, in fact for doing any fabrication or maintenance work. If the bench is made of the same wood as the rest of the furniture it will look smart and be relatively unobtrusive. The bench must be strongly fixed down, perhaps by bolts to an angle bar on the frames, or possibly by being glassed in, or possibly by hinges onto a strong locker front in the fo'c's'le.

To save money and save weight, instead of a conventional vice, which is bulky and will rust, a simple bar-type clamp is shown here. It consists of a wood, metal or strong plastic bar fixed to the bench by two or more long bolts. One of these clamps may be fitted at each end of the bench, and they are used to pin down onto the bench whatever is being worked upon. In this case the work-piece is shown as a wood plank, but it can be a splice, a manifold, or a seacock.

More common than a work bench aboard is a tool rack. This too should be made early on, so that it can be used during the construction period. Professional shipwrights tend to set aside one particular locker on board for their tools and each evening put everything back into that locker. They may select another locker, preferably one with its opening on top rather than in a side, for storing odd scraps of wood, which are needed throughout construction for such jobs as packing up cleating and sole bearers to the correct alignment, and for putting between the jaws of cramps and the work-piece to prevent the fine surface from being dented and damaged.

Nothing holds up production like frequent trips out of the hull to the stores or timber mill. For this reason a supply of all the commonly used fastenings is kept inside the hull. Those miniature chests of drawers made from metal or plastic are handy as each drawer will hold a full box of screws. Roundhead as well as countersunk fastenings are needed. Besides a broad selection of bolts, I like to have lengths of threaded bronze rod with the appropriate size of nuts and cap nuts. In that way I never find myself short of a bolt of a particular length – I just make up the right size in a very few minutes.

After a few hours' work in the confines of a boat's hull the chaos of shavings and off-cuts becomes obtrusive. Regular cleaning up is worth the time spent, partly because it saves losing small tools like nail punches which love to lurk in the bilge, hidden by builders' rubbish. When glassing-in it is important that there is no dust about, so the removal of rubbish is doubly important, and it must be thorough. A vacuum cleaner is required, preferably the industrial sort with a powerful suction. Before using it, large rubbish has to be gathered up, then a brush taken through the boat to remove everything bigger than a coin. If this is not done even a powerful suction cleaner will get its pipe blocked.

It used to be the tradition in yacht yards that the apprentices swept up every Saturday morning so that the dust would settle over the weekend and make it possible to varnish on Monday morning. Nowadays the lucky amateur has an eager 8-year-old daughter or niece to help him clear up.

=3 Getting help with the work=

Boatbuilding is a tough business. It would be boring if it wasn't rugged, crisis-laden, breath-taking, exciting, maddening – all the things that make it worth while. But it has to be admitted that at times it can be overwhelming, or boring, or too difficult in certain branches for some people. The answer is to call in help.

This applies to amateurs and professionals alike. The former want their level of enjoyment to be held and the latter want their profits to be kept up, so both groups have a strong need for occasional outside assistance.

It is normally fairly easy to get help with finishing such work as painting, engine installations, electrical work and rigging. It may take a bit more searching around to get help with furniture components and glassing-in work. The purchase and fitting of masts, spars and sails is easy as these items are made by specialist manufacturers and so this gear is almost as easy to get as deck fittings and such like, which are bought from chandlers. Some chandlers even act as agents for spar makers and sail-lofts.

The first source of help is in the classified advertisements of the technical and boat magazines. In some regions where boatbuilding is a noticeable industry the local newspapers carry classified advertisements offering help with different jobs.

In addition, certain parts which used to be made individually and specially for each boat are now available as standard items from manufacturers and wholesale chandlers. Their catalogues are essential for any serious boat-building project because so often time and money can be saved by studying these tomes. For instance, it is possible to buy standard rudder stocks for dinghies and small cruisers, whereas a few years ago these were made up specially for each boat. Similarly, book racks, crockery shelves and grab-rails can be bought in. Even when a standard fitting is not exactly right, it is often best to buy a standard fitting and modify it, or possibly change the boat to suit the component. Typical of these fittings are ballast keels, mast steps and steering gear assemblies. The latter are now available in a great range of types and sizes so that the best chandlers such as Simpson-Lawrence have a service which helps the builder select the right components and marry them all together into a compatible set of parts.

Amateurs can save themselves a lot of time and sweat by purchasing timber already planed. However, this puts the cost up noticeably and for a big boatbuilding project it may be cheaper to buy a planing machine, new or second-hand. It can always be sold when the job is complete. A disadvantage of buying a planing machine is that its blades are sensitive and need regular sharpening or changing, or both. One small piece of metal in way of a blade and the operator must stop and either fit a new blade (assuming he has one available) or sharpen out the nick left by the offending metal. Naturally everyone takes trouble to ensure that nothing damages plane blades, but it's amazing how often a tiny nail or screw or even metal swarf gets in the wrong place.

There are snags to buying wood already planed from a timber merchant. Some are careless about final finished dimensions so precise instructions have to be given. A more usual problem is plane 'chatter' which leaves the wood planed smooth but with undulations. When ordering planed timber, insist the wood be so smooth that a set square blade edge can be laid on each piece with no daylight showing under it. If in doubt, ask to see a sample of the planer's work.

To save money, timber can be ordered with only the two widest faces planed; this is in some regions called 'Dressed two sides', shortened to 'D2S'. A more expensive finish leaves the wood planed on all four long sides (but not the ends) and this is sometimes referred to as 'Dressed four sides' or 'D4S'.

A good timber merchant will be copious with his advice provided he is approached when he is not busy. One of the cardinal rules of boatbuilding is: 'Keep clear of professionals at their busy times' which are:

Friday afternoons,
During all the Spring fitting out season,
Just before the Christmas and Summer holidays,
Prior to taking a new curvaceous girl-friend out to dinner.

It is easy to get advice from every sort of professional from putty-maker to paint-mixer, from surveyor to sailmaker because all these people wish they too had the guts and gumption to build or improve a boat. The important thing to remember is that advice takes time to impart and these people are working in a low-profit industry. So don't ask for advice free, always cap it with an order. If you want help changing the sail plan and spend time with a sailmaker but do not like his products, at least give him an order for the storm sails, or the sail covers and the lee-cloths for the berths.

An amateur taking on a freelance shipwright to help with an awkward job such as glassing in some big heavy bulkheads may be tempted to rely on written references but these are not much good because people's standards vary so much. What one owner thinks is a superb job because the final finish is neat, another owner might think is skimped because he wants to sail in the Roaring Forties. Shipwrights, engineers, painters and riggers all vary in their approach to work. It is important to get one who not only does an elegant job but also gives the standard of strength needed for a cruiser, or lightness for a racing boat, or crash-resistance for a fishing boat; and all within the available money.

This means that before taking on any craftsman, his past work has to be examined. It is seldom enough to look at just *one* boat, or talk with *one* owner; the ideal is to discuss past boatbuilding projects with three or four.

Another way to assess a shipwright's talents is to look at his tool chest. A row of neat, sharp chisels, each in its own socket is eloquent, though it may mean the man is more interested in his tools than in the job they do.

A professional or amateur helper who never goes to sea is a mixed blessing. He may do fine workmanship but may not fasten everything together with a factor of safety of 3 or 5 (or 10 for ocean cruising). This ability to work with a severe gale constantly in mind is an asset in any craftsman. If the plans and specification are fully detailed, then the workman's experience and feeling for rugged safety is less critical – always provided he keeps referring to the drawings.

One thing is certain – whether the help is a painting contractor, a roving shipwright, a mast-maker, a company offering to install an engine provided it is purchased from them, an industrial joiner who wants to contract for all the internal furnishings, it is very seldom the best policy to go for the cheapest just because it is cheap. There is no part on a boat which cannot be spoiled by someone more interested in saving money than in doing a proper job.

When an amateur builder employs a professional, there should be a contract. One way to get a ready-made contract is to write to the Ship and Boat Builders National Federation at Boating Industry House, Vale Road, Oatlands Park, Weybridge, Surrey KT13 9NS, England. They have standard forms for boatbuilding and, though not all the paragraphs may be needed for a particular job, the basic form can be changed to suit circumstances. Even outside Great Britain the form can be modified to suit local circumstances. Above all, the arbitration clause should be left in to save legal expenses if there is a disagreement.

Should the owner and his professional help fall out over some aspect of the work, the last thing either side wants (or can afford) is escalating lawyers' bills. The way round this is to call in a designer or surveyor who is used to arbitrating. He has the technical knowledge to understand the work done, he may well recognise the cause of the disagreement and he should be able to settle the problem, often within a matter of days. In contrast a legal battle is fought out, usually over months but sometimes over years, by two groups of lawyers who often do not understand the technical aspects of the case. To assist them designers and surveyors are called in by both sides, costs rocket upwards – in bad cases senior and junior counsel are called in – there have been cases where the legal costs have been many times the cost of the original work. Compared with this overwhelming assembly of expensive brains trying to grapple with something they only half understand, a good arbitrator is like a sharp knife as he cuts through to the nub of the problem and gives his decision; then he divides his total fee and expenses exactly in two, and each side pays half. This is perhaps the biggest cost-saving technique in the whole of boatbuilding.

When drawing up a contract, both sides must agree who pays if anything goes wrong, so it is sensible to bring in the insurance broker who covers the boat. He will normally recommend a 'building' contract, not a standard boat insurance cover which relates to craft in commission and laid up. All the obvious risks have to be considered, such as accidents to anyone on or under the boat, serious damage to the boat when the professional is working aboard, fire which may break out after the professional help has gone home for the night, and so on. The insurance for building should extend to trials and moving the boat to the water, also launching and all the other perils attendant on this sort of job.

Of course, most amateur builders get other amateurs to help them. The man or woman to select should be good at working rather than celebrating – it takes determination to complete a major job on a boat. Some of the best help I've had have been children. They have so much enthusiasm, at least for short spells. Just as important, they fit into small spaces. They are unrivalled when putting on deck fittings because they have nimble fingers which can reach into small spaces under the deck edge with washers and nuts. They love to layer on the waterproofing 'goo' in copious dollops and then to clean off the surplus. I once completed a little ocean cruiser with a whole batch of children and the only trouble was the complex wage system – so many packets of sweets for an afternoon's work, depending on the age of the 'employee'.

The most sophisticated amateur builders have a batch of friends carefully selected for their special skills. One will be an engineer, another an electrician, another a joiner and so on. Sometimes they stay with the ship after she is launched and retain their 'departments' each year, so that during fitting out time the boat has all the right sort of treatment in each branch of the fitting out. Even with an all-amateur team of builders, there should be insurance to cover accidents to humans and the boat.

There is a shortage of really skilled amateur painters, so it may pay to call in a paint contractor. This is especially true if the paint is to be sprayed on, as it usually is on the topsides of a fibreglass boat. It is quicker to spray on rather than hand paint the barrier coats of epoxy resin which are put on the bottom of a new fibreglass boat to prevent osmosis. The cost of hiring a spray painter and buying the paint may not be all that much less than having a professional do the job. Here, as elsewhere, the trick is to find out when the firms are short of work and keen to give low quotations.

Painting should be done when the rest of the craftsmen are off the boat. On professionally built boats the painters should move in at the weekends and on amateur built ones the painters should come in midweek.

Whoever is going to help work on the boat – amateur or professional, skilled or beginner, child or grandfather – the owner should pander to them. Make sure they have plenty of light and warmth. If anyone has to get into an awkward corner, provide old cushions to soften the sharp protrusions on which they have to squat. If the job is not perfectly straightforward, provide a drawing or at least a sketch.

When it comes to moving heavy weights, amateurs should pause before taking on the job. Even in this technological age, shifting heavy ballast keels and engines is not to be lightly undertaken. Almost always the ideal arrangement is a surplus of lifting strength, so it may be best to use a crane. This will cost far more than rigging up scaffolding sheerlegs or using an overhead beam suitably reinforced.

To keep the cost down, the lift should be carried out when the crane is already in the area for another job. Plenty of yacht clubs hire cranes for group launchings and lifting-out at the beginning and end of each season. The boatbuilder who wants to lift a big engine or heavy tank can often use the same crane on one of these occasions.

If a crane is not available at a reasonable price, there are hire firms which supply lifting tackle like chain blocks and gantries. Incidentally, these firms also hire out things like extra-powerful drills which are so valuable for drilling or reaming holes through ballast keels and thick stem bands. They also have lists of professional firms who can help on boatbuilding projects.

4 *Better performance under*
sail

To make a boat go faster under sail, it is just necessary to increase the power and reduce the resistance. Sail power can be increased by adding to the area and making the sails more efficient. To lower the resistance of the hull, the wave-making must be cut down and the factors that make for frictional resistance reduced as much as possible. It's all so easy in theory and much of it is simple in practice. The only snag is that no one action is likely to make more than a tiny difference. A few changes just occasionally do make a dramatic improvement, but mostly each improvement gives less than a 1% increase in speed.

The conclusion is that everything possible has to be done, if a noticeable speed increase is required. And this calls for an expenditure of time, effort and money. The more of these which are poured into the boat, the more sensational the results will be.

More sail area

It is easy to increase the sail area on a boat. The mast can be made higher or the boom lengthened, either by getting new spars (which tends to be expensive) or by splicing new lengths on the existing spars. To lengthen a wood spar, the end is cut to a scarph slope of about 1 in 12 which matches the scarph on the new piece and the two parts are clamped together while the glue sets. If the mast is given extra length at the bottom, the gooseneck will need lowering, the spreaders will have to be brought down a percentage of the additional length, the running rigging will be too short and much, if not all, of the standing rigging will have to be replaced. If the addition is put on the top of the mast, the total number of alterations is likely to be less, so this is the favoured way to make the change, provided the mast section is large enough to carry the extra sail area.

Changing the length of an alloy spar is quicker. The mast is cut straight across at a strategic point below the tapered top section and a piece is inserted, with internal sleeves at each end of the new section. If the mast already has a join, it is sometimes straightforward to take off the bottom part and put on a longer one.

Changing a mast is not cheap and it is generally best to get a proper plan from a yacht designer who is used to this sort of surgery. Lengthening the boom is easier, but even here, as a generalisation, it is better to have a new longer spar than to lengthen an existing one. Admittedly a change to a new spar is likely to be more expensive.

There are other ways to increase the sail area without changing the spars. The bottom of the forestay can be moved forward, perhaps out onto a bowsprit (see Chapter 20), or the forestay can be raised further up the mast, if it is not already at the top. On a boat with the necessary space a mizzen can be added, or the headsails can be given a greater overlap aft of the mast. In all these changes the feel of the helm and the strength of weather helm have to be taken into account; this is so important, and Chapter 6 explores this factor further.

It is broadly true that only rarely are the spar lengths increased, partly because of the cost but more importantly because few boats can lug around longer sticks. If a change is being made from heavy wood spars to lighter aluminium ones, then an increase in length is permissible. Otherwise there is a penalty to pay: the crew have to be extra alert and reef earlier, because the boat will be more tender. On the other hand a turgid motorsailer with an inefficient low rig would be given a real 'shot in the arm' by a new powerful one, matched by a change in ballast ratio.

Shifting the forestay forward is often cheap, especially if the same deck fittings can be used. Even if a bowsprit is being added, it is sometimes possible to use the same fittings, modified maybe, and the same forestay. It may be necessary to add a short length of chain or a pair of metal straps or a couple of rigging screw toggles to the bottom of the forestay to make it slightly longer, but this is cheaper and quicker than buying a new stay. In the same way, the foresail halliards can often be used, but if they do need lengthening, it is probably better to make up new ones.

In all matters where extra speed is required, it is worth having advice and properly prepared drawings from a naval architect. For anyone who feels he cannot afford the fees for this, there is often free advice from a mast-maker or sailmaker. Naturally there is a risk here, because anything which is free may be worth the money which is paid for it! There is no denying that a sailmaker will turn out hundreds of sails each year, whereas a naval architect will only design a few boats in the same time, so the sailmaker may know as much about getting that tiny bit of extra speed. Certainly when it comes to modifying sails, the sailmaker should be brought into the discussion at the earliest stage. He should be approached when he is not busy so that he can give time and thought to the problem. In the yacht industry, few people have to work such long hours as sailmakers. Much of the work involves kneeling down and crawling on the sail loft floor, standing up, then down again – it's often a long, gruelling day.

A sailmaker will almost certainly say that a given sail is not worth increasing in area unless it is almost new and the job is straightforward. The cost of a new sail is relatively small when compared with other running costs and is often not much over three times the cost of a major sail overhaul. So bearing in mind that sails have a definite life (which varies between about 3 and 15 years according to quality and number of hours use each year), it is normally good sense to go for new mainsails and large genoas when making a radical change in the rig. The total cost is not all that great as the smaller headsails seldom need changing.

Increasing the overlap or the length of the foot of a headsail improves the boat's speed up to the point where about one third of the sail's foot length is aft of the mast. Thereafter the increase in speed brought about by lengthening the sail's foot length is not greatly noticed, except on a reach. Even on this course, the speed increase will be small.

Once half the sail's foot is aft of the mast, the extra area has little effect on speed and because the sail's foot starts to curl round inboard, it may even begin to slow the boat when close-hauled.

Lowering the foot of a headsail has a beneficial effect, partly because the extra area gives extra push, partly because the gap between the bottom of the sail and the deck decreases, so there is less chance of the wind escaping under the sail's foot. For the maximum efficiency, the foot of the sail should touch the deck along its whole length, then the whole airflow on the windward side must run aft to meet the lee side flow at the leech. This ensures that the pressure difference between the windward and leeward sides is maximised and so the pull of the headsail is as big as possible, provided the curvature of the sail is right. There's the rub! This curvature varies from boat to boat, and it varies with wind strength and other factors like air density, boat speed, wave height and frequency, and so on. To get the curvature of the sails correct, they have to be cut just so. In time, they stretch and the shape is wrong. A good sailmaker can modify sails to get the best shape back into them, provided they are not too old and over-stretched. This is where a sailmaker can undoubtedly work a little magic. It is not much good taking the sails to him in his loft. (All sail factories are called lofts even though the majority are now at ground level. In the old days it was usual to make sails in a loft above a shipyard and there is no industry so wedded to tradition as boatbuilding, so the name sticks.) Get the sailmaker out on to the boat on a weekday so that he can relax and concentrate on the faults in your sails. And on your whisky.

Saving weight

To reduce the resistance of the hull as it passes through the water, the wave-making is minimised by taking weight out of the boat. There are various approaches to this operation. A fanatical race-winning crew will get rid of every item which is not essential and may even dispose of the cabin floorboards, so that they have to walk fore and aft along the top of the keel, which may not even have the keel bolts recessed. They will carry just enough water in a lightweight container to see them fairly safely to the next port. They will go for lightweight plastic seacocks and try to do without these plumbing items entirely by using a chemical toilet, and by having a portable sink which they empty overboard by lifting it out and tipping the contents over the side (with only a very few spoons we hope). More seacocks are eliminated by making the cockpit drain out through the transom, well above water level.

The second level of weight-saving is keen but requires the expenditure of less money. Lightening holes are drilled in bulkheads and furniture, and some of these parts are taken right out of the boat. When the time comes to renew the ship's battery, the lightest possible type will be bought and it will be stowed as low as possible, in a plastic container. When any new item is purchased the alternatives will be weighed to discover which is the lightest. The crew will be told what weight of personal gear they may bring on board and their full kit-bags weighed every so often during the season. Only essential equipment is carried, so spare parts for the engine are left ashore unless the boat is on a major race or cruise. The galley is stripped of inessential cutlery, pans, plates and containers. Those which are kept are mostly of lightweight plastic.

The various lockers are checked to make sure that there is just one pair of pliers on board and not one in the engine tool kit, another in the bo'sun's bag, a third on someone's hip in a sheath containing knife and spike and a fourth in the ship's tool drawer.

The third level of weight-saving is at what might be called 'club racing' level. Here the attitude is that racing is for fun and it is widely considered that fun melts away when drinking, hi-fi and good eating stop. So though this level of weight-saving is serious enough, it does not take precedence over other forms of enjoyment. In practice, this means that the spare propeller is put ashore but not the second anchor. The fishing gear may well be kept on board because it weighs little and it makes calms amusing. The various spare ropes will be reduced to one spare sheet for use on headsail or spinnaker and perhaps two warps. The dinghy inflation pump will be kept aboard, but spare oars taken ashore, and so on.

At whatever level weight-saving is pursued, there are basic rules for the operation:

1 It is always possible to save a bit more weight, even if it only involves having the crew cut their hair.
2 The most effective way to reduce the total displacement of a boat is to start by cutting down the biggest weights. The ballast keel should be drilled out and plugged with wood dowels or lightweight filler to the limit recommended by the boat's designer. The engine is the next biggest weight and that should be changed for a lighter one, or just altered as much as possible. Castings are changed for fabrications and fabrications for plastics. The cooling water pipes should be reduced in diameter, provided they have the usual over-large bore to deal with tropical climates, and the pipes changed to plastic ones where this is safe.
3 Often the best way to save weight is to leave an item off entirely. For

example, during some inshore races a lower guardrail is not needed, so port and starboard bottom wires are taken ashore. This is much more effective than merely reducing the diameter of the wire.

4 If an item is essential on board, it is often possible to make one part do two jobs. One winch with a batch of sheet stoppers is much lighter than two winches and, instead of carrying a boathook, a dinghy oar with a hook one end can be adequate, even though it is less than ideal.

5 Metal things tend to be heavy. Drilling lightening holes in them helps, but where possible a lighter material should be used.

6 To save weight effectively a knowledge of modern materials is important. Spinnaker poles have gone from solid Douglas fir to hollow spruce, to aluminium, to carbon fibre, and so on.

7 Weight-saving requires continuous vigilance because weights creep back on board. The sump below the engine gets half full of water; blocks which break are not taken out of the boat; a torn sail is heaved into a cockpit locker and forgotten beneath other sails in constant use; and so it goes on.

Reducing hull drag

Hull resistance is also cut down by reducing the wetted surface and smoothing the flow of water. Radical changes in the wetted surface are seldom possible or advisable, though there have been some dramatic alterations, mainly on boats which are being very intensively campaigned in a series of races, or on boats which are being changed from a low-speed role to a more exciting one. For instance, a converted fishing boat or motorsailer can occasionally be given an improved performance by changing the rudder, cropping back the bilge keels and perhaps fairing off the aft deadwood. On a few racing boats the rudder may be cut down in area, or the keel changed, but to achieve success here in light airs, medium winds and gales, needs skilful naval architecture and possibly help from a towing tank which specialises in this type of work.

Though it is usually difficult and costly to make a radical change in the wetted surface, small improvements in the way in which the water slides over the hull are often simple. Trailing edges of keels and rudders can be made narrower and sharper, rudder hangings can be faired over with filler compounds, the smoothness of the hull bottom is improved by constant rubbing down with wet-and-dry glasspaper, seacocks are recessed or changed for the flush closing type and, when used for discharge, may be raised above the load waterline, and so on.

A two-bladed propeller makes less resistance than a three-blader, but when at rest it should be aligned vertically behind the stern post. To do this, the propeller shaft has to be marked with paint so that the propeller alignment can be seen from inside the boat. Better still, the propeller should be changed for a folding one. Where there is not space to fold the propeller blades back because there is a rudder or skeg in the way, a feathering propeller may be fitted. It has blades which turn to align with the flow of water and this does make a significant difference to the speed of a boat; in one case we recorded a half knot gain at 7 knots on a 60 foot cruising ketch with a big propeller.

A boat with no reduction gear on its engine will have a smaller propeller which gives improved performance under sail, but less efficiency and probably less speed under power. However, the absence of a reduction gear on the engine saves weight and also means the propeller is lighter. The stern gear will probably be lighter as well. All this is important when putting an engine into a boat, or changing engines.

When viewing the underbody of a boat with a view to getting more speed, the main principle to keep in mind is: 'Water hates sudden change of shape'. Anything which sticks out or is indented into the hull makes for extra resistance. Fish which swim fast have eyes which do not protrude, tails which are thin in plan and elevation, bodies which are sleek from every angle.

The one exception is the trailing edge of the keel or the rudder, where there should be a sharp cut-off at right angles to the line of flow. This is to get good separation of the water from the hull and avoid 'burbling'. But even here, it is really better to have a tapering aft edge so that the edge is as sharp as a knife. A principal reason why so many boatbuilders go for the blunt cut-off is that it is so expensive to get a fine taper which is strong enough. So often a tapered trailing edge gets broken if it is as thin as a knife blade.

5 Minimising upkeep, chafe
and wear

Whether a boat is new, middle-aged or old, a lot can be done to reduce annual refitting work. There are some owners who think that modern boats need little or no maintenance. They get a shock when, without warning, a bilge pump fails to work, a sail rips right across, or the mast falls down. These dramatic events usually occur in bad weather, maybe off a lee shore, probably when the crew is seasick, or tired, or hungry, or late getting back to port with some critical appointment to be kept next morning. The happy phrase 'a stitch in time saves nine' applies so well to boat maintenance – so far as sail maintenance is concerned it is literally true.

Many modern boats, that is those built since the mid 1970s, are built on the 'motorcar principle'. They are made as attractive to the new buyer as possible, with no thought as to long life, ultimate reliability, good factors of safety and good long-term value. They are built as cheaply as possible and if an item is out of sight, it is made just adequate for its job for a limited period. Even things which are not out of sight are selected for cheapness, not because they are the best for the job. Sheet winches, bilge pumps and rudder bearings are almost always undersize on the principle that the buyer of a new boat only looks carefully at the upholstery, the fancy furniture and the racing record of the Class. Even that minority of boats in current production which are built to high standards need plenty of maintenance every year because the sea (and all lakes, canals and rivers, for that matter) are harsh places where materials corrode, bearings seize and weathering occurs, even when the boat is moored.

Winter storage

A first principle of maintenance reduction is: 'Always haul a boat out every winter and put her in a weatherproof shed'. This raises a derisory cheer because so many boat sheds have roof leaks and cracked windows. But it is better to have a yacht under cover, even if there are a few drips on the deck, than have her out in the open. A waterproof sheet or two can be rigged to divert drips from overhead clear of the deck. Careful owners put on complete covers extending from beyond the bow to aft of the stern, even when the boat is under cover. They are right, because such covers keep off dust, bird droppings and visitors, quite apart from the infiltrating rain.

If a boat cannot be in a shed, she should be as well covered with waterproof tarpaulins as possible. A single cover tends to be heavy and make life awkward when working on a boat. Three overlapping covers are best, because they are not too heavy and usually only one needs to be turned back at a time when work is being done at the weekends. The bow and stern areas are left open in such a way that air and some light can sweep along the deck, but rain and snow cannot get in.

Tarpaulins need to be tied down at 18 inch (500 mm) intervals with ropes secured right under the boat. If the lashings are tied to the boat's supports and a severe gale vibrates the tarpaulin, the shores holding the boat up will be pulled out. It is usual for tarpaulins to have eyelet rings hammered in round the edges to take the lashings, but these little pieces of metal chafe against hulls whenever the wind blows and cause damage. The type of tarpaulin which has cloth loops for the lashings, or has the lashing sewn directly onto the tarpaulin, are best.

It is not a good idea to use the boat's mast as a ridge pole for the tarpaulin, though it is better than storing the mast in a jumble of others on the ground where people can, and probably will, walk over them or even drive over them, as does occasionally happen! The best type of ridge pole is supported every 6 feet (2 metres) and curves down at each end, with full headroom beneath for anyone standing in the cockpit.

Chafe and wear on deck

Boats are a bit like children – constantly getting into minor scrapes. They are also restless, never still for long, so there is always a chance that one 'moving part' will touch another . . . and repairs will be needed.

Some problems are not hard to foresee and precautions can be taken. For instance, virtually every boat which is frequently anchored suffers from chips and scratches on the bow. These usually occur when the anchor is being pulled aboard, especially if the sea is rough, or the crew are short of muscle-power, or they are working in the dark or the rain. Even slight contact between a small anchor and a fibreglass hull results in some damage. A defence against this trouble is a pair of big, thin, flat fenders, made from a heavy Terylene, PVC, or canvas cloth. Each fender is like an envelope with an insert of that closed-cell foam plastic material as used inside modern lifejackets. For boats up to about 30 feet (9 metres) length, the plastic will be about ½ inch (12 mm) thick and for every 10 feet (3 metres) increase in length the padding thickness will go up at least ½ inch (12 mm).

These fenders will extend from near the waterline almost to the sheer. Their fore and aft length will be about 1/15th of the boat's length.

The two fenders are joined down the forward edge and hung on each side of the bow by lines from strong eyes at the corners. For large boats it is necessary to have upper and lower fenders each side; otherwise each one will be too large to handle.

The fenders, which can also be used when lying alongside as back-ups to the ordinary sausage-shaped protectors, should be designed to fit the boat's bow rake and be double stitched with 2 thicknesses of cloth for every 30 feet (9 metres) of boat length. A local sailmaker will produce the fenders and wise owners hang these 'mats' over the bow every time the anchor goes up or down. For stowage, they can be rolled up, and when not in use they come in useful as deck cushions for sunbathing purposes.

The foredeck is likely to be chafed by the anchor chain if there is any great distance between the winch and the stemhead roller. Some builders put Treadmaster or a similar industrial flooring material on the deck, but this particular cork-and-resin sheeting is not ideal if there is constant harsh wear from the chain. However, it is good for preventing anchors chipping a fibreglass deck when put down carelessly. Heavy duty rubber flooring material is slippery when wet but is better for resisting wear. If there is likely to be a lot of chafe from the chain, a strip of metal sheet is needed. It will normally be of stainless steel these days, but in the old days bronze was used and sometimes, to save money, heavy gauge copper sheeting nailed inside a shallow hardwood trough was laid fore and aft between the winch and the stemhead.

The widely used aluminium alloy slotted angle-bar toerail is vulnerable, especially as it is common practice to shackle blocks directly onto the up-standing flange. In a few hours the hard metal of the shackle will gouge the softer alloy of the toerail. Careful crews secure blocks with a loop of nylon or Terylene rope, but in time even rope may chafe aluminium, which is why the most cautious crews use plastic piping to guard the toerails.

A piece of this pipe as long as the slot in the toerail is slit lengthways, slipped through the slot and held in place by several tight lashings of light line or hose clamps. To stop the lashings wearing, they may be soaked with epoxy resin. When the plastic piping is worn it is easy enough to cut it off and fit a new piece.

Once a toerail has been badly worn, the best cure is to fit a new length of the angle bar which can be bought from the original builder or from a wholesale chandler. If the deck edge has much curvature, it is usually worth while having the correct bend put in the bar by the supplier. If these people cannot do this bending, metal-working firms with pipe and bar bending machines will do it. It is best to supply a pattern of the deck-edge shape so that the exact curve can be worked into the new length of toerail.

Where renewal is too difficult or expensive, it is often possible to bolt or rivet a new length of angle bar or flat bar inside or outside the worn toerail. Very often there will only be a few slots which have become worn and it does not look unsightly if a piece of metal strip is fixed in way of the damage with at least two fastenings each side of each slot. The doubler bar will have a slot cut in it for securing blocks and so on and the new metal will be carefully rounded at all edges and corners and finished off with a coat or three of paint to match the toerail.

The cockpit zone

The whole area round the cockpit is liable to chafe. Sheets, reefing lines and halliards led aft from the mast as well as such ropes as tiller lines, all give trouble where they touch the structure. When buying a new or second-hand boat it is worth looking at sister ships to see where they have been chafed and take due precautions. A trial sail under gentle conditions just to see where chafe is likely is also a good idea.

To prevent the chafe, the fittings for the ropes such as winches and leads should be moved, or tilted, or blocked up on wood chocks. When working out how to avoid having ropes touch coamings it has to be remembered that the lead of sheets port and starboard is not identical, because virtually all winches work clockwise. This means that a rope coming from a *forward* sheet lead block on the *starboard* side arrives at the *outboard* side of the winch and probably clears the coaming. On the *port* side the rope leads to the *inboard* side of the winch and may well chafe the cockpit or cabin coaming. This explains why many boats have extra lead blocks aft and outboard of the sheet winches.

Incidentally, these lead blocks are often of the 'cheek' type, with bolts through one side of the sheave cage; they are designed to fit flat on deck, but this gives a foul lead up to the winch so a tapered wood wedge has to be fitted between the block and the deck. Occasionally the wedge on the port side has to have a different athwartships bevel to the one opposite, even though its fore-and-aft wedge shape is the same.

If chafe on the coamings has already occurred, it is best to apply a new gelcoat without delay and remove the source of wear. If future wear is expected, a wood pad may be bolted over the affected area and renewed every year or two. If half-round metal strips are screwed to the wood roughly at right angles to the run of the rope, this should reduce or even eliminate the need to renew the wood protectors which, incidentally, should be of teak or at least a reliable hardwood.

Cockpit locker lids get chipped at the edges. It is always difficult to match up a new gelcoat and, even if a repair is unnoticeable when new, it may well fade to a different colour in a few months. Often the best repair is a normal re-gel followed by the fixing of a teak batten over the edge of the lid to hide the mend. If the batten is held by screws put in from behind, no dowels are needed and the fastenings are not seen. It may be necessary to fit a row of battens if the damage is at the outboard edge of the locker lid; otherwise the cockpit seat will not be comfortable for sitting on. Battens about 1½ inches (40 mm) wide with ⅜ inch (8 mm) gaps between look right. The thickness of the battens will depend on the length of available screws, but should not be less than ½ inch (12 mm). All the edges and corners of the battens need careful rounding or at least bevelling.

This use of teak or a lesser hardwood to cover damage is most convenient and can be used in many situations. I once was involved in the repair of an

These cockpit seats have been protected with teak slats; however, the gap between the strips of wood is too wide for comfort. These slats can be added to protect seats, or to cover chafe marks and other damage. The plastic pouches in the foreground are for winch handles but can also be used to stow flares.

attractive dark blue fibreglass cruiser which had been badly chafed amidships on the topsides near the deck. For a variety of reasons it was impossible to get the repair to match the hull colour and there was no money available for a full topsides re-paint. The unsightly blemish was covered by a neat name board, lovingly made and varnished to a deep sheen. It took a lot of time and innumerable sketches before the nameboard looked just right, but once it was made and fitted no one ever guessed what was underneath, whereas lots of people admired the way the boat carried her name.

Below decks

Cabin steps get chipped and chafed; sometimes heavy loads get dumped on them and in time the constant coming and going causes wear on the treads. Some types of steps are made so that the treads are easily renewed. There is the kind seen on racing boats, made from a standard aluminium ladder with hardwood treads fixed at each crossbar. Usually each tread is held with four screws or bolts so it is easy to renew or even turn all the treads upside down.

For more conventional steps, the best plan may be to fit Treadmaster or Trakmark on the treads. Metal protector strips are not good because they make the steps slippery, especially when wet. Some people do not like coverings such as Treadmaster on the steps because it does not accord with the decoration and style of the cabin. In such a case the best repair may be the fitting of a set of doublers on top of all the treads, with facing pieces on the forward edges so that the steps will simply seem to have extra thick treads. This is cheaper and quicker than making up a new set of steps.

The hull underwater

Below the waterline, it is to be hoped that chafe does not happen often. Naturally boats operating in shallow water 'smell' the ground, as they say on the East Coast. If the bottom of the keel is of fibreglass, as with an encapsulated ballast keel, or on a fibreglass power boat hull, a guard is needed. Sometimes a metal keel strip is fitted, but it seldom works well for long because the fastenings fail. If they are screws, they cannot get a good grip in the fibreglass and if their heads are rubbed as the boat grounds, the tearing force usually bends them and rips them at least partly out. Bolts are much better, especially if the heads are deeply counter-sunk; very deeply. Also the bolts need to be closely spaced so that they work in unison. This spacing should be of the order of ⅟₆₀th or certainly ⅟₅₀th the length of the boat. Bolts ½ inch (12 mm) diameter on a 30 footer (9 metres long) and ¾ inch (20 mm) on a 40 footer (12 metres) long may sound massive, but when touching the ground the whole weight of the boat tends to tear the keel band off.

Another way in which the hull bottom can be defended is by fibreglassing on a wood 'shoe'. This is seldom seen but it is a logical idea. The main hull is not pierced by bolts or screws so there is no chance of it being damaged unless the grounding is dramatic. The wood shoe is shaped to fit, with a moderately thick layer of fibreglass protecting it and bonding it to the bottom of the hull.

When the boat grounds the shoe compresses, distorts slightly and chafes away, so there are three ways in which the unwanted energy is absorbed. If the shoe can be designed so that it has a slope aft, it will also act as a wedge. As the boat grounds she will be forced upwards and this too will take up some of the momentum and so reduce the damage. This is why boats built with a long keel, which has the traditional 'drag' or slope down and aft, can often be run aground and suffer little or no damage. Modern keels, shaped like aeroplane wings, are vulnerable and a protective shoe carefully designed and fabricated may save expensive damage.

Rudder problems

Because it is a moving part, it is inevitable that the rudder suffers from wear. The first way to minimise trouble is to stop the rudder from turning more than 35° each way. If the rudder is forced over beyond this angle, it acts more as a brake than a steering instrument. This braking ability is handy, especially on a small boat with no engine, or on a vessel which has to be brought into crowded harbours; but rudders are seldom designed to act as brakes and it is inevitable that when they are used for this extra purpose there will be extra trouble.

Limit stops to prevent the blade from going over more than 35° can be fitted on the outside of the hull in the form of chocks or brackets provided the slight extra hull drag is acceptable. It is more usual to have limit stops on the tiller, often with some semi-hard pad of a tough rubber to prevent a sudden bang when the rudder is forced right over. This happens if the boat goes hard astern, a time when ideally the tiller should be held well clear of its 'full-over' position.

It is this full-over position which so often causes damage if there are no tiller stops. The blade sides chafe on the aft edges of the skeg or keel; the bearings are forced sideways and sometimes the vertical edge join of the blade is opened.

Nearly always it is best to take the rudder off to repair it. Where chafe has indented the blade sides, extra glassing is needed and when the blade halves have started to come apart, the open seam needs glassing over. If the crack is 12 inches (300 mm) long, re-glass for at least 3 feet (900 mm). Good shipwrights tend to re-glass all round, even if the blade halves appear to have opened up only down the bottom aft edge, where trouble often starts.

Repairs in this area are always a worry. If the job is done with enthusiasm and without stinting the materials, the result is a rudder which is thicker and less hydrodynamically shaped than before. This is not acceptable to racing owners. People who cruise offshore are naturally worried when they see a rudder which has been patched. Hollow fibreglass rudders are a source of constant worry, with too many failures. It is for this reason that my firm often recommends wood rudders made in the traditional way and sheathed in fibreglass for serious offshore work.

Guiding rules

When making *any* repair, the best shipwrights pause for a moment and consider the reason why the job is being done. Was the component strong enough in the first place? they ask themselves and anyone else concerned. When it looks as if a freak accident caused the damage, it often makes sense to put back the same size part as the original one. But if a quite minor thump makes a fiddle or bookshelf, or spar, or even a part of the hull crumple, then it is madness to rebuild with no more strength than before.

Modern boats are built with the thinnest, lightest parts which their designers and constructors think will be acceptable to the boat-buying public. Partly this is a good attempt to reduce the total weight of the vessel so that she is fast, easily handled and a joy to own, partly it is a grim plot to make the boat cheap, even if this makes her short-lived and bordering on the flimsy.

Rough rules of thumb are:

1 If the boat was built after about 1972 she is probably on the light side – increase the size of parts being repaired.
2 If she is being (or has been) changed from a racing boat to one more biased to cruising, increase thicknesses.
3 If she was built of wood or steel, she was probably stout enough so far as the basic structure is concerned when she was new.
4 If anything has broken more than once, it needs 'beefing up', but it is also time to look for the basic cause of the trouble. Hatch tops, for instance, must have stops to prevent them from being opened further than the hinges can accommodate. If the top is allowed to open beyond this, the hinge pins will sheer or the hinge straps will be torn off, even if bolted on.
5 A glued join may be perfect and a bolted one may be superb, but there is nothing like a combination of glue and bolts for real strength. Yes, we all know that in theory the two should not be combined because they have different characteristics. But at sea it is the combination of these contrasting abilities which defies wind, weather and crashes.

=6 *Curing weather helm*=

If a sailing boat tends to pull at her helm and tries to come up into the wind, she is said to have weather helm. A little of this tendency is widely believed to be good in that it helps a boat make progress to windward. But if the tiller tugs and jerks the helmsman's arms till they ache, something is badly wrong. The trouble is caused by the total thrust on the sails being well aft, whereas the centre of resistance on the immersed hull and keel is too far forward. This results in a couple which twists the boat into the wind. It all sounds straightforward but getting rid of this defect can be hard. Often there is no single cure, so the best approach is to try all the alternatives, starting with the easier ones, which are cheap and simple to apply.

If the pull on the helm is rather unpleasant but not truly serious and if the boat is performing well, it may be enough to lengthen the tiller. This will not alter the external forces on the boat but the helmsman will no longer feel as if he is fighting the boat; there will be a firm but not irritating pull on the helm which can be managed comfortably. This technique is worth trying by tying a temporary extension to the tiller. It can be a simple bar of wood well lashed on, giving say a 12 in (300 mm) extension. If this is not enough, perhaps double that length will do the trick.

The limitation here may be the space in the cockpit. A long tiller which bashes all the jib-sheet hands in the kidneys at every tack is unpopular. If the idea is right but space is restricted, it may be worth fitting wheel steering. Certainly this will pay off on a boat more than 35 feet (11 metres) overall. The gear chosen should not be the smallest available for the size of boat because, if there is a tendency to weather helm, the strain on the steering components will be high. Therefore a set of parts with a good reserve of strength should be chosen, and all the linkages and fastenings carefully checked, locked on where appropriate, fully lubricated and examined every few weeks.

The next logical move is to get the sails further forward. Small changes are easy: the mast is made more upright and slid as far forward as it will go in its step; the forestay is moved to the end of the stemhead fitting; and the leech of the mainsail is cut away to reduce the foot length. If there is a mizzen, the boat should be tried with this sail lowered. When this cures the problem, it could be worth leaving the whole mizzen mast ashore and in due course perhaps going for a larger mainmast. On boats which have a divided rig because the crew are light the increase in mainsail and headsail size is counterbalanced by fitting larger, more powerful winches and possibly leading a mainsail down-haul line through metal rings sewn down the luff at 6 foot (2 metres) intervals. In a real squall this line can be led to a winch and the sail brought down with force.

On ketches and yawls a moderate tendency to weather helm in strong winds can be counteracted by taking in the mizzen as the first sail change. The second alteration will be a deep reef in the mainsail, so that the area of the total sail plan is being progressively shifted forward.

Whatever the rig, a sailmaker can often help and compared with other charges his work is likely to be relatively cheap. Flattening the main and headsails will reduce weather helm, though no dramatic change in the pull on the tiller is to be expected. If the sails have no Cunningham holes, these can be added, together with winches or tackles and lead blocks to pull the eyes down tight.

If none of these changes produce the required results, it is time to start spending money. Moving the forestay fitting forward should not be wildly expensive, even if it is necessary to fit a bowsprit. How this is done is described in Chapter 20. The cost of making and fitting a bowsprit will be kept down if standard parts are used as far as possible. For instance, on a wood plank bowsprit the outer end fitting for the forestay and bobstay can be a pair of four-bolt eyeplates, as sold by chandlers.

Before going to the expense of fitting a proper bowsprit, a temporary one can be rigged up to see how effective is the idea. Using a stout piece of pipe or a wood pole well lashed in place, a temporary forestay is secured outboard. To keep the outer end of the rough bowsprit from bending up, a lashing is put right round the girth of the hull up forward and from the bottom of this a tackle is taken forward to the bowsprit end. The tackle is pulled tight and this should bend the temporary bowsprit down slightly before the headsail sailing load comes on it. Bowsprit shrouds are rigged port and starboard from the outer end of the pole to the toerails and these too are drawn up tight before sail is hoist. Then all the crew have to do is to wait for a fresh breeze . . . but conditions should not be too boisterous for these trials!

Moving the mainmast forward may be the next move but this is not something to do without a good knowledge of boat structures. As well as moving the mast step forward the structure which supports it has to be extended, the chain plates have to be moved and sometimes the main sheet horse has to be shifted. This is the time to call in a naval architect, if one has not already been asked to help with the problem.

The outstanding feature of excessive weather helm is the constant pulling on the rudder. In squalls this may result in the boat soaring up to windward until her sails flap and she comes to a standstill, or, in extreme cases, even gets round on to the opposite tack. What is needed here, apart from strong arms on the tiller, is a better rudder which will prevent this occurrence. This rudder may also reduce the pressure on the tiller when the wind is not gusting.

A rudder which is high and narrow is the most effective for a given area, so the blade should be modified to this end by maximising the vertical dimension. This usually means continuing the blade right up to the underside of the counter and the bottom down, until it is level with the sole of the keel. At the top the clearance should be as small as possible without risking the blade

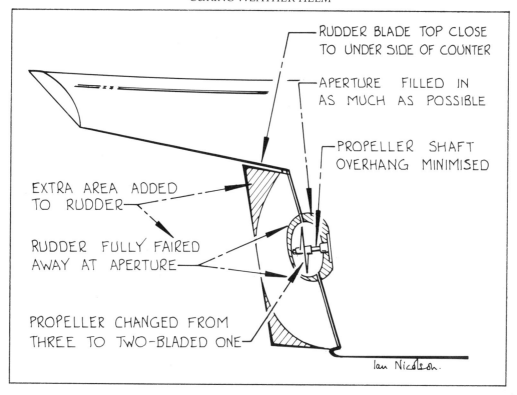

RUDDER BLADE TOP CLOSE
TO UNDER SIDE OF COUNTER

APERTURE FILLED IN
AS MUCH AS POSSIBLE

PROPELLER SHAFT
OVERHANG MINIMISED

EXTRA AREA ADDED
TO RUDDER

RUDDER FULLY FAIRED
AWAY AT APERTURE

PROPELLER CHANGED FROM
THREE TO TWO-BLADED ONE

Ian Nicolson.

Fig. 4. Rudder modifications

The alterations shown here will not only help to reduce weather helm, but will often improve the all-round performance of a boat. Making these changes by themselves is not likely to cure weather helm completely because some boats have this defect to such an extent that they can never be made pleasant and easy to sail. Nevertheless there have been interesting cases where reducing the propeller aperture and improving the blade shape of the rudder have made remarkable differences and changed an awkward boat into a sweet-tempered one.

touching the counter and the clearance can be as little as about ⅛ inch (3 mm) if the stock has no tendency to move vertically on the bearings. This small gap prevents any significant quantity of water burbling over the rudder. If the underside of the counter is not flat, water will flow over the rudder when the blade is off centre but this can be prevented by 'bumping' the counter locally with a swelling added on so that when the rudder blade goes over, its top edge remains very close to the counter.

At the bottom of the rudder it is usual to keep the blade a significant distance above the keel to ensure that if the boat runs aground, the keel takes the blow whilst the rudder is still safe at a slightly higher level. However, if the weather helm is really problematical and the owner is constantly aware of the urgent need to prevent grounding, and if he sails in waters good and deep, a case could be made out for having a rudder which extends *below* the keel bottom – always provided that the lower part of the blade is made fail-safe. This is achieved by having the lowest portion made of softwood with four light screws holding it on to a wood blade. In the event of a grounding the bottom 'sacrificial' section will tear off easily leaving the rest of the rudder operational. There are other techniques which can be used. For instance, a fibreglass rudder might have an extension glassed on to the bottom with about three layers of 1½ oz chopped strand mat so that the lower section is sacrificed to save the rest. Boats over 40 feet (12 metres) will need four or five layers of glassing.

When the depth is increased, the width may sometimes be reduced. This has the effect of moving the centre of effort of the rudder forward and so the pull on the tiller is reduced. Slicing the trailing edge off a hollow fibreglass rudder is seldom straightforward, but a wood blade is often easily altered even if there are metal fastenings extending the full width.

Another way to lessen this unwanted tiller pressure is to fill the propeller aperture between the rudder and the stern post. The only way to do this is to remove the propeller, which means that the boat can no longer use her engine. It is necessary to slip the boat and take off the propeller, then fill the aperture with temporary blanking-off pieces of wood or steel or fibreglass, according to the materials available and those used to build the boat. She is then taken out and tried in all wind strengths. If the cure is dramatic, the owner has a choice: he can either sail with no engine (and incidentally discover a whole new world of fun and skill and excitement), or he can change the line of the propeller shaft to an offset one; alternatively he can fill the aperture as much as possible and have a feathering propeller. This has blades which turn fore and aft, when not in use. The propeller is set with blades vertical so they fill most of the aperture not already blanked off by fairing pieces of wood or fibreglass, or metal, or a combination of these. This ploy works by preventing water on the high pressure side of the rudder from pouring through the aperture to the low pressure side and reducing the rudder's efficiency.

Just to confuse the whole matter, it is sometimes best to increase the total rudder area by adding to the width alone, if the depth is already as large as possible. Or where the depth can be increased, it may still pay to increase the width to get a larger total area. The way to tell if a rudder is too short of total area is to compare its size and proportion with boats of similar size and type. A loss of area of 10% is significant and should normally be corrected by adding extra area. If underway, the boat does not answer her helm instantly and reliably, if she hesitates or feels 'woolly' when in the hands of an experienced helmsman, the chances are that the blade area is too small. Unless, of course, the boat's underbody is badly fouled with weed.

There is another rudder fault found on boats which might be described as traditional, that is, boats with the rudder attached to the aft end of the keel. Sometimes, to reduce wetted surface area, the rudder stock is raked steeply with the bottom end far forward of the head. When the helm is put over to make the boat turn off the wind, the water flow on the rudder pulls the stern down and the steep rake contributes to a lack of turning efficiency. To correct this fault the stern post is extended aft at the bottom to give a more upright rudder stock. This is a major job and to make the finished alteration work well and look good it is necessary to employ more than average skill and cunning. The new post has to be smoothly faired in and strongly secured which is not achieved cheaply.

A change at the bow which may have a modest effect consists of fairing off the forward end of the keel and stem. Much depends here on the material used for construction and on the shape. On a beefy wood boat or a steel one changes are often made fairly easily, especially if only a small modification is wanted. Where the stem and keel leading edge is sharp, it is reported that rounding off will reduce weather helm, so even on a fibreglass boat it may be possible to double up inside the keel or hull with extra layers of glassed-in cloth, then fair off on the outside. The aim here is not to shift the centre of lateral resistance further aft noticeably, but to change the characteristics of the underwater shape by rounding the leading edges to produce a change in hull behaviour.

Of course there are times when it pays to move the centre of lateral resistance further aft by extending the fin back. The job varies very much according to the material of construction used. On a fibreglass boat with a separate fin the mechanics of the job may not be too hard, but the actual shift of the centre is likely to be small, because the additional area will be so far forward. It may be more effective to add area to the front of the rudder skeg provided there is room for this clear of the propeller. On a steel boat the work is often easy because this is such an adaptable material. On a wood boat using epoxy resin and a good shipwright it is not too hard to increase the area by cutting away the trailing edge of the fin to get a flat aft surface, then gluing on laminates which are gradually narrowed to give a taper. The work is likely to be slow and it takes a lot of patience to achieve a worthwhile increase in area. This is not a job for beginners.

It is well known that weather helm gets worse as the angle of heel increases, so any change which keeps a boat more upright will improve matters. Clearly the first move is to improve the reefing facilities then the sail can be reduced swiftly and certainly. For anyone who is unsure when to reef, two simple rules of thumb are offered, because they are easy to follow and because they have won races, got boats out of nasty situations and comforted a lot of worried owners. They are:

1 Put a reef in when the first person aboard wonders if it is time for one. By the time the job is complete the chances are that the rest of the crew will agree that it was opportune. Virtually no one reefs too early.

2 Reef when the waterline on the lee side is within a hand's span of the deck edge. The odd thing about this rule, which is as crude as the first one, is that it suits so many different sizes and types of boat. Of course, it does not apply to one-design inshore racing boats which seldom reef and are so small that the water is *always* about 8 inches (200 mm) below the sheer line

in any breeze. But it suits a variety of cruisers and racing machines from beamy beasts to long, elegant, eel-like old-timers.

There are other cures which can be tried, often with uncertain success. Reducing the top weight so that the boat heels less is a good idea in theory. But it applies to few boats because most boats built in the last twenty years, and virtually every one built in the last ten, is as light aloft as prudence will allow. A few old-timers with massive spars and over-thick rigging are still churning the seas and they can be modified by fitting modern spars, but their owners usually feel that this will spoil the character of the boat and they are probably right.

Adding or shifting ballast is another cure which has to be approached thoughtfully. Part of the problem here is that extra ballast almost always increases weather helm and few modern boats have much ballast inside. To make matters worse, the shift of ballast follows no definite rule, because sometimes moving the weight aft makes things worse, sometimes moving it forward makes it worse. This is easy to understand in theory, less easy to apply in the water. In a nutshell, if a boat has a tendency to lift her stern when she heels, she will tend to bury her bow and the immersed shape of the hull is then such that she wants to surge to windward. Shifting ballast forward will merely push the bow down deeper, so the tendency to go to windward will be worse. But if the ballast is moved aft, this will put the stern deeper into the water. This may result in a worse immersed shape vis-à-vis the tendency to charge off upwind.

An answer to this dilemma is to use the crew's weight as shifting ballast. Try the pull of the helm, using a spring balance to get a dispassionate assessment of the true load on the tiller. Sailing a straight course in a steady wind, send the crew forward one by one. If the spring balance shows the load is decreasing, a little ballast and movable gear like anchors are shifted from the stern or amidships forward. In practice the shifting of ballast is something which should be done circumspectly. Like a lot of weather helm problems, it is worth getting the help of a naval architect who specialises in this type of problem. If he is old and wise, he will probably say, 'as he takes his fees, there is no real cure for this disease . . .' Then he may add: 'The best thing you can do is to sell your boat and buy a well-mannered one. But before you buy, take your choice out in a real breeze for a trial sail . . . just in case *she* has weather helm.'

=7 *Changing the cabin plan*=

The best advice for anyone thinking about changing a cabin plan is to spend a month considering the idea and have the courage to leave things as they are unless the arguments in favour of changing are massive. It is so easy to rip out furniture and fittings, but putting back a new interior which looks good, stands up to rough conditions offshore and keeps up the value of the boat calls for many virtues and skills. These include:

- Patience and a lot of time (about 3 times the original estimate).
- Ample cash (about 4 times the first estimate).
- Skills with tools, paint brushes and glue applicators.
- Skill in planning and negotiating. For instance, the cushions and backrests are usually made by an upholsterer and these items are needed when everything else is finished, which is inevitably in the spring, just when the cushion-maker is frantically over-worked. It takes the patience of a diplomat to get the cushions measured and made in time for the re-launching.

Other people have to be talked into helping, including:

1 Timber suppliers. The wood needed is not the usual rubbish sold to handymen. Good quality hardwood, free from defects, needs careful selection and this is a slow job, best done by the buyer, who has to gain the timber merchant's confidence.
2 Wholesalers of fastenings, plumbing fittings and so on. Anything made of metal, whether it be a bolt or a pipe joint, costs so much it must be bought to advantage, which means in bulk, from the source as near to the manufacturer as possible. Some amateur boat re-builders set up private companies so as to be sure of getting full trade discounts.
3 Tradesmen, especially fellows who can do the jobs you cannot do well yourself. If you are red hot with wood tools, the chances are you are not so good when it comes to putting in the electrics, or plumbing, or getting a good polish on the furniture. If itinerant specialists cannot be found, it is worth getting a boatyard to do the jobs you cannot do expertly, but be sure to get a full *quotation*, not just an approximate *estimate*.
4 Friends. Only the most patient and skilful re-fitter can hang a door unaided, or lift a long berth front from the interior of a car up into the cabin without chipping the edge of the woodwork. This is what friends are for.
5 Family. Friends sometimes let you down, so wives, children and grandchildren have to be cajoled into helping when all else fails.

All this planning and preparation work is needed if the finished alteration is to look right, feel right and be a success at sea. If the new work is a different colour, or is in a style contrasting with the unaltered parts of the boat's interior, the boat's value may drop and the alterations are unlikely to be a complete success. The furniture and fittings must match the unchanged parts. If the woodwork has rounded edges in the galley, but there are bevelled edges in the adjacent open plan saloon, it looks wrong. If the new drawers and lockers have chrome-plated fittings but they are bright brass elsewhere, it is not only the professionals who will be disappointed.

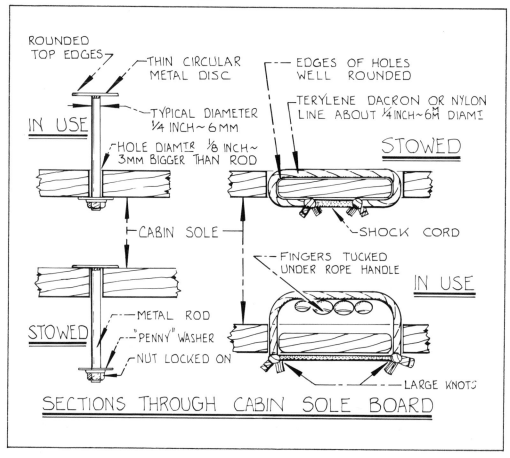

Fig. 5   To lift cabin sole boards

The two drawings on the left show a sole board lifting device found on Camper and Nicholson built boats. It lies flush, very nearly, on the sole when not in use. It is easy to pick up and gives a good grip but it should not be used on sole boards weighing more than about 50 lbs. This kind of lifter is normally used in pairs, and is usually of stainless steel.

On the right a cheap kind of sole lifter is shown, made of a short length of thin rope which is kept flat by a piece of shock cord on the under side of the board. The top sketch shows the rope recessed into the board top, but this indent is not essential. What is important is that the knots onto the shock cord are big, and if there is even a slight chance they may pull through the holes, washers should be put on the rope.

It is worth making drawings of even a simple improvement like this before you start work.

To get the whole concept right, as well as the minor parts, a full set of drawings is essential. Drawings are also needed for predicting the time and cost of the job, for listing the materials; and they also show up deficiencies in the original ideas. They will show if a berth is going to be less than 6 feet 5 inches (1.96 metres) and this matters because, although the family who own the boat may all be small, the next buyer may have a family of tall children. Other deficiencies which plans show are:

1   Lack of foot room, especially around galleys and chart tables.
2   Lack of 'put-down' space in galleys, fore cabins, toilets, etc.
3   Lack of grab-rails throughout the boat.
4   'Arm's reach' problems, such as into those distant galley lockers and down to the toilet seacocks.

Drawings should be in plan, elevation and section, to ensure there is ample headroom where it is needed. Just what constitutes headroom varies according to the size of the person involved, the size of his crew and the size and purpose of the boat. Generally speaking there must be full headroom of 6 feet 3 inches (1.91 metres) in the aft part of the saloon of a cruising boat 26 feet (8 metres) long. In a boat 30 feet (9.15 metres) long this headroom should extend to the toilet, galley and ideally over a small area of the fore cabin too. For a boat 35 feet (10.7 metres) long, the headroom should be general all over the main part of the cabin area. This is the current fashion and if a boat has less room she will be hard to sell. In pure racing boats headroom is ignored very largely, but in a racer/cruiser the same criteria apply as in cruising boats.

It is a tremendous advantage to have the original drawings of the boat when planning the new accommodation. If these are not available the first job must be to set down the hull shape in way of the cabins being changed. This involves taking a large number of vertical and horizontal measurements and transferring them onto paper. Some amateurs like to use graph paper to save a lot of work with T-square and set-square whilst others get a naval architect or draughtsman to carry out this part of the job for them.

Anyone unused to taking dozens of dimensions for making up a plan can make the job simpler by using chalk lines on the sole, on bulkheads, across the cabin deckhead – in fact right through the boat. These lines are made with sharpened chalk to keep them narrow and they are drawn parallel to such 'base-lines' as main bulkheads, the centre line of the boat and the top of the cabin sole. If a piece of structure like a bulkhead is going to be left in place during the reconstruction, some people put on lines of masking tape. Each length of tape has a base-line accurately pencilled on, which is parallel to the centreline or the waterline or the sole. Unfortunately, masking tape cannot be left on for more than 3 or 4 months or it will be hard to remove and may leave permanent marks. The edge of the tape cannot be used as a base-line because it will undulate – at least slightly.

The new plan can be based on another similar boat, or even a production boat of the same class which has a different layout. Dimensions are taken from the other boat in the same way as they are lifted from the yacht being changed.

For minimum sizes of berths, tables, galleys and so on, consult my previous books *Boat Data Book* and *Build Your Own Boat*, where there is copious information. Where possible, allow a few spare inches for comfort and to give the boat a pleasant feeling of spaciousness.

A centreline is drawn down the sole and up each bulkhead. If there is a doorway at the centreline, a batten is secured by clamps down the exact centreline. Soft padding protects the woodwork from the clamp jaws. The batten must be planed on all four long faces and one edge of the wood is located exactly on the centreline.

At equal distances down the centreline pencil marks are made and the 'distances off' are measured at each mark. These distances will be to berth fronts, berth backs, to the inside of the hull shell, to the galley front, galley outer edge, to the front and back of the sink, cooker, plate racks and so on. (This is similar to marking out a bulkhead, as detailed on page 56 of the companion book to this one, *Build Your Own Boat*. This book has many chapters relevant to changing a cabin plan.)

Using all these dimensions, a scale drawing of the new cabin plan is drawn up, modified by the owner, criticised by the crew, re-drawn several times over and then taken to the boat to see if the ideas will fit. It will probably need redrawing yet again. Because a boat is not box-like but slopes inwards, so that the beam at berth level may be less than the beam at deck level, and down at cabin sole level the beam is certainly much less, it is essential to draw athwartships sections every 3 feet (1 metre) or so, to show if there is going to be room for the proposed new layout.

When the drawing has been fixed, the interior furniture is taken out, preserving as much of the material as possible for future use. Wood parts are unscrewed or unbolted. If they are held by nails, these are carefully extracted, one by one. Fibreglass parts are separated, using an electric jig-saw with a fine-tooth blade. Plenty of spare blades are needed as more break than wear out.

Now that the cabin is empty, the plan is re-checked to confirm that everything will fit and the new locations for the furniture are marked, using pencil if the marks are on anything which will be covered later on; otherwise chalk is used since it can be rubbed off without leaving a blemish.

From now on the work is ordinary boat-building and there is a choice of techniques. Some people like to make each little part inside the boat and assemble every component as it is made, piece by piece. Others, including most professionals, use what might be described as the prefabrication approach. They make up quite large 'carcass' units such as a complete galley bench, or a settee front. It might be thought that the latter is just one or two pieces of wood, but in practice it tends to be a fairly elaborate assembly, what

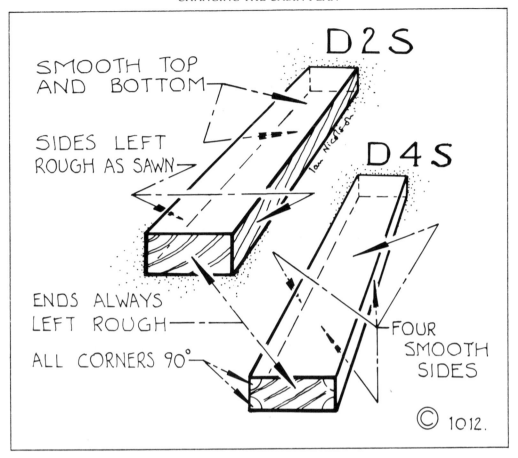

SMOOTH TOP
AND BOTTOM

D2S

SIDES LEFT
ROUGH AS SAWN

D4S

ENDS ALWAYS
LEFT ROUGH

ALL CORNERS 90°

FOUR
SMOOTH
SIDES

© 1012.

Fig. 6   Buying prepared timber

To save time and work, it is often a good idea to buy timber in planed on either two or four sides. This preparation is sometimes shortened to D2S or D4S. As much timber as possible should be bought all of the same thickness and, where possible, all of the same width, since this saves money and time.

with the vertical and horizontal stiffeners, the framing around the drawer apertures and the cleatings. Cleatings, or cleating pieces, are sometimes called fillets; they are usually of cheap soft wood and they join one part of a 'carcass' to another, or the 'carcass' will be fastened to them and the cleating in turn secured to the hull or sole, or a bulkhead. My own preference is for using rot-resistant hardwood for the cleatings and, where possible, I prefer to use offcuts of the main furniture material.

For an amateur it is almost always best to make up the furniture units at home right up to the second or third last coat of varnish or polish. This procedure means that the work can be done in the evenings during the week, leaving those limited weekend hours to get on with the work which can only be done actually on the boat.

Anyone who wants to change a cabin but feels he cannot achieve a sufficiently high standard of woodwork can get a boatyard or joinery contractor to make up the furniture units. These are made slightly too long and cut to fit inside the boat, then bolted to bulkheads and glassed in to the hull. Each carcass should be secured along at least three edges. Components have to be made small enough to get through the hatches, so it may be necessary for them to be made up in relatively long, narrow sections. They may be bolted together during the prefabrication stage so that the assembly can be checked, the drawers and locker doors fitted, and so on. Then the bolts are withdrawn, the 'carcass' dismantled into small sections and eased into the cabin for re-assembly. This sounds complex but it is better and quicker than working in the confines of a small cabin.

If a furniture contractor is used, he has to be made to swear he will never, never, use steel nails, screws or hinges. Of course his men will, so the boat owner has to re-check each furniture part all over before paying for it.

8 Extra bunks

(This chapter should be read in conjunction with Chapter 9.)

We raced all morning and we raced through the afternoon. When we crossed the finishing line we cruised to the club rendezvous far up a remote Scottish loch where normally only the curlew call disturbs the quiet. But this evening there were lots of cruisers and cruiser-racers, also a few half-deck day racers, all drifting in on the last of the evening breeze. Some used engines but on our 28 footer we enjoy the difficulties of working into a crowded anchorage, finding a good spot and letting the anchor go in just the right place all under sail. So we crept into the bay, weaving in and out of the moored craft, while our friends called across from other boats.

Each year two clubs race to this rendezvous on a summer Saturday for a Sunday of rowing races, dinghy tug-of-war competitions, sailboard racing and other inter-club rivalry. Some of the boats are not cruisers with cabins, just semi-open boats. A few have boom tents, some have no cover over the 'sleeping area' at all, so if it rains – and in Scotland rain is a speciality – the sleepers may get a little damp.

As our anchor went over, the heavens opened and torrents of rain came down. It went on, hour after hour. Later one of our crew put on oilskins and rowed around the fleet of open boats, collecting friends. The dinghy came back laden and when it was time to turn in, we covered the cabin sole with the driest of our sails, put oilskins on top, pounded the whole lot down into a fairly even cabin-wide mattress and that is how we turned our five-berth cruiser into an eight-berth boat.

There is no doubt that the cabin sole makes one of the best spare berths. I've got through long bad gales far offshore by putting a settee cushion on the sole and sleeping moderately comfortably for days. The sole is a cheap spare berth and, if it is softened by an inflatable mattress or even one of those semi-soft thin plastic 'bed-rolls' which campers use, it is not too rugged; except for arthritic seamen.

For a more comfortable berth and one which does not obstruct the passage through the boat, settee backs can be converted so that they swing up to form upper berths. There has to be sufficient height under the deckhead to allow this. Most people agree 2 foot 3 inches (675 mm) is the minimum. The existing backrest is removed together with any panelling or lockers which may be in the way. The berth can be made up in the form of a shallow box with no lid. The box sides are lower than the cushion is thick, for comfort; otherwise when anyone sitting on the settee leans back, he will find the edge of the wood will

43

dig in and anyone sleeping on the upper berth will suffer bruising from the box sides when rolling over in the night. The outboard edge of the box, which also forms the top edge of the backrest, is strongly hinged to a stiffened shelf which in turn is well secured to the hull. Though even a heavy man only weighs about 200 lbs, he puts a greater load than this if he heaves himself up into the bunk with a jerk. Also all the load may come at one corner of the berth,

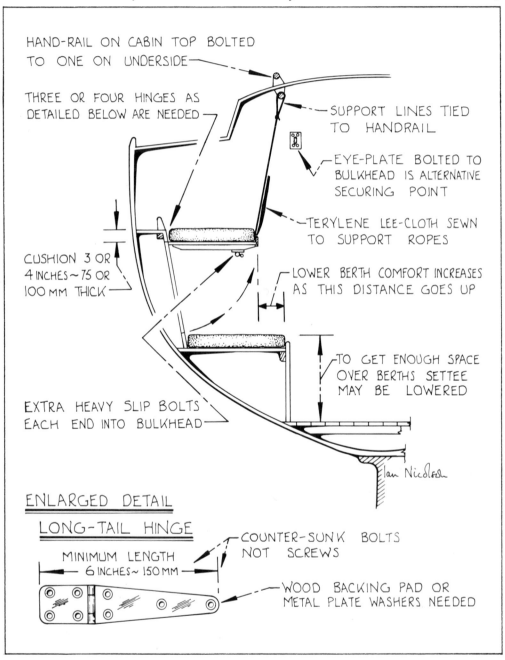

HAND-RAIL ON CABIN TOP BOLTED TO ONE ON UNDERSIDE

THREE OR FOUR HINGES AS DETAILED BELOW ARE NEEDED

SUPPORT LINES TIED TO HANDRAIL

EYE-PLATE BOLTED TO BULKHEAD IS ALTERNATIVE SECURING POINT

TERYLENE LEE-CLOTH SEWN TO SUPPORT ROPES

CUSHION 3 OR 4 INCHES ~ 75 OR 100 MM THICK

LOWER BERTH COMFORT INCREASES AS THIS DISTANCE GOES UP

TO GET ENOUGH SPACE OVER BERTHS SETTEE MAY BE LOWERED

EXTRA HEAVY SLIP BOLTS EACH END INTO BULKHEAD

Ian Nicolson

ENLARGED DETAIL

LONG-TAIL HINGE

MINIMUM LENGTH 6 INCHES ~ 150 MM

COUNTER-SUNK BOLTS NOT SCREWS

WOOD BACKING PAD OR METAL PLATE WASHERS NEEDED

so the hinges should be secured with bolts. The inboard edge is supported by slip bolts or ropes. It may be necessary to fit a step or two under the berth and a grab-handle over it to help older people to get into the berth. This applies to any high berth.

As a general rule, all berths should be made 6 feet 5 inches (1.96 metres) long, but it is unlikely that everyone on a four berth boat will be that tall, so on some craft there are three full length berths and one only 6 feet (1.85 metres) long. On old boats a berth or two 5 feet 10 inches (1.78 metres) may be found, but with the average height of the population increasing, this is no longer acceptable.

To gain an extra sleeping place, a settee can be turned into a double berth. One way to do this is to have a hinged flap on the inboard edge of the settee. The flap is like a table leaf and when up is held up by supports on the under side. The cushion may be portable or fixed to the flap, but the latter is obtrusive when the flap is folded down and the settee used as a seat.

Another technique is to have a portable extension to the settee which bolts or clips into place. This movable part is stowed in the fo'c's'le or some other place where it will not be in the way. Alternatively, a sliding extension which pulls out from under the settee cushion can be fitted. This needs supports, which may be portable legs or ropes taken from eyeplates on the cabin top, or ropes from eyeplates bolted to the adjacent bulkheads.

Whichever form the extension takes, it is a good idea to make it up in the form of a shallow box as this gives the required rigidity. A flat sheet of ply is not satisfactory as a berth extension because it will bend and twist too much as the sleeper climbs in and lies down. The box bottom will be the berth base and this will often be of ½ inch (12 mm) marine ply or, to save money, exterior grade ply.

The sides and ends of the box will be of hardwood which will seldom be less than 2½ inches × ⅝ inches (65 mm × 15 mm) in section. All joins must be screwed and glued because stiffness is needed here. Some builders save the high cost of plywood by going for ⁵⁄₁₆ inch (8 mm) ply with stiffening battens glued to it at 15 inch (375 mm) intervals. If ever there was a place where epoxy glues should be used, this is it. Anyone who has crashed to the floor out of a high berth will know how bruising it can be.

◁   *Fig. 7 Using a settee backrest as an upper berth*

A backrest may be designed to hinge up into the horizontal position to form a berth. When anyone is climbing into this upper berth it is likely that much of his weight will come on one corner and therefore all the supports of the berth must be extra strong. For this reason there should be three, and better still four, bolted hinges. The inboard side of the berth may be supported by slip bolts into bulkheads. Alternatively there may be support ropes, similar to those which hold up cot berths. Sometimes a combination of support ropes and slip bolts is used. If the berth is to be used when the yacht is sailing, it can be a great advantage if the angle of the berth is adjustable to suit the angle of heel. In any case there should be a lee cloth for it is most uncomfortable to fall out of a high berth and not much fun for the person below!

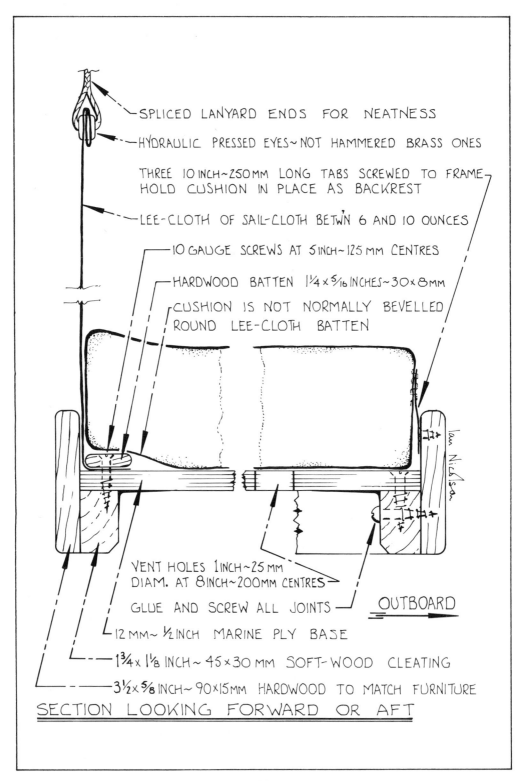

SPLICED LANYARD ENDS FOR NEATNESS

HYDRAULIC PRESSED EYES~NOT HAMMERED BRASS ONES

THREE 10 INCH~250MM LONG TABS SCREWED TO FRAME HOLD CUSHION IN PLACE AS BACKREST

LEE-CLOTH OF SAIL-CLOTH BETW'N 6 AND 10 OUNCES

10 GAUGE SCREWS AT 5INCH~125 MM CENTRES

HARDWOOD BATTEN 1¼ × 5/16 INCHES~30×8MM

CUSHION IS NOT NORMALLY BEVELLED ROUND LEE-CLOTH BATTEN

VENT HOLES 1INCH~25 MM DIAM. AT 8INCH~200MM CENTRES

GLUE AND SCREW ALL JOINTS

OUTBOARD

12MM~½INCH MARINE PLY BASE

1¾ × 1⅛ INCH ~ 45×30 MM SOFT-WOOD CLEATING

3½ × 5/8 INCH ~ 90×15MM HARDWOOD TO MATCH FURNITURE

SECTION LOOKING FORWARD OR AFT

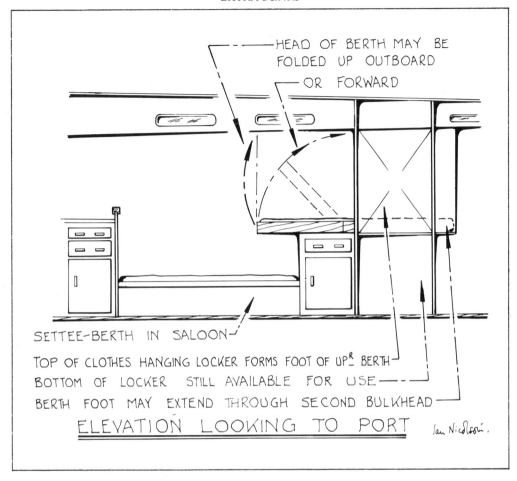

HEAD OF BERTH MAY BE
FOLDED UP OUTBOARD
OR FORWARD

SETTEE-BERTH IN SALOON

TOP OF CLOTHES HANGING LOCKER FORMS FOOT OF UP^R BERTH

BOTTOM OF LOCKER STILL AVAILABLE FOR USE

BERTH FOOT MAY EXTEND THROUGH SECOND BULKHEAD

ELEVATION LOOKING TO PORT   Ian Nicolson.

Fig. 9   Fitting an extra berth in the saloon

There are lots of clever ways of fitting in extra berths. Just one is shown here; the space above the side-board is 'stolen' and a folding shelf (with deep fiddle to retain the mattress cushion) fitted over it. This forms the head of the berth. The foot is a box in the top of what was a clothes hanging locker and, though it is not shown in the drawing, this might still be used for clothes. Either the lower part can be fitted with coat-hooks, or the berth can be hinged up, to allow clothes to be hung in the locker until the berth is needed.

◁   *Fig. 8   Hinged-up backrest forms berth*

To make an upper berth, a piece of plywood of the correct size is framed all round, the outer parts of the framing matching the other furniture in the cabin. The whole assembly must be glued and screwed together so that it is very strong. For comfort, the frame does not extend right to the upper surface of the cushion which forms the backrest when hinged down and the mattress when hinged up.

It is important to have separate slip bolts or suspension straps for the berth and not use the leeboard lanyards for holding the berth up in position. Also the cushion must be secured in place, otherwise it will fall out when it forms a backrest and when the boat heels.

Other places where extra berths can be worked in are:

1   Over the chart table, possibly with the end of the berth extending over a settee, or into an oilskin locker.
2   Over the top of a sideboard with the foot extending through a bulkhead into an adjacent toilet compartment.
3   Partly in the cabin with the foot extending into a cockpit locker which has to be sealed off in a watertight way.
4   Out in the open on a cockpit seat, possibly with boards to widen or lengthen the seat, with a cockpit tent over.
5   On deck located where there is not too much camber and where necessary with precautions to prevent falling overboard when asleep, even if this is only a safety harness with a short lead.

If all else fails and it seems impossible to work in an extra berth in the available cabin space, there are several tricks worth trying. The first is to inspect sister ships and similar craft to see their cabin layouts, and note where they have their berths. Some boats have sail lockers quite big enough for a bunk, but it can be hard to work in the required ventilation. One has to remember that in spite of appearances to the contrary, tough young crews need oxygen as well as beer to survive.

Another way to find a place for the extra berth is to get a naval architect or yacht yard manager or draughtsman, or a yacht surveyor to look over the boat and make suggestions. These people spend their lives in and around boats and they are used to seeing clever arrangements and subtle contrivances for achieving the basic 6 feet 5 inches × 1 foot 10 inches (1.9 metres × 0.56 metres) needed for a night's rest.

Once an area has been selected, it is often necessary to cut an aperture through a bulkhead. The first job is to remove all fittings, obstructions, decorations, clocks, barometers, shelves, panelling, everything which is portable or unscrewable. The shape to be cut out is marked lightly, using a sharpened chalk because this is easily brushed off if a mistake is made. The chalk has to be sharpened, otherwise the line will be too thick. By measuring to the nearest doorway, across the boat, and down to the cabin sole, the vertical and horizontal distances of the shape to be cut out are established and marked on the opposite side of the bulkhead. A critical look is now taken at the proposed modification. How will it affect other parts of the furniture? Will important lockers be lost? Will the oilskins have to be found a new home? Will the man sitting on the toilet be able to lean back? All these are the sort of questions which have to be asked.

Once the proposed shape of the cut-out has been marked on both sides of the bulkhead, holes are drilled at each corner, using a bit about $\frac{1}{16}$ inch (1 mm) diameter. This size of hole is easily plugged and hidden if a mistake has been made. If all is well, the holes are enlarged for a jig-saw and the piece is cut out of the bulkhead, then the berth built on each side. It is usual, but not universal, for a berth foot which obtrudes into a toilet space or hanging locker, or over a chart table, to be boxed in. This is partly for neatness, partly because the box is so handy for stowing bedding. It should be well made and sealed against drips. It is known in some circles as a 'trotter box' because pigs' feet are trotters.

When making a berth, or indeed any piece of furniture, it is worth making a rough pattern of scrap wood. This helps with ordering the new materials but more important, it provides a chance to see what the alterations will be like in place before the change is made.

If the berth is in two compartments, it will almost certainly be necessary to make up the two parts separately. Suppose the bulkhead at the aft end of the main cabin is being pierced and a new berth extending under a cockpit seat is being formed:

1   The requisite hole through the bulkhead is cut.
2   Battens are laid through the hole on the inboard and outboard sides, so that the edges of the berth can be marked on the ship's side etc. These battens must be carefully levelled up, or the final berth will not be exactly horizontal.
3   If the area under the cockpit has a locker lid over it, this is removed until the berth has been completely made. When the job is finished the lid is bolted down with ample sealing or bedding all round to keep out water.
4   With the long battens as guides, the length and width of each part of the berth is measured and rough templates are made up.
5   The patterns are tried in place and wood chocks are glassed to the hull sides as supports. Typically these chocks will be 8 inches (200 mm) long with 6 inch (150 mm) gaps between, each chock being about 1 inch (25 mm) thick and extending down the hull 2 or 3 inches. Four layers of 1½ oz chopped strand mat hold these chocks along the sides and bottom. There is no glassing along the top because the pattern is in the way. To prevent the pattern being glassed in accidentally there is polythene sheeting on it.
6   The patterns are lifted out and the berth base parts are made up to the same shape. If in doubt, add stiffeners to the base parts. These should be deep rather than wide, say 2 inches vertically × ¾ inches (50 mm × 20 mm) and spaced less than 15 inches (375 mm) apart. The base parts are glassed in, provided that in future it is easy to get at the spaces beneath for cleaning, drying out – or, *crisis of crises* plugging a serious leak.
7   If the parts have to be lifted out for access, finger holes 1 inch (25 mm) diameter are made about 6 inches (150 mm) from each corner. Additional holes at about 8 inch (200 mm) centres staggered are made if there is a risk of water accumulating under the cushion from condensation or drips through a hatch.
8   The part of the berth under the cockpit is glassed to the vertical side of the

cockpit well, and also onto the side of the boat. Typically, 4 runs of 1½ oz chopped strand mat 8 inches (200 mm) wide is used here. Glass in the bottom end too. If the end does not come up against a bulkhead or the transom, it will be necessary to either put in a bulkhead, or form a barrier across the end of the berth to prevent the mattress and blankets from slipping off the end.

9   The forward end of the berth which is in the cabin is made next. Its inboard edge will be made up like any berth, with a wood leeboard which must match the rest of the furniture. The forward edge may be lodged on a partial bulkhead or onto a piece of furniture.

10   If a berth is to be joined to a piece of furniture which is not very strong, additional strengthening is put in. If in doubt, add stiffeners because they take little making, whereas a splintered galley side will not be mended in half an hour. Typical stiffeners are 1½ inch × 1½ inch (40 mm × 40 mm) spaced about 7 inches (175 mm) apart and secured with ¼ inch (6 mm) diameter bolts at 6 inch (150 mm) centres. If the stiffeners are inside the furniture unit, they can often be glued as the internal wood is commonly untreated. On the outside, however, there will be a polish, or varnish, or a plastic such as Formica, which will make the glue at least partly ineffective. If in doubt, put the stiffeners on horizontally *and* vertically, but normally vertical ones are all that are needed.

11   The final job is to make the heavy paper patterns, for the cushions.

12   Sleep well!

=9 *An extra cot in the fo'c's'le*=

(This chapter should be read in conjunction with Chapter 8.)

The forward cabin or fo'c's'le of most boats is a narrow, tapering compartment used mainly for sleeping. Because it is so far forward, it is uncomfortable at sea and so the berths here tend to be used mainly when the boat is in port. Even so, the berths need lee-boards to prevent sleepers from falling out if a vessel under power goes storming past and causes frantic rolling. Besides, if a berth is made with a lee-board it can be narrower, so it can be squeezed in where a full width bunk will not fit.

Even if there are already two berths in the fo'c's'le, it is often possible to fit in at least one more and sometimes two.This can be done by having the upper berths within about 2 feet 3 inches (675 mm) of the deckhead. This height may not look very comfortable but it gives room to turn over in the night and that is all that is needed. (If anyone complains that he cannot sleep aboard, tell him it is obvious who has not been doing a fair share of washing up, cleaning, winch work, and so on.)

If a berth is diagonally over a lower one, so that only the foot of the upper berth extends over the lower, the distance between the berths can be reduced to 16 inches (400 mm) since that is enough for the sleeper on the bottom berth to turn his feet over. On beamy boats it is therefore possible to have a pair of lower berths set well inboard with perhaps 2 feet (600 mm) between them and the upper berths angled further outboard at the head, with 6 feet (1.8 metres) between them at the head end.

There are two types of cot berth: the true cot which is an all-round metal frame (roughly rectangular in plan) with canvas stretched across it, and the Root berth which has a metal tube down each side, but none at each end. The Root berth tubes are slid into seams down the sides of a long strip of canvas or Terylene, or similar strong cloth. Both tubes are supported at the ends by wood chocks with slots, or metal sockets, or notches in the tops of partial bulkheads, or similar devices. The outboard edge may not have a tube, but instead may be a wooden batten screwed or bolted to structure on the ship's side or a piece of furniture, or a tough shelf.

The base of the cot may not be of canvas because it mildews, so many people prefer a man-made cloth. Another choice is strong, non-stretch leather-cloth to give an easily cleaned surface and a smart appearance. There is also new-style canvas made from a synthetic material which looks traditional and is wonderfully strong, also rot-proof. Nowadays most people like a coloured cloth, not just because it shows the dirt less, but also because it makes the inside of the boat more cheerful and even luxurious . . . or at least less 'grotty'.

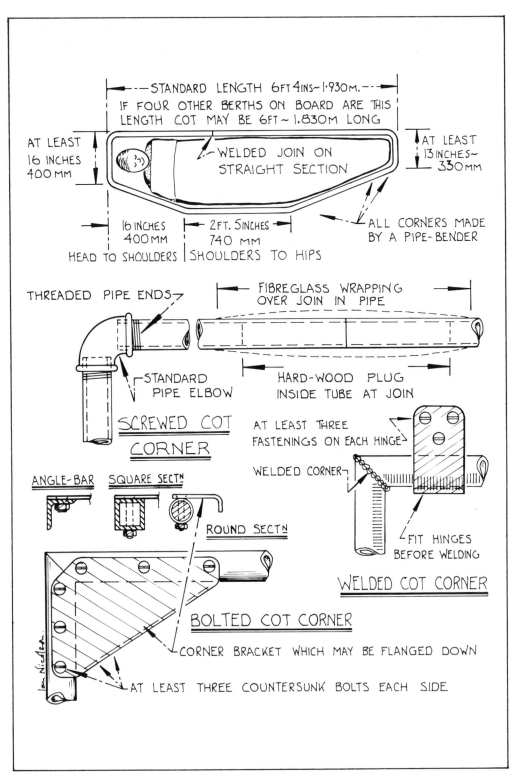

STANDARD LENGTH 6FT 4INS ~ 1·930M.

IF FOUR OTHER BERTHS ON BOARD ARE THIS LENGTH COT MAY BE 6FT ~ 1·830M LONG

WELDED JOIN ON STRAIGHT SECTION

AT LEAST 16 INCHES 400 MM

AT LEAST 13 INCHES ~ 330 MM

16 INCHES 400 MM
HEAD TO SHOULDERS

2 FT. 5 INCHES 740 MM
SHOULDERS TO HIPS

ALL CORNERS MADE BY A PIPE-BENDER

THREADED PIPE ENDS

FIBREGLASS WRAPPING OVER JOIN IN PIPE

STANDARD PIPE ELBOW

HARD-WOOD PLUG INSIDE TUBE AT JOIN

SCREWED COT CORNER

AT LEAST THREE FASTENINGS ON EACH HINGE

WELDED CORNER

FIT HINGES BEFORE WELDING

WELDED COT CORNER

ANGLE-BAR   SQUARE SECTN

ROUND SECTN

BOLTED COT CORNER

CORNER BRACKET WHICH MAY BE FLANGED DOWN

AT LEAST THREE COUNTERSUNK BOLTS EACH SIDE

The advantages of a cot are:

1   It is cheap and easy to make even with limited facilities (see sketch).
2   It can be made off the boat and carried aboard easily. For cleaning out or painting the inside of the boat it is easily taken ashore.
3   It can be used without a cushion which saves money and weight aboard; in practice most people like at least a 1 inch (25 mm) thick foam plastic cushion, or one of the bed-roll type of thin mattresses.
4   It can be swung up against the ship's side when not in use and this gives access to sail stowage bins, or the toilet, or a work bench.
5   The angle of the berth can be adjusted to suit the angle of heel of a boat going to windward. With proper gear, the berth angle can be altered up or down by someone already in the berth.
6   If the boat is dismasted, the tubes can be used as part of a jury rig.

A Root berth had all these advantages except 5, and now we have designed a gadget to adjust the end supports of the inboard tube without climbing out of the bunk. In addition, a Root berth is easier to get in and out of a cramped cabin since, when dismantled, it consists of just two straight tubes, whereas a cot is a roughly rectangular frame.

Whatever type of berth is favoured, it always makes sense to assemble a rough pattern so that the exact length and width and taper towards the foot is established by trial and error right inside the cabin where the cot will be. Also the precise height below the deckhead, or above the cabin sole, sometimes matters a great deal. With a mock-up of the berth this height can be fixed by thoughtful consideration and with the help of crew members who may have to use the berths. When the precise size and location have been fixed, the full-size pattern is eased out through the doorway and main hatch – provided it fits.

It has to be admitted that a cot in the fo'c's'le can be very uncomfortable if it is not well planned. A principal source of discomfort is the tilt of the berth fore and aft. If the fitting is done when the boat is ashore, it is probable that when the boat goes afloat the berth will be found to be too high at the head or foot. It is no good fitting the berth parallel with the cabin sole because that could be slightly sloped. It is just as useless to set the berth at right angles to a bulkhead, because it may well be slightly out of plumb.

◁   *Fig. 10   Cot berth fabrication*

Cot berths are usually made from steel or aluminium alloy tube, although they could be made from wood or heavy duty plastic tubing. If made from metal tubing, the neatest way of forming the cot is to bend each corner, using an ordinary pipe bending tool. If this is not available, plumbers' standard elbows can be bought, together with threaded pipe which is screwed into each elbow. The final join is made by inserting a hardwood plug on a straight section of the piping and binding this with wrappings of fibreglass tape.

Where welding facilities are available, but no pipe bender, each corner can be welded up. As a last resort, for anyone very short of facilities, the sketch at the bottom of the left-hand side shows how a simple corner bracket can be made up and each corner bolted together.

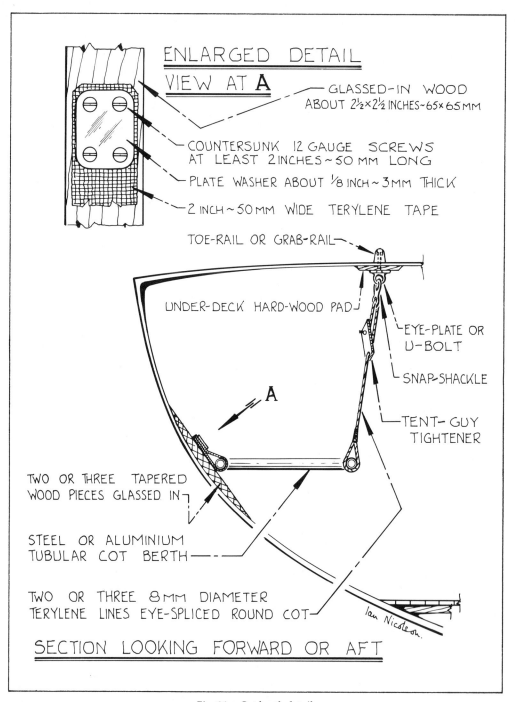

ENLARGED DETAIL
VIEW AT **A**

— GLASSED-IN WOOD
ABOUT 2½×2½ INCHES~65×65MM

— COUNTERSUNK 12 GAUGE SCREWS
AT LEAST 2 INCHES~50 MM LONG

— PLATE WASHER ABOUT ⅛ INCH~3MM THICK

— 2 INCH~50MM WIDE TERYLENE TAPE

TOE-RAIL OR GRAB-RAIL

UNDER-DECK HARD-WOOD PAD

EYE-PLATE OR
U-BOLT

SNAP-SHACKLE

TENT-GUY
TIGHTENER

A

TWO OR THREE TAPERED
WOOD PIECES GLASSED IN

STEEL OR ALUMINIUM
TUBULAR COT BERTH

TWO OR THREE 8MM DIAMETER
TERYLENE LINES EYE-SPLICED ROUND COT

Ian Nicolson.

SECTION LOOKING FORWARD OR AFT

Fig. 11 Cot berth details

The type of Terylene webbing used for dinghy toe straps makes good hinges for cot berths, provided it is well secured. The detail at the top shows how at least four screws with a washer plate at least 2 inches (50 mm) long are used. It is best to have three of these hinges, although two are acceptable, even if they are at the extreme end of the cot. The inboard side of the cot is usually supported by two ropes, although three are to be preferred. They are adjustable so that any stretch can be taken up. In this drawing the supporting lines are clipped onto eye-plates bolted through the main deck and to disguise the bolts, as well as spread the load, there is a toerail or handrail on deck.

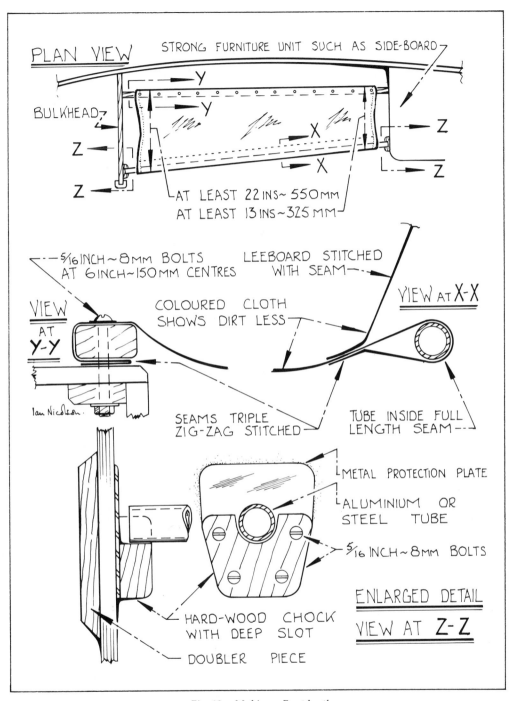

PLAN VIEW   STRONG FURNITURE UNIT SUCH AS SIDE-BOARD

BULKHEAD

AT LEAST 22 INS ~ 550 mm
AT LEAST 13 INS ~ 325 mm

⁵/₁₆ INCH ~ 8 mm BOLTS   LEEBOARD STITCHED
AT 6 INCH ~ 150 mm CENTRES   WITH SEAM

VIEW AT X-X

VIEW AT Y-Y

COLOURED CLOTH
SHOWS DIRT LESS

Ian Nicolson.

SEAMS TRIPLE
ZIG-ZAG STITCHED

TUBE INSIDE FULL
LENGTH SEAM

METAL PROTECTION PLATE

ALUMINIUM OR
STEEL TUBE

⁵/₁₆ INCH ~ 8 mm BOLTS

ENLARGED DETAIL
VIEW AT Z-Z

HARD-WOOD CHOCK
WITH DEEP SLOT

DOUBLER PIECE

Fig. 12   Making a Root berth

The berth shown here is secured along the outside by a wood batten, but it could have a metal tube in a sleeve, as on the inboard side. If two tubes are used the whole berth is portable and can be stowed in the fo'c's'le when not in use. Though no mattress is shown, one will make the berth more comfortable, and it need only be 1 inch (25 mm) thick. The base cloth must be rugged and strongly sewn with seams at the ends as well as each side. Chocks on the inboard side at different heights may be arranged so that the berth can be tilted for different angles of heel.

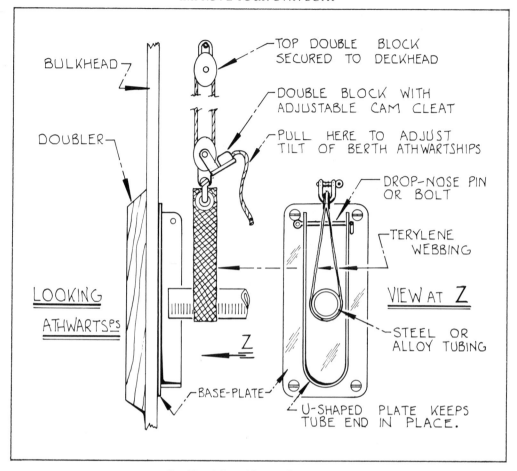

BULKHEAD

DOUBLER

LOOKING
ATHWARTS.P.S

TOP DOUBLE BLOCK
SECURED TO DECKHEAD

DOUBLE BLOCK WITH
ADJUSTABLE CAM CLEAT

PULL HERE TO ADJUST
TILT OF BERTH ATHWARTSHIPS

DROP-NOSE PIN
OR BOLT

TERYLENE
WEBBING

VIEW AT Z

STEEL OR
ALLOY TUBING

BASE-PLATE

U-SHAPED PLATE KEEPS
TUBE END IN PLACE.

Z

Fig. 13   Adjustable Root berth support
The inboard tube of a Root berth can be lowered or raised by the person in the berth, to keep the
berth level when the boat heels. This arrangement can also be used on a cot berth. An adjusting
tackle is needed at each end of the berth and a common small dinghy mainsheet tackle complete
with cam cleat is all that is needed. It is shackled to a length of toe-strap webbing which has a
strong eye each end. To stop the tube going too far down, if for instance the rope came out of the
cam cleat, there is a metal channel closed at the bottom. The top of the channel is blocked off with
a big split pin or bolt so that the crew cannot accidentally hoist the tube too high. The metal
channel stops the tube from moving outboard as would happen if there was no restraint.

When fitting a cot the choice is to fix one outboard support only and wait
until the boat is afloat before securing the other, or establish the boat at the
correct level by jacking her up. If she cannot be raised with a jack or two,
wedges driven in under the keel will raise her slowly. In *Build Your Own Boat*
there are details of how the job is done. Once the boat is level, the berth is
adjusted relative to the boat using a spirit level. This should be used on both
the inboard and outboard tubes of cots and Root berths.

A cot berth can be slung from metal hooks or Terylene straps screwed to
chocks which in turn are glassed onto the ship's side. Alternatively the

supports can be screwed to a strong shelf or even a lining which is massively reinforced and properly backed up. The screws need to be 2 inches (50 mm) long and buried fully in hardwood to carry the load of a cot. Just occasionally a cot is supported by wood chocks with deep grooves in the top, as for a Root berth.

When it comes to making up a cot or Root berth, the metal-work can be done by a garage or small steel fabricating shop. Some mast-makers will make up an aluminium cot if short of other work. If steel is used, it should be galvanised, but where this is impossible the metal should be burnished bright and fully treated with paint, preferably the epoxy sort. Even if galvanising is used, it is best to put paint on top.

If aluminium tube is used, it should be the seawater resisting type and ideally should be anodised. If anodising is not feasible, or if the aluminium is not the type which can stand up to salt water, then a full paint treatment should be applied.

One advantage of tubing is that it is available in so many thicknesses and diameters. Traditionally, cots were made of standard 1 inch (25 mm) so-called gas piping, but anything close will do, like heavy gauge ¾ inch (20 mm) diameter steel tube, though each rope or hinge support must be about one quarter of the berth length from the end.

For Root berths, 2 inch (50 mm) alloy tube is popular and aluminium scaffold poles have been seen on many boats. I understand quite a lot of them were not stolen from building sites!

10 *Nets . . . for safety*
and stowage

When ordering a net, four dimensions are needed. The first is the mesh size, which is the distance across the square holes which form the nets. When measuring an existing net, it is important to spread it out flat with no tension, otherwise the meshes will be elongated or made diamond shaped and cannot be accurately measured.

The second dimension is the thickness of the twine or rope or cord which makes up the net. This dimension is measured in millimetres. As a rough guide, 3 mm = ⅛ inch. Note that the *diameter* of the line is measured nowadays, but not so long ago it was the circumference.

The other two dimensions are the length and the width of the complete net. Here again, when measuring a net it is essential it is laid flat and not pulled out even slightly. A characteristic of all netting is that it is marvellously stretchy and this can be a great advantage on occasions . . . at other times it is a considerable nuisance.

Netting is in many ways an ideal material for use afloat. It is cheap and light, it encourages ventilation and it dries quickly. It does not matter if it gets wet, provided it is of man-made material, and it is easy to work. Its limitations are its stretchiness and its – shall we say – its 'nettiness'.

Net leeboards

For instance, in some ways it is great as berth leeboards, especially for a long quarter-berth where a cloth leeboard prevents the sleeper getting a good flow of air to breathe. Some sleepers find that they wake up with a headache in that long type of quarter-berth where there is a tendency for air to get breathed twenty times a night by the sleeper. A leeboard of netting would seem exactly right here, but there are snags. A quarter-berth is close to the main hatch and a PVC or Terylene leeboard will keep splashes off the sleeper. Also a net leeboard which extends right up to the pillow is uncomfortably rough against the cheek and nose, whereas a cloth one is tolerable.

For a leeboard, a net of between ¼ and 1 inch (6 and 25 mm) mesh size should be selected. The leeboard should extend at least 16 inches (400 mm) above the top of the berth cushion. Most people like the comfort of a leeboard which reaches from shoulder level down to the very bottom of the berth, but the last 18 inches (450 mm) should perhaps be left open so that anyone turning in can sit on the end of the berth to undress. A net leeboard needs four (better still, five) lashings extending upwards unless there is a tough wood or fibreglass batten along the top, in which case three lashings may be enough.

Netting for stowage

The principal use of netting below decks is for stowage. The usual technique is to fix the netting strongly along one edge, using a batten. The two sides

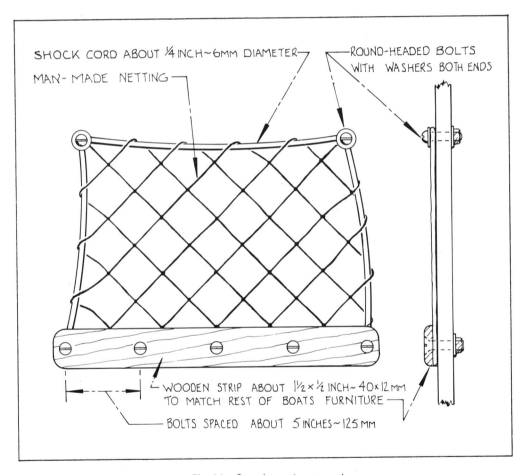

SHOCK CORD ABOUT ¼ INCH~6MM DIAMETER

ROUND-HEADED BOLTS WITH WASHERS BOTH ENDS

MAN-MADE NETTING

WOODEN STRIP ABOUT 1½ × ½ INCH~ 40×12 MM TO MATCH REST OF BOATS FURNITURE

BOLTS SPACED ABOUT 5 INCHES~125 MM

Fig. 14 Securing a stowage net

Some people screw in cup hooks, one row for the top of the net and one for the bottom and consider this to be adequate for fixing a stowage net to a boat. In practice the cup hooks are seldom strong enough and they project in a most inconvenient way. Shown here is the correct way of fixing a stowage net, with a strong batten along the bottom. This will not fail even if the net is overloaded. If the net is very long then two bolts at the top will not be enough and there will be intermediate ones located perhaps every 18 inches (500 mm). In the same way there may be additional bolts down the side.

lightly fixed, or maybe not secured at all, and the edge which might be labelled the entrance or opening has a piece of shock-cord threaded through it. Sometimes the shock-cord extends up the sides.

This type of stowage suits clothes (which should be encased in watertight bags), small items like flashlights, flares, the box containing the first aid kit, spare dry batteries in polythene bags and so on. Anything stowed behind a net is easy to see, which is why this is a good way to keep safety gear.

Netting is no good for some heavy weights. For instance, it is no good fixing a net up against the yacht's side in the fo'c's'le and putting an anchor behind it. When the boat heels with the anchor on the 'up-hill side' the net will stretch and the anchor flop away from the hull, only to bang back as the boat goes round on the other tack. Nor is it a good idea to stow things like safety harnesses and coiled rope behind netting – the end result is a jumble and a tangle.

Netting is often fixed up under the deckhead. It is useful over a bunk for holding clothes taken off before climbing into the sleeping bag. A net secured just inside the cabin entrance is handy for things like flash-lights. A net on the topsides beside the chart table will hold the books which will not fit into the adjacent book rack. For this sort of job, netting with a mesh size of about ⅜ to ¾ inch (10 to 20 mm) with a cord diameter of around 1/16 inch (1 mm) works well.

Above the chart table it is handy to have a net to take notebooks and the kind of chart which folds up like a map. In a crisis the same stowage can be used for a rolled-up chart which will be put away in its proper place later.

Netting on deck

Nets are used on deck particularly to keep headsails from going overboard after lowering. Usually the netting is fixed to the top lifeline and the toerail; it extends from the pulpit back to the second stanchion and further aft on large craft. The mesh size is often as large as 9 inches (225 mm) and the line size about ⅛ inch (3 mm). Ideally the two guardrail wires are threaded in and out through the top and middle of the netting, but in practice this is seldom convenient so there has to be a lashing at each hole. Naturally, the netting is on the inboard side of the stanchions and the middle wire, if the latter is not woven through the netting.

Boats with young children on board sometimes have netting right round the decks for safety. The size which suits a racing boat's fore deck is too big for this purpose because a 9 inch mesh pushed outwards by little hands may be big enough for a child to squeeze through. The mesh size has to be down to about 2 inches (50 mm) to be totally safe and the line diameter will be almost ⅛ inch (2 mm).

All nets on deck must be of Terylene or nylon, otherwise there is a risk of rotting and sudden unexpected failure.

Where a net is extended right round the deck to keep children aboard, there must be a portable section forward for getting anchors back aboard. On a cruiser, netting may be fitted if the guardrail wires are so far apart vertically that there is a risk that one of the crew may go between them in extreme conditions. This is the sort of safety device seen more on ocean cruisers than craft used for weekending.

11 *Making and fitting a*
book rack

The standard sizes of books are given in *Boat Data Book*, like so much basic information needed when making or mending anything on a boat. For anyone whose copy of *Boat Data Book* has been stolen, the dimensions of large books are about 11¾ inches (300 mm) high by 8½ inches (215 mm) deep and, on average, 1½ inches (38 mm) thick. Some are fatter and some thinner, however, for 10 books it is safe to allow 15 inches (380 mm). Paperbacks are about 7¼ inches (185 mm) in height, 4½ inches (115 mm) in depth and have an average thickness of ⅝ inch (16 mm). This does not take into account those very fat sagas.

The fiddle to keep the books in the case when the boat heels has to be above the half height of the books, so it is usual to have one low fiddle at the base of the books, perhaps one inch (25 mm) high and a second portable fiddle

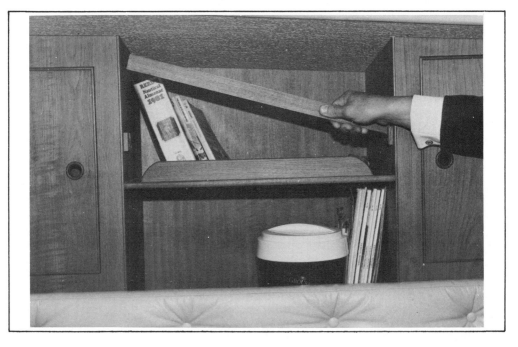

Most bookshelves have a simple lift-out top fiddle which rests in a recessed chock at each end. At the bottom there is a normal fiddle with a gap at each end to make it easy to clean the shelf. The bookshelf between two lockers has a magazine shelf below, with the settee backrest forming the fiddle which keeps the magazines in place.

three-quarters of the way up the average book height. There is no way of arranging the higher fiddle so that it does not obstruct the view of *some* of the titles on the spines of the books. A perspex fiddle can be used, but light reflecting off it makes it impossible to read the titles much of the time.

Looking around the cabins, it is usually obvious that there is not a lot of choice when it comes to locating an extra bookshelf. Books do not like drips, so they cannot be near a hatch or ventilator. An opening port above a row of books is almost certainly going to mean soggy reading sooner or later. Usual places for books are:

Alongside the chart table.
Outboard of the settees.
On the forward bulkhead of the saloon, right up high.
Outboard of the quarter berths and forward berths.
Over the ends of berths, extending athwartships.
Over the tops of hanging lockers.

Flat book holders, sometimes called 'magazine boxes' can be worked into quite small spaces and, even though it is hard to read the book titles, they are useful, especially in very small boats and for retaining specialist books for particular jobs. For instance, a flat holder near the galley for cookery books and another alongside the navigator's seat for his witchcraft, are most handy. Yet another in the toilet and even one by the engine (for machinery manuals) are useful.

It is almost always best to assemble a book rack off the boat and make it a self-contained unit so that it can be taken ashore every other winter for cleaning and varnishing or polishing. It should be made up in the form of a box with no top and be tough enough to stand up to the hurly-burly of life afloat. In one of those sick-making lurches when the boat goes off the top of a wave and there is nothing but a wide open hole the other side, someone is going to grab the bookcase because it is the only thing close by. If he ends up with a handful of splintered wood and a broken arm, the effective crew will be reduced by one, and this is especially inconvenient for anyone sailing single-handed.

The wood thickness should be ⅝ inch (15 mm) for most purposes, though on a racing boat where weight-saving is so critical ⅛ inch (3 mm) ply may be used with suitable edge stiffeners. Of course, the really ruthless weight-saver would make his bookcase up out of Terylene sailcloth sewn into a flat box shape, perhaps with a transparent plastic front. This book container will be like other 'furniture' made from cloth, secured to a bulkhead by rows of screws through battens.

When wood is used it should match the rest of the cabin furniture. Where this is inconvenient, a contrasting wood may be used, or the wood should be bleached and stained to accord with the cabin decoration. If there are difficulties getting things to match, it sometimes makes sense to take a completely different approach. For instance, a bookcase by the chart table can be painted to match the adjacent radios, or be made up of polished aluminium, because this fits in with the gadgetry round the navigator's nest. A bookcase in

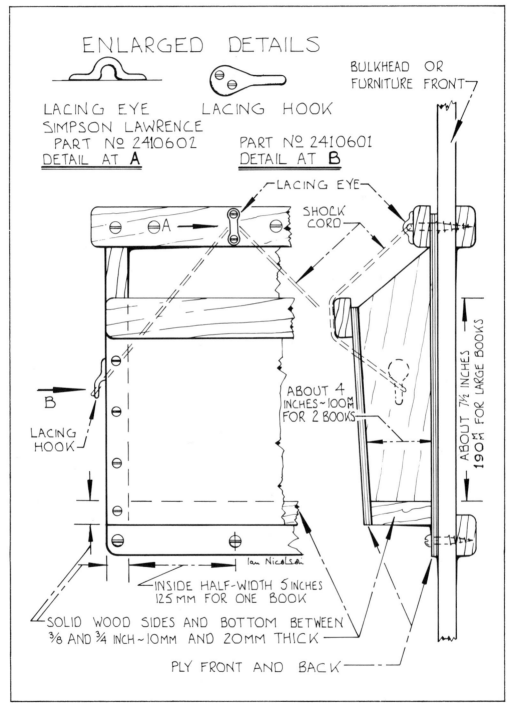

ENLARGED DETAILS

LACING EYE   LACING HOOK
SIMPSON LAWRENCE
PART Nº 2410602   PART Nº 2410601
DETAIL AT **A**   DETAIL AT **B**

BULKHEAD OR FURNITURE FRONT

LACING EYE
SHOCK CORD
A
B
LACING HOOK

ABOUT 4 INCHES ~ 100 M FOR 2 BOOKS

ABOUT 7½ INCHES 190M FOR LARGE BOOKS

Ian Nicolson

INSIDE HALF-WIDTH 5 INCHES 125 MM FOR ONE BOOK

SOLID WOOD SIDES AND BOTTOM BETWEEN ⅜ AND ¾ INCH ~ 10MM AND 20MM THICK

PLY FRONT AND BACK

the saloon can be padded and covered with the same cloth as the back rests of the settees, or covered with a toning leather-cloth.

Generally speaking, plywood should not be used for bookcases because it cannot take screws driven in at the edge and it is not good at holding screws near its edge. If ply is used, its exposed edges must all be fully covered.

When the shipwright has decided where the case is to be located and has measured up the space, he should cut out the base and hold this in position, with a few books on top. All sorts of crises may now thrust themselves forward. The sharp outer edge of the bookcase may be well placed to scalp anyone sitting down on the settee, or a cupboard door may be obstructed, or the level of the bookcase may be out of line with adjacent furniture and therefore look wrong.

When the base is right, the ends, back and front are all fixed on, using screws and glue. An amateur is well advised to hold the bookcase in two hands when the glue is dry and gently twist to see how stiff the structure is. Not so good? I do hope you stopped exerting force before there was a horrid splintering. To make the piece of furniture stronger, bolt short lengths of metal angle-bar at the joins of the bottom and ends, of the bottom and the back, and even between the bottom and the front. By putting the metal inside the case it will not show once the books are in place. This trick of using metal angle-bar to stiffen up a wood structure is a handy one which can be used on everything from vent boxes to folding berths.

Just before the case is assembled, it should be given a critical look. If it seems heavy, increase the bevels on all the exposed edges, or round the edges down some more. The top inboard corners of the ends may be rounded too and, if the case still looks slightly massive, the ends can have lightening holes cut in them. During assembly, all sharp edges are faired off.

The high portable fiddle is often in the form of a wood bar, typically 1–1¾ inches (25–45 mm) deep, also between ⅜ and ¾ inch (10 and 20 mm) thick. Each end rests in a wood chock with a recess cut in it. If the boat turns keel upwards, this type of bookcase lets the contents fall out; so for boats which do that, instead of an upper fiddle there may be a net held with shock-cord over all the books, or the case may have a solid top and a front which is complete

---

◁   *Fig. 15   Magazine rack style bookcase*

Where there is not space for a normal bookcase, this thin rack can be fitted, up against a bulkhead or on a furniture front. It can be made to hold two large books, as shown here, or the width can be doubled to hold four, or the thickness doubled, according to the available space.

The lacing eye at the top holds a length of shock-cord which has a loop each end to slip over the lacing hooks. This prevents the books from coming out of the rack even if the boat lies on her side. To save weight and space the front and back of the case are made of thin marine ply, with battens to stiffen it and to cover the ply edges. The top batten has screws right through it, through the bulkhead and into a doubler strip beyond. The bottom of the back has no batten provided that the case is fitted low and that the bottom edge of the ply cannot be seen; and here again the screws which hold the case in position go through the bulkhead into a backing strip or doubler.

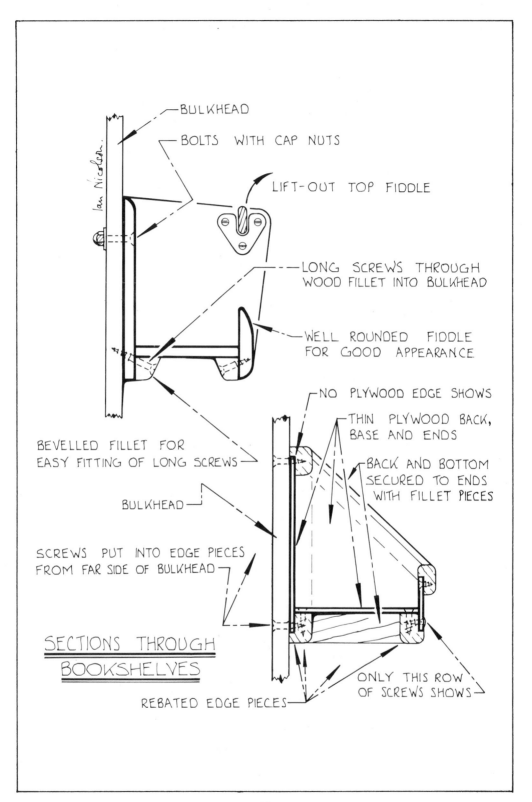

BULKHEAD

BOLTS WITH CAP NUTS

LIFT-OUT TOP FIDDLE

Ian Nicolson

LONG SCREWS THROUGH
WOOD FILLET INTO BULKHEAD

WELL ROUNDED FIDDLE
FOR GOOD APPEARANCE.

NO PLYWOOD EDGE SHOWS

THIN PLYWOOD BACK,
BASE AND ENDS

BEVELLED FILLET FOR
EASY FITTING OF LONG SCREWS

BACK AND BOTTOM
SECURED TO ENDS
WITH FILLET PIECES

BULKHEAD

SCREWS PUT INTO EDGE PIECES
FROM FAR SIDE OF BULKHEAD

SECTIONS THROUGH
BOOKSHELVES

REBATED EDGE PIECES

ONLY THIS ROW
OF SCREWS SHOWS

apart from a slit showing the book titles. This front will be hinged and secured by a pair of barrel bolts, so these books are safe in all circumstances.

Securing a bookcase to a bulkhead can only be done with screws if there is a wood pad on the far side to take the screws. Bolts through the bulkhead are better in many ways, especially if the case is going to be removed every few years. As the bolts on the bookcase side will be hidden by the books, the nuts go this side and the heads on the far side of the bulkhead where they show. If the case has to be fixed to the boat's topsides and the hull is of fibreglass, it will be necessary to glass in a piece of wood which should be almost as long as the case and at least 1½ inches (40 mm) thick to take screws 1½ inches long.

There should always be at least five fastenings for a bookcase and at least one fastening for every three large books. When making the flat type of case, that is the 'magazine rack' style, the front is kept lower than the back so that fastenings can be put in above the front. Better still, if the back is made extra wide, fastenings can go in all round.

◁ *Fig. 16   Bookshelf in solid wood and ply*

A bookshelf is more than an open-topped box fixed onto a bulkhead. It should be an attractive piece of furniture which matches the rest of the woodwork in the cabin. To make it strong enough it is advisable to glue it together and use screws. The top sketch shows how the screws go through the back and into the bottom fiddle are hidden from view, yet are easy to drive in due to the way the wood fillets are bevelled.

The bottom sketch shows a lightweight bookshelf made from ply, perhaps from off-cuts. It is poor boatbuilding to leave a ply edge showing, so rebated hardwood is used along the top and bottom, as well as down the ends. The ply is too thin for dowels so the screws are mostly put in so that they do not show. That single row of screws along the front should be decorative such as the type which have an antique coppery finish.

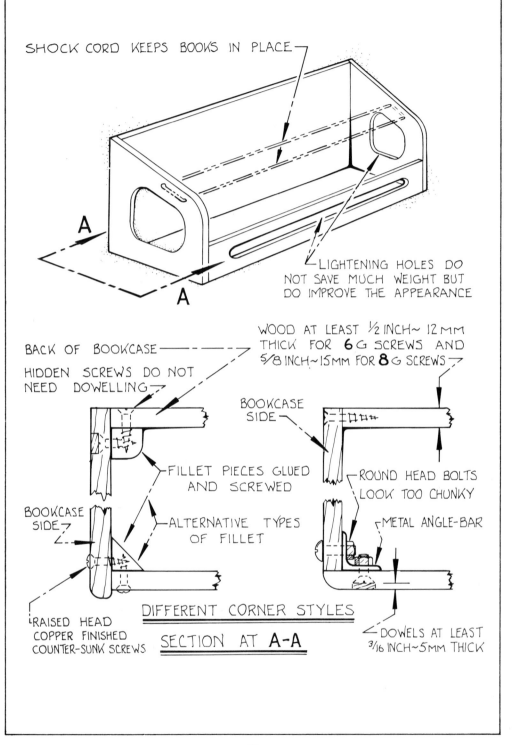

SHOCK CORD KEEPS BOOKS IN PLACE

A

A

LIGHTENING HOLES DO NOT SAVE MUCH WEIGHT BUT DO IMPROVE THE APPEARANCE

WOOD AT LEAST ½ INCH ~ 12 MM THICK FOR **6** G SCREWS AND ⅝ INCH ~ 15 MM FOR **8** G SCREWS

BACK OF BOOKCASE

HIDDEN SCREWS DO NOT NEED DOWELLING

BOOKCASE SIDE

FILLET PIECES GLUED AND SCREWED

BOOKCASE SIDE

ROUND HEAD BOLTS LOOK TOO CHUNKY

ALTERNATIVE TYPES OF FILLET

METAL ANGLE-BAR

RAISED HEAD COPPER FINISHED COUNTER-SUNK SCREWS

DIFFERENT CORNER STYLES

SECTION AT **A-A**

DOWELS AT LEAST ³⁄₁₆ INCH ~ 5 MM THICK

Fig. 17   Adding interest to furniture

A bookshelf which is rectangular is boring and tends to look amateurish. This one has the ends cut at a slope and lightening holes cut out of the front and ends. If the object was mainly to save weight, the ends would be made lower, and the lightening holes would be in the back and bottom too.

Four different ways of making corner joins are shown, all easy, and none need special tools like a rebater. At the bottom on the left there are two forms of fillet which have screws staggered otherwise a screw coming in from the side will meet one coming in from the back or front. The front edge of the end is neatly rounded and extends beyond the fiddle so that very precise fitting is unnecessary.

On the right at the bottom there is a piece of non-ferrous angle-bar used to hold the front and side together. This makes a strong job and the metal is hidden by the books. The alternative, shown above, of screws driven into end grain is not wonderfully strong and must be used with a good glue like epoxy resin.

12 *More and better stowage*
space

We used to cruise in a converted 6-metre, a racing boat which was lengthy and slim. She had so little beam, freeboard and headroom that one of our crew said: 'If she wasn't so beautiful and so fast she'd be like a drainpipe – long and thin and very wet'. The usable cabin space was the length of a berth and the cabin sole was half that length. In quite a moderate sea there was always a wave tumbling along the deck, deep, green water which cascaded into the cockpit. As the 'pit drained into the bilge, we sometimes pumped for twenty mintues each hour when going to windward.

In spite of all her disadvantages, we loved that boat and four of us went off in her every weekend through the summer and autumn. There was no engine, no echo-sounder, not even a radio receiver for weather forecasts, and the only electrical items were the three flash-lights – three because we expected one or two to get drowned between Friday evening and Sunday.

We went offshore and along the coast, up rivers and into little creeks where we were only able to turn by nudging the bank on one side, then with the helm hard over and the jib aback we would just squeak round and creep out of the entrance. Of course, we got into awkward situations. We had to reef in a hurry at night in frightening squalls. We had to kedge off. Sometimes we had to tack back and forward outside a haven until the tide slackened. Sometimes we picked up our home moorings after dawn on Monday, but we were never late for work. We seldom broke anything and when we did, we had spares on board as well as tools for mending whatever needed repairing. We never went hungry or thirsty, and once moored up we were always able to produce dry clothes from some carefully contrived stowage space.

One reason that boat gave us such pleasure was because we worked out the stowage plan in great detail. So far as possible, wet things stayed on deck. When we hauled down a saturated genoa we either lashed it in a long sausage along the lee toerail, or we put it in a bag and stowed it in the capacious cockpit. By keeping wet things *out of the cabin* we kept the living space dry – well, fairly dry. When we came off watch, or arrived in port, we put wet oilskins on hooks in the cockpit. This is a trick which can be copied on quite a few boats. On big boats especially, a row of oilskins can be stowed in a cockpit or counter locker, or on the bulkhead at the fore end of the cockpit.

Wet clothes are as much a menace in the cabin as wet oilskins. Some people stow them at the bottom of the oilskin locker; some boats have hooks near the engine so that warmth from the machinery dries them out. On some boats the procedure is to put them into plastic bags and stow them in the bilge or under a forward berth, or even in a counter locker.

Bulky things are always a problem, especially in boats under about 30 feet (9 metres). Sails take up a lot of room, but worst of all, they need stowage spaces with extra big openings. If a cockpit locker is used, the seat top will usually not suffice as an opening lid – part of the cockpit well side must also fold open to allow a full sailbag to be thrust below. In the same way, if sails are stowed under a forward berth, there must be some way of lifting up a long length of the berth, and some of the inboard berth side too. It is a good idea, where possible, to have a side which does not extend up to the berth base. If a distance of about 8 inches (200 mm), or even 14 inches (350 mm) is left between the berth base and front, there will be good ventilation to dry out wet sails and getting the bulky bag into its resting place will be much easier.

For a cruiser, there is a good case to be made for carrying storm sails permanently on deck ready to hoist, though this does risk losing these sails in extreme conditions when heavy waves sweep the deck. The storm jib is hanked onto an inner forestay and lashed tight down on deck, with a cover to keep the sun off it. Sheets and halliards as well as tack pennant may be permanently clipped on ready for instant use.

The same arrangement can be organised for a small mainsail or trisail. It is fitted into a special track running up the mast beside the main track and again, a cover is kept over the sail to preserve the cloth from the damaging sun's rays. Another location for stowing sails is in the counter, though it will often be necessary to have one or more special hatches made. I have seen a clever double-hinged hatch which could be half opened to get at minor items on one side or the other. When one of the two sails stowed aft was wanted the whole width of the hatch was folded back and the sailbag hauled on deck easily.

It is rare these days to find stowage beneath the cabin sole except aboard craft which are large. This is partly because so many modern yachts have little volume beneath the sole and partly because stowage containers for this area usually have to be specially made. However, all boats need more stability and one way to get it is to put gear low down, so under-sole stowage is sensible.

One technique is to make up baskets or boxes which fit neatly into the spaces between the sole bearers. Baskets made of galvanised steel mesh, or of marine ply with ample drain and ventilation holes, or made with a rigid top frame and lower part formed from netting, all work well. Such things as tins of food (with the labels peeled off and a note of the contents marked on indelibly) and some bo's'un's gear can be stowed here, even though there is a chance water will invade the storage occasionally. If the bilge is well ventilated and the boat is in port for long periods, vegetables (especially root vegetables) may be stowed below the sole. Some people put items like dry batteries, packets of dried food, spare sailcloth and even tools into inner *and outer* plastic bags and stow these low down. The plastic bags are tightly sealed and must be wedged in place, otherwise when the boat lurches about they will chafe through.

Stowage in the bilge is seldom convenient, which is why gear needed often or urgently should not be put here. Spare blocks and shackles are traditionally strung on string and hung below sole bearers, but a good case can be made for having at least some of these items more accessible.

Gear which is seldom used and is heavy, such as the No. 3 anchor, the emergency tiller, spare oars and boathooks, can all be stowed low down if some of the sole bearers are made portable. Of course, those of us who have grown old and cunning through many miles of sailing, know that all these items can be needed in a sharp panic – so access to them has to be reasonably easy. Probably better than portable sole bearers are extra deep ones with recesses cut in the top for long, narrow items such as the emergency tiller.

The area round the galley never has enough space for all the tools of the cook's trade as well as the spices and condiments, the ready-use food, the spare matches and that half bottle of scotch which is the best cure for so many of the cook's problems. The first answer to the infinite problem of galley stowage is to accept that there never can be enough room near the centre of operations. I've drawn out vast galleys for motor yachts which can only be described as being beyond the dreams of most people, and still we found that the cooks complained they were starved of storage space. We have had occasion to point out that the space available was better than in many houses, but we only got one of those sophisticated shrugs which chefs use with such effect.

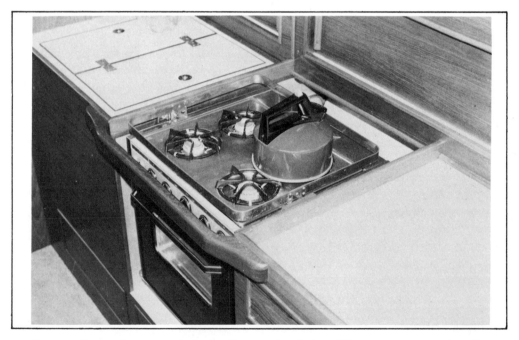

On many boats, drying-up cloths are hung on hooks but, if they are spread out on the handle in front of the cooker, they will dry more quickly. The main purpose of this wood hand-grip is to give the cook something to hold onto, and prevent a collision between cook and cooker in rough weather.

If there is not sufficient space around the sink and cooker, at least there should be as much as possible close by. Modern boats tend to have space below settee berths which is only accessible by lifting the cushion and hidden locker lids. If a drawer or two is worked in at the galley end of each settee, the cook will suddenly find that he has much more space.

There are often void spaces each side and in front of the sink and, by cutting through the fibreglass galley mould, all sorts of small spaces can be discovered. These crannies may be left open-fronted, with neat frames round the apertures, or drawers or locker doors may be fitted. The same technique may apply to the moulding which surrounds the cooker or 'fridge.

Sometimes the drawers are made unnecessarily short, even though there is ample room outboard of them. This may be because it suited the builder to fit standard size drawers throughout and so the lowest one, which is located where the hull curves inwards, decided the length of all the drawers. It may be worth the effort involved to rebuild some drawers to maximum length.

For small items, shelves on the inside of locker doors are most useful. Shelves fitted along the inside of cabin coamings are good because although they have to be kept narrow, they can be made long, extending well beyond the galley.

Most tools, stores, emergency equipment, spare clothes – in fact just about everything – are wanted near the main hatch. Almost everything is ideally stowed well aft and as a result many boats are down by the stern. The clever owner realises that there is bound to be a conflict of interests as every piece of the yacht's gear demands that it be stowed within a few feet of the busy working area by the main hatch. A conscious effort must be made to stow things forward, but of course, not too far forward where they would cause the boat to be bow heavy. A mass of gear in the fo'c's'le causes a boat to hesitate when she should be rising to a sea, which makes her wet, given to taking waves over the bow too soon, and slowed by waves more than she should be.

We conclude that all sorts of things must be stowed somewhere about the forward end of the main saloon, neither near the cabin entrance nor yet so far forward that they are unavailable in the usual crises which afflict every boat at intervals.

Things like lifejackets, fire extinguishers, food needed soon but not immediately, dry clothes, spare batteries, those ship's tools not used every day, books, charts not needed immediately, spare water, beer and stronger fluids, all these and more can be located forward – but not too far forward.

What really *must* be near the cabin entrance is the full range of panic tools like a sharp knife, a Mole-grip, an adjustable spanner, a shackle opener, white flares to scare off big ships, two or three or four waterproof torches, binoculars, pencils, the deck-log (to record the log readings, the characteristics of the next three lights expected on the horizon and so on), also sweets and tobacco for the watch on deck. This gear is best stowed in special racks or shelves with extra deep fiddles, or in PVC pockets made deep so that nothing ever falls out, or similar safe stowage. This special secure home for these items is arranged on the bulkhead just inside the main hatch, or under the top steps of the cabin ladder, or under the bridge deck, or in nets under the aft end of the cabin top. It is virtually impossible to make this stowage neat so most people accept a slightly chaotic appearance near the cabin doors and feel that it gives the yacht a feeling of tough, deep-sea, go-anywhere-ability – it implies that the boat is crewed by people who like to nip round Cape Horn before breakfast most weekends – and that makes everyone aboard feel good.

Of course, meticulous owners do not like the clutter of slightly rusty knives, bent spikes and sea-worn spanners clustered round the entrance. They arrange attractive fully closable lockers of ½ inch (12 mm) thick wood which matches the rest of the adjacent furniture, with reliable large turn-buttons or similar closures and separate compartments which exactly fit each item. One advantage of this arrangement is that if any item is missing from its correct storage place, the gap is immediately noticed. This is certainly the efficient way to stow tools, and is similar to what is seen in aircraft hangars where each item is on a brightly coloured board outlined in black so that if anything is missing the size and type of tool which is astray is obvious to everyone. A few yachts have this type of stowage in the main cabin and plenty have it in the engine compartment.

13 *Cave lockers*

A locker with an open front, that is with no door, is called a 'cave locker'. Sometimes the clumsier phrase 'Open-fronted locker' is used. The fashion for cave lockers started in the 1930s.

Cave lockers have so many advantages that it is not surprising they are favoured by designers, builders and owners. Having no door, they are cheap and the total of a lot of doors plus their hinges, locks and handles, can add up to an appreciable weight, especially on a small racing craft. The cost savings in hinges, screws, locks, handles, bolts and the time taken to fit the door, all add up to ample money. This is especially true when the hinges are small so that their screws are fiddly little scraps of metal which a horny handed wood-worker can scarcely grasp in his calloused talons.

A special advantage of cave lockers is that they can be fitted in all sorts of awkward corners. There may be no space for a locker door to swing open, or a door may be hard to fit because the locker is in some cramped space. In the galley it is sometimes inconvenient to have a locker door because the work-bench has to be cleared of dishes before the door can be swung open. Or the locker may be below the counter top and a door here cannot be opened until the cook has moved aside . . . and if the cook is wearing a galley strap to prevent being flung about in rough weather, moving out of the way of a door becomes a major operation.

Cave lockers are especially good for clothes because of the ample ventilation. If clothes are hung up, a simple bar or two across the opening will stop things swinging out when the boat heels and the bottom makes a great storage space for shoes and boots. These will stay safe behind the fiddle which may be 8 or 12 or even 18 inches (200 mm or 300 mm or 450 mm) high. The front opening of a locker holding 'shore-going' suits on clothes hangers can be as small as 2 feet 6 inches (750 mm) even though the locker is deep enough for long overcoats. And the width need be no more than 8 inches (200 mm) even though the inside of the locker is far wider, so that it holds a whole rack of clothes.

Small cave lockers for rolled up sweaters, shirts, socks and towels are useful because the clothes can be jammed in tightly and they are not likely to fall out even if the boat capsizes. For this sort of use, or for toilet gear, an individual locker or two for each member of the crew is popular. The access hole must be at least 5½ inches (140 mm) in diameter to allow a large fist to get through.

It has to be admitted that a plain cave locker has disadvantages. Gear tends to fall out when the boat heels, rolls or flings herself about in severe conditions. Also, the contents of the locker are open to view and some people think this is untidy. I used to have a little cruiser with cave lockers all round the cockpit which was great for the quick stowage of fenders, warps and spare line. Being open-fronted, the lockers let the air blow through and anything stowed wet soon dried. But nowadays there are so many robbers about that a cave locker in a cockpit is too tempting for thieving fingers. Also my little cruiser was only used for coasting – for deep sea work it is better to have the deck gear secured inside closed cockpit lockers. A compromise might be: cave lockers for the fenders (which will be hanging over the ship's side when in port and therefore vulnerable to thieving anyway) and for minor pieces of line which are so essential on any boat for lashings and so on. These cockpit cave lockers will usually be inboard of the cockpit well and coamings, so that they are self-draining with the rest of the cockpit space.

A good way to avoid the problem of gear falling out when the boat heels is to have the locker entrance at the forward or aft end rather than on the inboard side. However, modern craft are so light and lively that gear may still jump out when the boat gets really skittish in a seaway. Other ways to stop gear falling out are:

1   Fit a net across the entrance, perhaps with shock-cord to keep it in place.
2   Have several lengths of shock-cord stretched across the opening. The cord may be vertical or horizontal or diagonal, or a combination of these.
3   Have a closure made of a flexible material such as sailcloth, PVC, towelling or a transparent material such as is used for windows in folding hoods.
4   Keep the entrance small, with a high fiddle and wide sides.

If a net is used, it can be left off when the boat is not at sea. Naturally, small objects can slip through a net, but it is poor policy to stow small things in cave lockers anyway. A net is often kept in place with cup hooks, but these are not strong and they protrude too much. A much better type of fitting is the Boat Cover Fastener which comes in two forms, the hook and the eye (see Fig. 18). Incidentally, these little fittings are handy for a great variety of jobs ranging from holding canvas berth bases to keeping cockpit cushions in place. (Simpson-Lawrence Ltd, Catalogue Numbers are SL 152702 for the hooks and SL 152704 for the eyes.)

If the closure is made of a cloth, it is usual to have either a zip or a lacing up one side and across the top and half or two-thirds down the other side. The remaining edge is screwed to the locker front. When a zip is used, a plastic one is much to be preferred to a metal one, here as elsewhere in a boat, to avoid seizure due to corrosion. Instead of a zip, Velcro may be used, but it is not particularly strong.

A cloth closure is normally made by a sailmaker. It does not have to be made to a precise size as it is fitted inside the locker front, so the measurements can be taken off a plan instead of the more time-consuming job of measuring on the boat.

The opening of a cave locker should have well rounded corners and the ends may be semi-circular, partly to give the best appearance, partly because sharp

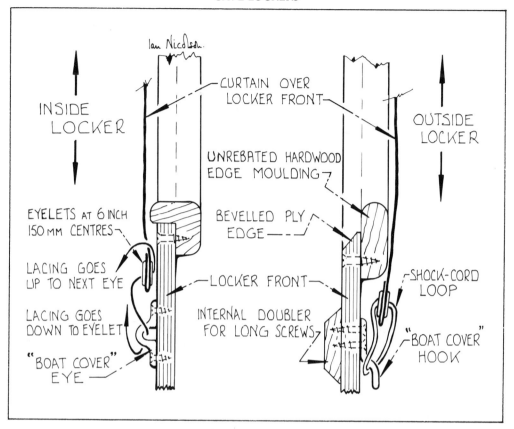

Fig. 18 Closures for cave lockers

The left sketch shows a curtain secured inside a cave locker, and the right side shows a contrasting way of fixing a curtain, on the outside. These sections through the fronts of two lockers also show how the ply edge is covered in alternative ways; the one on the right is cheapest and because the ply is well bevelled there is no chance that the coarse edge will be seen.

The metal eyes and hooks which hold the curtains can be used for many jobs afloat and are available from chandlers. The hooks have the Simpson-Lawrence catalogue number 2420600, and the eyes 2420700 when chromium plated. They are also available in plain brass.

angles are a source of weakness and the locker fronts are usually thin, and partly to prevent gear falling out. The depth of the fiddle at the bottom is critical at sea when gear is so likely to tumble out, but a high fiddle prevents the crew from seeing what is in the locker and good visibility is such an asset. Fiddles made of perspex or luctite or some similar transparent material make sense here. The top edge of the perspex must be well rounded, otherwise anyone plunging his hand into the locker may get a cut wrist. The perspex is best secured with bolts and the holes for these are drilled one size too large to prevent splitting when the bolts are tightened.

The front of the locker may be of fibreglass, ply or aluminium, or even of perspex. On a racing boat the material will be as thin as possible to save weight. It is not unusual to find 6 mm ply used even on large racing machines and on small boats the ply thickness may be down to 4 mm. Fibreglass down to 1.5 mm is sometimes found. All these thin materials need some form of stiffening round the opening and this is usually made of a hardwood. It may be

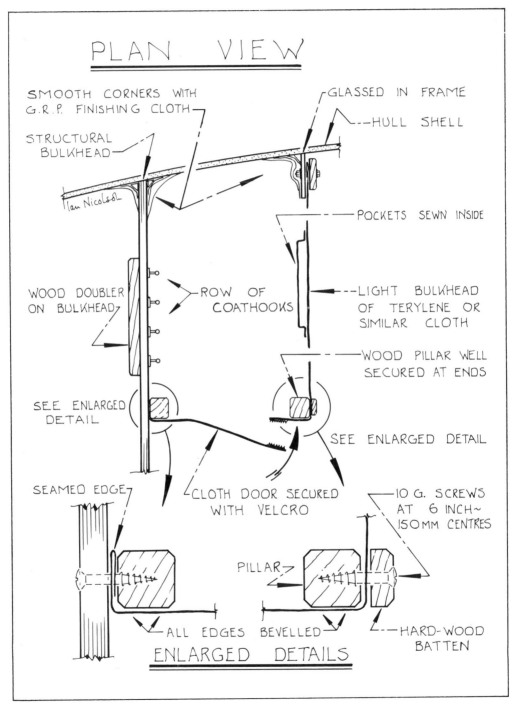

PLAN VIEW

SMOOTH CORNERS WITH
G.R.P. FINISHING CLOTH

GLASSED IN FRAME

HULL SHELL

STRUCTURAL
BULKHEAD

Ian Nicolson

POCKETS SEWN INSIDE

WOOD DOUBLER
ON BULKHEAD

ROW OF
COATHOOKS

LIGHT BULKHEAD
OF TERYLENE OR
SIMILAR CLOTH

WOOD PILLAR WELL
SECURED AT ENDS

SEE ENLARGED
DETAIL

SEE ENLARGED DETAIL

SEAMED EDGE

CLOTH DOOR SECURED
WITH VELCRO

10 G. SCREWS
AT 6 INCH~
150 MM CENTRES

PILLAR

ALL EDGES BEVELLED

HARD-WOOD
BATTEN

ENLARGED DETAILS

made up like a picture frame of rebated section, or from wood having a square or rectangular section with the corners well rounded (see Fig. 18). These frames are either bolted to the locker frame or screwed from inside so that the fastenings do not show. Fixing from the inside is only possible if there is space inside the locker to wield drill and screwdriver, so it is essential to discover this first at the planning stage. Here, as elsewhere throughout every boat, ten minutes spent with rule and pencil making a fairly accurate sketch will avoid a hundred minutes wasted in frustration and mistakes, not to mention broken drill bits and bashed knuckles.

The corners of the framework may be cut from the solid or mitred or laminated. Even though this is interior furniture it must still be made up with waterproof glue. There are times when water runs deep inside a boat and there is seldom a day when the moisture level in the cabin is less than soggy.

One marvellous thing about cave lockers is the way they can be used to increase stowage capacity quickly and cheaply, often in unexpected parts of the boat. Few galleys have enough lockers, but there are often narrow spare spaces beside or below the sink, under the cooker and into the adjacent engine casing or bridge deck, or the cockpit. In the forward cabin, available spaces are likely to be triangular in plan and section, odd shapes indeed, but useful nonetheless. In a toilet compartment it is sometimes possible to steal a little space for extra lockers by cutting through the forward bulkhead under the forward berths, or high up above the berths, close below the deck and right outboard. Cutting through the aft bulkhead may be possible to grab some little used volume beneath a settee or behind a back rest. When searching for extra lockers it is usually best to sit in a cabin and look thoughtfully around, rather than stare at a boat's plan which may well hide rather than reveal usable spaces.

◁ *Fig. 19 Cloth furniture*

Furniture made from Terylene (Dacron) or PVC needs no painting or varnishing, and it is very light. It is used particularly on racing boats. This sketch shows an oilskin locker or wardrobe made up of a structural bulkhead and the ship's side, with the aft side and inboard face made of cloth.

Instead of a Velcro strip to secure the door, a zip may be used, or hooks and shock-cord. The entrance should be made as large as possible otherwise it is difficult to get clothes into the locker. In order to be strong enough to stand up to someone falling against it the pillar should be at least 1½ × 1½ inches (40 × 40 mm) even on a small boat, and 2 × 2 inches (50 × 50 mm) is really better. The pillar can be of aluminium or steel tube, in which case the batten will be bolted on. In the sketch all the wood sections are the same width to speed up manufacture, using a circular saw and a mechanical planer.

14 *Building a wardrobe or*
════oilskin locker════

(With general notes on fitting furniture)

On even the smallest cruising yacht it is convenient to have somewhere to stow smart shore-going clothes so that they do not get wet from drips through hatches or from contact with foul weather gear. Similarly, wet oilskins need a stowage space where they can drip and dry off without wetting the crew, the bedding, the charts or any of the other vulnerable things in the cabin.

Deciding the position

If the boat is very small, or filled with other things, it may be impossible to find room for an oilskin locker. In this case wet oilskins may be thrust into a cockpit locker. On quite large motor yachts the oilies are sometimes hung on hooks aft of the wheelhouse, sheltered under an overhanging deck, as if in an open porch. Here they are handy for anyone coming out on deck. However they cannot be left in this position when the boat is unattended because they are visible to anyone passing and may be pilfered, but then they can be hung *inside* the wheelhouse when the boat is not in use.

Logically a wardrobe is put in the most convenient place for the crew when they are changing clothes. In a boat with an aft cabin it is usual to fit in at least a small wardrobe here. Another is often located between the saloon and the forward cabin so that it serves both compartments. On craft big enough to have several separate cabins it is the universal practice to have at least a minimal wardrobe in each cabin. It may be a locker from the deckhead down to about 15 inches (380 mm) above the mattress at the bottom of the berth, giving just enough foot-room under the wardrobe. It may be a corner of the cabin, with a door extended diagonally from one bulkhead to an adjacent one at right angles, giving a wardrobe which is triangular in plan view.

Normally, the designer will have shown on the boat's plans where the oilskin locker and wardrobes are to go. If he has not, then he can be asked for his recommendations on this. It is best to study the plans painstakingly before starting construction, making a list of all the questions for the naval architect then setting them out in related groups in a single letter. Naval architects are extremely busy and are not likely to be everlastingly co-operative if they are bombarded with a constant fire of questions spread out over weeks. But if they are consulted every two months or so and sent carefully paragraphed letters with groups of the problems met by the builder, they will be helpful.

When the designer cannot be consulted, it is a good idea to get suits of oilskins and hold them up in places where the locker might be situated. For a wardrobe, a man's suit on a hanger is a useful dummy. First it is held up behind a cabin door to see if there is ample space for it, then tried in that awkward corner outboard of the head of the fo'c's'le berth, next in the odd-shaped space behind the cabin steps, and so on.

Typical spaces needed are:

An overcoat or long, full-length oilskin coat:
4 feet 7 inches (1400 mm) long,
2 feet 1½ inches (650 mm) wide.

A jacket or short oilskin coat on a hanger:
2 feet 7½ inches (800 mm) long,
1 foot 11½ inches (600 mm) wide.

A jacket or oilskin coat hanging on a peg will be the same length, but between 6 and 12 inches (150 and 300 mm) wide. These dimensions tend to be the minimum and some extra space is needed to get clothes into lockers. The heights are from the neck of the garment downwards so extra space is needed for coat-hooks and hangers.

When searching for a suitable space for stowing clothes it is worth remembering that:

1   Oilskins must be near the cabin entrance so that anyone coming off watch puts dripping oilies away immediately without trailing them all over the cabin and wetting everything.
2   Where there is insufficient space in small craft for a proper hanging locker, oilskins can be stowed in awkwardly shaped spaces, if necessary lying on their side.
3   A good place for wet clothes is a space near the engine which will be warm and dry when the engine is running – provided that the heat is not excessive.
4   When the boat is small, clothes stowage should not take up valuable space where there is headroom or cabin sole space.
5   Although access does not need to be very easy for shore-going clothes, it must be easy for oilskins, because these will be wanted by tired, sea-sick crew. If they cannot get their skins back in place when they come off a gruelling watch, they will leave them lying on the cabin sole.
6   If women are to be on the boat and are to enjoy being aboard, there must be additional wardrobe space.

If a large space is available, it may be split into two: a wet locker for oilskins and garments which have become saturated, and a dry one for shore clothes. Sometimes the dry compartment is lined with PVC or a similar waterproof material to keep gear dry regardless of conditions aboard. On a long range offshore racer there will be times when there seems to be as much water inboard as outside, so somewhere that is reasonably dry for clothes stowage is a boon.

There are four types of clothes locker:

(a) The rectangular box-shaped one, similar to a domestic or landlubber's wardrobe, as sold in furniture shops.
(b) The commonest type in small boats is a space along a short length of the ship's side, bounded by a forward and aft bulkhead with the shaped curve of the ship's side outboard and a full or partial bulkhead or closure on the inboard side.
(c) An enclosed or semi-enclosed oddly shaped space, which is not designed so much to conform to the shape of garments hanging up as to use some otherwise unimportant space.
(d) A row of coat-hooks in the open on a bulkhead, or along one side of the fo'c's'le, or under a bridge deck, or even in the toilet or saloon.

Choosing the materials

Any piece of furniture in a boat should match the rest accurately or contrast with it in a way which makes it look attractive. This means that the wood or fibreglass has to be exactly the same as the surrounding furniture and decoration, or have compatible colour, texture, graining and so on.

Plywood is widely used for furniture because it is easy to buy and work. It comes in 8 feet × 4 feet (2440 mm × 1220 mm) panels so a bulkhead can be made up of one or two pieces, and this saves time. Small offcuts can be used for minor parts and the joiner is sure that they will all match. There is little contraction or expansion with changing moisture content in marine ply, and there is ample strength in even the lightest gauges. For instance in a racing craft, where lightness is so essential, a locker can be made up of 4 mm ply, provided there are stiffening pieces at all boundaries.

The main disadvantage of ply is that it is not cheap when compared with solid timber, measuring cube for cube. However for the professional builder who counts every hour of his labour dearly, ply is the material to use because it is quick to work. The amateur who is bent on saving cash may find that it is cheaper to make up the sides and front of a clothes locker using solid timber. A visit to a wood-yard may reveal that there is some timber on offer at an attractive price but be careful that it is not material that shrinks when near a warm engine or cooker then expands when damp from drips through a hatch.

In the long run it may be best for even the most hard-up amateur to go for ply. But which ply?

Wise men, looking ahead, always use the very best marine ply. It is costly but it will have a 10 year guarantee. A second choice is the type of marine ply which bears the country's stamp of quality rating, showing that it is waterproof, but even this cannot always be taken as the gospel truth. In UK the stamp shows: BSS 1088. This should mean that the ply will not deteriorate when used as furniture inside a boat, but there have been some imported materials with this stamp which have been defective and after two or three years the moisture from deck drips or from bilge water has attacked the ply edges causing delamination, blackening, then softening and eventually rot. It is the old story: what is most expensive in the first instance is often the cheapest in the long run. Anyone who cannot afford the best should go for the lower grade of marine ply such as 'painting grade' instead of 'varnishing quality' or, as a poor third choice, for 'exterior' grade. When using ply, whatever the quality, the edges should be well protected from moisture by fibreglass or well bedded edge mouldings or at least by a full paint regime. Edges which will show must be covered with mouldings which are usually wood but may be plastic or, just occasionally, decorative metal strip.

It may be necessary to order the ply with an exterior veneer to match the surrounding woodwork in the boat. The edge moulding can be of the same or of contrasting wood – availability is often the dominant consideration. Before designing the furniture it is advisable to have a talk with the timber merchant. He may advise ply with exterior veneers on one or both sides, or Formica or a similar hard plastic with a maintenance-free surface. This is expensive but it needs no painting or varnishing, so for a professional (or an amateur in a hurry) it is perhaps the best choice.

Unless a boat is being built with ruthless insistence on weight-saving, the ply used will be at least 5 mm (³⁄₁₆ inch) thick and on boats over 30 feet (9 metres) it will seldom be less than 8 mm (³⁄₈ inch). Where furniture is to form part of the hull stiffening structure, it will commonly be 12 mm (½ inch). This thickness is widely used because it can be fitted with little or no additional stiffening at all.

For economy furniture is made so that it is not necessary to buy an extra sheet of ply and end up with most of it unused. For example, a wardrobe may be made 2 feet 4 inches (710 mm) wide so as to be comfortably big enough for clothes on a hanger. This dimension subtracted from the standard 4 feet (1.22 m) width leaves 1 foot 8 inches (510 mm) so this dimension is selected for the depth of the locker. One cut of the ply panel gives both the side and the front of the locker with no waste of time or material. In practice, the edges will need planing, so the finished dimensions are marginally less before the edge mouldings and corner pieces are added.

Whether solid timber or ply is being used, much of the finishing work should be done before it is put into the boat. Painting or polishing is far easier on flat panels laid on a work-bench in a warm atmosphere. The final coat of paint or varnish, and perhaps the previous one too, will have to be deferred until the components are fitted in the hull and probably until the boat is almost

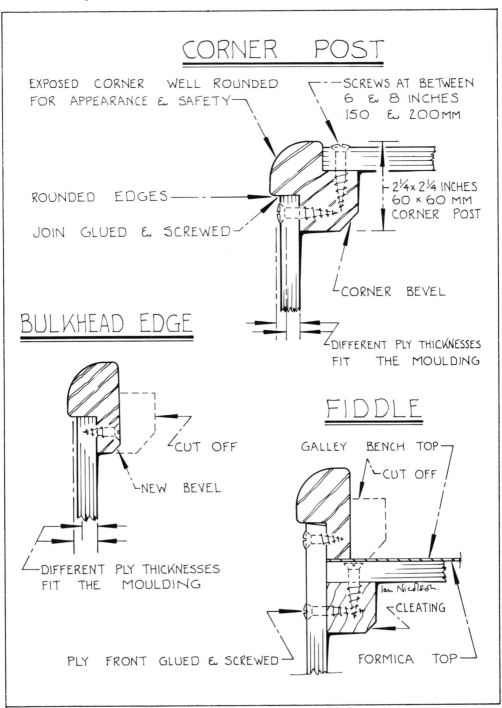

CORNER POST

EXPOSED CORNER WELL ROUNDED FOR APPEARANCE & SAFETY

SCREWS AT BETWEEN 6 & 8 INCHES 150 & 200 MM

ROUNDED EDGES

JOIN GLUED & SCREWED

2¼ x 2¼ INCHES 60 x 60 MM CORNER POST

CORNER BEVEL

BULKHEAD EDGE

DIFFERENT PLY THICKNESSES FIT THE MOULDING

CUT OFF

NEW BEVEL

DIFFERENT PLY THICKNESSES FIT THE MOULDING

PLY FRONT GLUED & SCREWED

FIDDLE

GALLEY BENCH TOP

CUT OFF

Ian Nicolson.

CLEATING

FORMICA TOP

84

complete. A few scratches may be found on the woodwork after the parts have been trimmed and secured in place, so there may be some touching up to do before the last coats of finish but it is still worth doing as much finishing as possible before putting parts into the hull. This applies to waterproofing the edges of ply as well as the decorative finish.

Sometimes it will pay to go even further. The whole wardrobe or oilskin locker may be made up as a unit outside the boat and lifted in complete. It has to be made small enough not only to go through the hatch but also to twist round and fit into its final place aboard. It will need at least 5 bolts or heavy screws, well spread out, to hold it in place.

Some professionals order their boat furniture from industrial joiners, as they find this the most economical way of getting interior components. They have to be watchful that the joiner uses no ferrous fastenings or hinges and this needs careful policing. Amateurs can also buy furniture in and sometimes save money as well as time, because industrial joiners buy their materials in bulk and cheaply. Sometimes a firm will be glad to have a small job to fill in between major contracts, so it may be possible to negotiate a good price. This is one of the many reasons why it is best to order well in advance.

If solid timber is used, it will seldom be less than ⅜ inch (10 mm) thick and for amateurs, who are not fully skilled in woodworking, it will be best to use ⅝ inch (15 mm) thickness to avoid splitting. On very simple, cheap boats the timber may be standard tongued and grooved softwood, but the appearance will be workmanlike rather than elegant. There are plenty of people who find the current fashion of styled boat interiors too delicate, too similar to boudoirs, and too little in accord with harsh conditions at sea. For such people plain timber of the cheaper sort has everything in its favour including a low price. It is sad that boats fitted out in this way are hard to sell unless they are commercial craft.

Inside a fibreglass boat with fibreglass lining or furniture it is often best to make the wardrobe of the same material. It is strong and, provided that it is thin, it will be fairly light. Typically fibreglass is between 1½ and 2 times the weight of water, whereas wood is generally between ½ and ¾ times the weight of water. Fibreglass panels will probably be about ⅛ inch (3 mm) thick, with glassed on stiffeners about $1 \times \frac{1}{2}$ inch (25×10 mm) thick every 10 inches (250 mm).

Where weight is a critical factor, the oilskin locker or wardrobe may be made

---

◁   *Fig. 20a   Standard wood mouldings*

The top sketch shows a corner post machined from hardwood, designed to take different thicknesses of marine ply. The post can be used for furniture or to join two bulkheads at right angles. The rebate at each side is deep and leaves an exposed corner which looks smart.

The same moulded section can also be used as a bulkhead edging piece, simply by cutting off one side, as shown in the left hand drawing. A new bevel is planed along the new sharp edge.

Using the same technique of cutting off part of the moulding, it can also be used as a fiddle (bottom right). In this case a galley bench is assembled and the ply front is shown planed away at a slight bevel so that the visible edge lies tight up in the rebate of the fiddle.

of a cloth with just a simple wood or aluminium framework. The cloth should be a sea-going one like PVC or one of the modern sailcloths such as Terylene or nylon. For hard usage a 10 oz tanned (that is, dark brown) Terylene is smart because it does not show the dirt. It is not tanned as in the old days, when

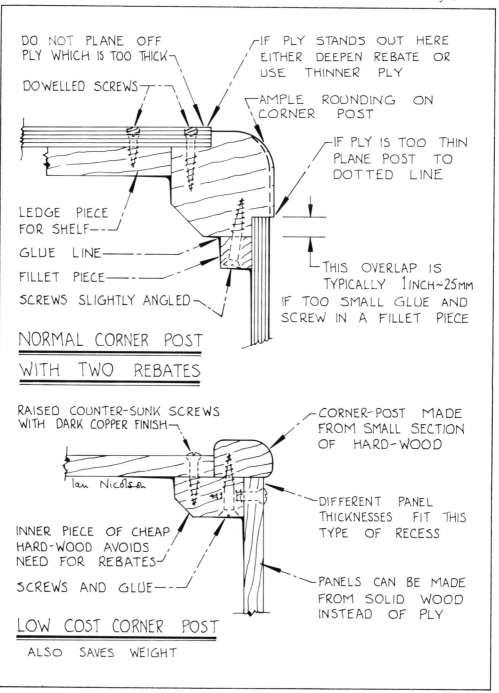

DO NOT PLANE OFF PLY WHICH IS TOO THICK

DOWELLED SCREWS

IF PLY STANDS OUT HERE EITHER DEEPEN REBATE OR USE THINNER PLY

AMPLE ROUNDING ON CORNER POST

IF PLY IS TOO THIN PLANE POST TO DOTTED LINE

LEDGE PIECE FOR SHELF

GLUE LINE

FILLET PIECE

SCREWS SLIGHTLY ANGLED

THIS OVERLAP IS TYPICALLY 1 INCH ~ 25MM IF TOO SMALL GLUE AND SCREW IN A FILLET PIECE

NORMAL CORNER POST WITH TWO REBATES

RAISED COUNTER-SUNK SCREWS WITH DARK COPPER FINISH

Ian Nicolson

CORNER-POST MADE FROM SMALL SECTION OF HARD-WOOD

DIFFERENT PANEL THICKNESSES FIT THIS TYPE OF RECESS

INNER PIECE OF CHEAP HARD-WOOD AVOIDS NEED FOR REBATES

SCREWS AND GLUE

PANELS CAN BE MADE FROM SOLID WOOD INSTEAD OF PLY

LOW COST CORNER POST

ALSO SAVES WEIGHT

canvas was dipped in a vat of waterproofing brown dye, but the colour of the modern equivalent is the same rich red brown which so many people find attractive. It is now possible to buy Terylene dyed in other colours and it makes excellent lightweight furniture, not least because it needs no finishing. It is disconcerting how long it takes to build up the four to six coats of paint or varnish on wood that are necessary for the best finish.

Cloth furniture is bought from a sailmaker, and it is generally best to have him measure the space inside the boat and make up the unit to his own dimensions. This can be the cheapest way of obtaining furniture as it is easily fitted using screws through wood battens round the top and bottom of the cloth bag which forms the locker. Typically the battens will be $1\frac{1}{2} \times \frac{5}{8}$ inch (40 × 15 mm) hardwood with the edges bevelled, secured with 8 or 10 gauge screws at about 4 inch (100 mm) centres. If pillars are needed to keep the vertical edges of the bag in position these will be about $1\frac{1}{4} \times 1\frac{1}{4}$ inch (30 mm × 30 mm) hardwood or 1 × 1 inch (25 × 25 mm) square section or round tube, aluminium or galvanised steel.

Whatever the oily locker or wardrobe is made of it may have a cave-front and Chapter 13 deals with the design features of this. A fibreglass or wood locker may have a cloth door such as a panel of PVC or man-made canvas with a plastic (never metal) zip round the top, one side and bottom. Another way of closing a cloth door is with 1 inch (25 mm) wide Velcro strip round three sides. The cloth is screwed down one side of the doorway, usually on the inside of the locker so that the fastenings and the batten through which they go do not show.

If a wooden door is fitted, it should have a ventilation slot or grating at the top and bottom. At least two other vent holes are needed in each locker and to be effective they must be at least 6 × 2 inches (150 × 50 mm) otherwise they will only work when there is a howling gale through the boat and this is rare, whatever the weather outside.

⊲   *Fig. 20b   Corner post techniques*

The disadvantage of the common type of corner post shown in the top sketch, is that it is costly to make. This is particularly true if only a small number of posts is needed. Cutting rebates by hand is slow and making them by machine involves setting up the machine just exactly right, perhaps for only ten minutes' actual work. If the rebates are not deep enough, the ply cannot be planed off to fair in with the corner post, so if in doubt make the rebates slightly too deep and then later plane off the corner post, as shown on the right side.

The panels must fit with a good lap which even on quite small boats is typically about 1 inch (25 mm) for a strong join. A fillet piece should be added if, in practice, the join is too narrow or too weak. When the fillet is added after the ply is in place, it is a good idea to angle the screws slightly so that the new wood is pulled tightly into the corner. Plenty of glue is used here, as elsewhere, and it should spew out all along the join. The surplus is cleaned off with a rag before it hardens.

The bottom sketch shows a cheaper type of corner post. When the inner piece does not show it can be made of cheap hardwood. Whenever possible the two pieces should be both glued and screwed together. The adjacent panels, which can be solid wood or ply, may be held by raised countersunk decorative screws to save using dowels. When putting these screws in care must be taken to avoid hitting existing screws joining the two parts of the corner post together.

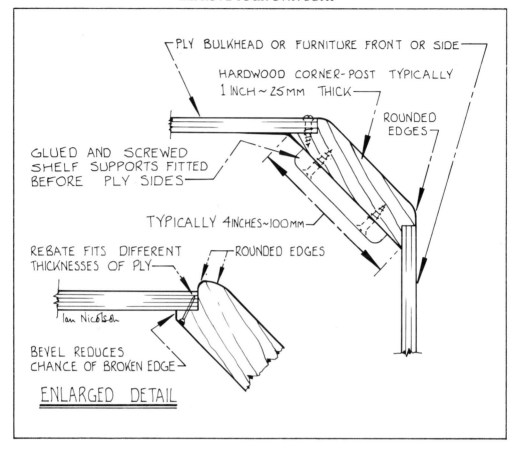

PLY BULKHEAD OR FURNITURE FRONT OR SIDE

HARDWOOD CORNER-POST TYPICALLY
1 INCH ~ 25 MM THICK

ROUNDED
EDGES

GLUED AND SCREWED
SHELF SUPPORTS FITTED
BEFORE PLY SIDES

TYPICALLY 4 INCHES ~ 100 MM

REBATE FITS DIFFERENT
THICKNESSES OF PLY

ROUNDED EDGES

Ian Nicolson

BEVEL REDUCES
CHANCE OF BROKEN EDGE

ENLARGED DETAIL

Fig. 20c Special corner post

This type of corner post can be used between two bulkheads at right angles, or at the corner of a piece of furniture. It gives a modern appearance, often slightly improves the foot room when the cabin sole is cramped and it avoids sharp corners which so often cause bruises in bad weather. The post is made from a relatively thin piece of wood, so it is economical in material. It consists basically of a piece of wood set at 45° (or a similar angle if 45° does not suit) with a rebate at each end.

The bulkheads or furniture panels are normally of plywood and these are glued into the rebate. It is a help if screws are used while the glue is setting, but sometimes nails driven from the inside, as shown bottom left, are used. The enlarged detail shows an extra deep rebate which will take a variety of different panel thicknesses.

The inside of these lockers must be smooth to avoid damage to clothes by chafe when the boat rolls. In an extreme case a sleeve was worn right off a jacket when a boat rolled downwind week after week on a long passage in the Trades. Occasionally shock-cords are stretched across lockers both athwartships as well as fore and aft to keep clothes and oilies firmly in place and prevent them from swinging out of lockers into passage-ways.

In a wardrobe (but seldom in an oilskin locker) there will be a hanger bar which is made up of a length of 1 inch (25 mm) diameter wood bar or ¾ inch

(20 mm) diameter metal tube, usually secured by chocks at each end. These chocks are held by at least three 8 gauge screws into at least ⅝ inch (15 mm) of hardwood. A space 1¾ inches (45 mm) is needed above a hanger bar as a minimum to get the hanger hook over the bar. The distance down from the top of the hanger bar to the neck of the garment on the hanger is about 4 inches (100 mm) so this distance has to be added to the length of the garments stored.

Coat-hooks are best made of non-ferrous metal or wood since so many of the plastic type cannot stand up to the tough conditions aboard a small boat. If plastic hooks are used, they should be the strongest available with at least four 8 gauge screws into ¾ inch (20 mm) wood. Metal hooks with only two similar screws survive . . . usually.

A shelf above the locker is popular because it is a logical place to stow hats and gloves. In the oily locker there will be woolly caps and wet weather towelling scarves as well as safety harnesses on this shelf. If there is no space for a shelf, a net or Terylene bags may be fixed up either under the deckhead, on the back of the door, or down the face of a bulkhead.

In the bottom of the locker there is often an awkward tapering space which is no use for hanging clothes. This is good for stowing boots and shoes, provided there is enough ventilation. Boots need a height of 1 foot 5 inches (430 mm) but they can lie on their side. They have a foot length of about 13 inches (330 mm) and two together have a width of about 9½ inches (235 mm) but these dimensions are not important in a small boat as boots will often be thrust in, squashed up, to get them into a tiny space.

In a wardrobe the aim will be to keep all water out so the bottom may be sealed with fibreglass and more of this material will be put in to form a shield against drips from chain plates which are so seldom 100% watertight. In an oilskin locker there is a dilemma because water is required to drain away, but bilge water may slop up. In the main it is best to have two or more drainage holes at least 1 inch (25 mm) diameter and hope that little water comes in.

In passing, it is worth remembering that sea-cocks, piping and electric cables should be located where the crew can get at them. Inside *small* lockers access varies from poor to lousy, so the relatively spacious interiors of oilskin lockers and wardrobes make them good for these items. The clever designer gets his sea-cocks just below the level at which the clothes hang. Wiring and piping is run along in the recess between the ship's side and the bulkhead. On some of the best cruisers there are internal lights in these lockers, which may be arranged to come on automatically when the door is opened.

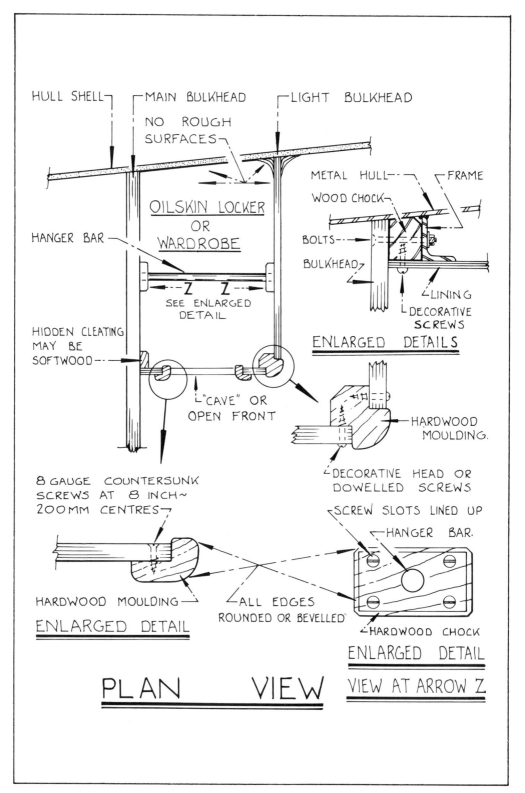

HULL SHELL — MAIN BULKHEAD — LIGHT BULKHEAD

NO ROUGH SURFACES —

OILSKIN LOCKER
OR
WARDROBE

HANGER BAR —

Z — Z
SEE ENLARGED DETAIL

HIDDEN CLEATING MAY BE SOFTWOOD - -

L "CAVE" OR OPEN FRONT

METAL HULL — FRAME
WOOD CHOCK —

BOLTS - - - -
BULKHEAD —

LINING
DECORATIVE SCREWS

ENLARGED DETAILS

HARDWOOD MOULDING.

DECORATIVE HEAD OR DOWELLED SCREWS

8 GAUGE COUNTERSUNK SCREWS AT 8 INCH ~ 200MM CENTRES —

SCREW SLOTS LINED UP
HANGER BAR.

HARDWOOD MOULDING —
ALL EDGES ROUNDED OR BEVELLED

HARDWOOD CHOCK

ENLARGED DETAIL

PLAN VIEW

ENLARGED DETAIL
VIEW AT ARROW Z

Fig. 21   Oilskin locker or wardrobe construction

It is common practice to use a main bulkhead as one boundary of a wardrobe. The outboard side of the wardrobe is usually the ship's hull, possibly lined with a suitable material to give a good decorative finish and protect the clothes. A lightweight bulkhead forms the second athwartships boundary and this is usually made of plywood, often glassed along the outside to help stiffen the hull.

A corner post, which is well secured at top and bottom, joins the light bulkhead to the front. The corner post shown has a well rounded inboard corner and its rebates are extra deep, so that it is unnecessary to ensure that the rebate is precisely the same depth as the ply thickness. This means that one standard section of corner post can be used in a variety of different places on the boat.

The cave or open front is described in full detail in Chapter 13. If the locker is very small inside, the hanger bar can be fitted through holes in the bulkheads with external wood pads to stop the bar sliding out. At the top right an enlarged detail shows how the locker bulkheads are secured in a metal boat.

When making a clothes cupboard it is sensible to design it with a shelf on top. This gives extra stowage space, and avoids the need to make a precise fit at the top. Besides, a clothes cupboard does not need to be higher than the length of a suit on a hanger, plus the necessary 2½ inches (60 mm) clearance above the top of the hanger bar.

15 *Making and fitting*
a table

A table tends to dominate the cabin so it has to be a well made piece of furniture. In another way it is obtrusive . . . it is in the target area for anyone who falls across the cabin when the boat crashes off a wave-top and throws her crew about. So while a boat's table must serve the same broad function as one ashore, it has to be tougher. At the same time it should be elegant and interesting.

It is the one piece of furniture that gives the designer, boatbuilder, joiner, timber merchant, owner, his wife and children, the crew, and everyone else a chance to show their talents. To get ideas for tables a tour round a boat show is worthwhile and at a show anyone looking for some fun can 'accidentally-on-purpose' lurch against a cabin table and see if it creaks or splinters apart!

A boat's table, besides being stronger than a house table, should have unobtrusive legs to avoid taking up foot-room in the cabin. It has to be secured with total certainty and it has to have fiddles. Like everything in a boat it should be designed with a Force 11 storm in mind. All the joints should be glued as well as screwed or bolted. If the table is portable, the temporary holding bolts or clips should be at least three in number and each capable of holding the table on its own.

The type of table depends very much on the size and purpose of the boat. Craft under 30 feet (9 metres) often have portable tables which tuck away into some unobtrusive stowage space when not in use. But larger craft also make use of portable tables, or at least the kind which fold out of the way. On every size of boat it is common to find tables which have both a standard and a lower height so that they can be used for meals or as a coffee table for more casual occasions, or even for converting into a double berth.

Some portable tables can be used in the saloon or in the cockpit; some are designed for meals and also for chartwork; some form the top of the engine-box; and some have as their basis the centre-board casing.

Some are in the middle of the saloon and get in the way too much; others fold down across the middle of a settee, so that only two people can use it, and then only by turning sideways. This form of table is quick to get in use and fold out of the way and it takes up no floor space, so though it has limitations its assets are just as important.

A popular design of table stands on a single tubular leg or slides up and down a pillar extending from cabin sole to deckhead; a better design is on two such pillars and three or four pillars are even better. The pillars also strengthen the boat if they extend down from the deckhead to the hull and are most useful grab-handles in severe weather. The pillar idea needs cautious use because there have been instances of heavily stressed mast-support pillars being used to hold up a table. The pillars were under-designed but would have worked

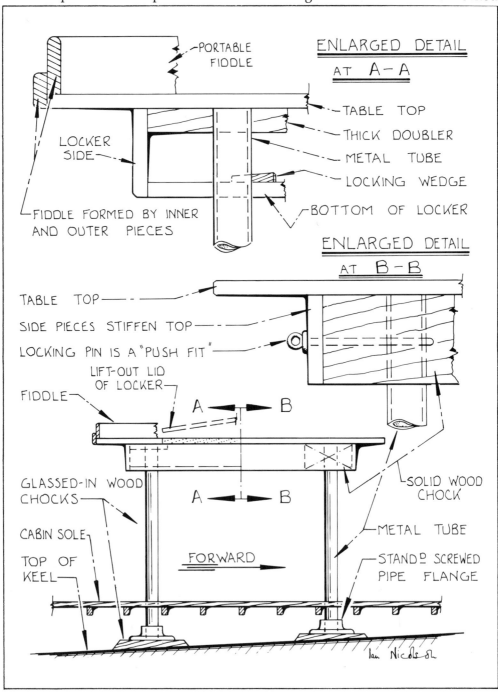

94

well enough if there has been no accidents. On two occasions someone fell against the table when the mast loading was near its peak. The twisting side load on the table transmitted to the pillar (which was straining under the downward force of the mast) was too much and the pillar buckled.

When designing a table the people who will sit or stand round it have to be remembered. They need space to put their feet down, room for their knees; they do not want their plates too far away and they will hate sharp edges which cause bruises. On the other hand there is usually space to fit in drawers, bottle racks or trays for condiments. When designing the table, the type, location and basic outline are decided first and the details like the storage compartments worked in later.

A first decision concerns gimballing or swinging. A table which is fixed will have a sloping top surface when the boat heels or rolls so everything tends to fall off. To defeat this, gimballing is arranged by fixing a pivot at each end and the table is ballasted well below the pivot line so that the top surface is always horizontal . . . well, nearly so! In practice the table often has trouble keeping pace with the gyrations of the boat so precautions are needed. These include:

1 A design which suits the type and size of boat.
2 A good safety factor, so that there is ample reserve strength and weight in the table's ballasting.
3 Pivots which do not flex or bend or twist but which have some damping to prevent overswing.
4 Fiddles 3 or 4 inches (75 or 100 mm) high to hold plates and mugs when the gimballing is defeated by very severe conditions.
5 Sea trials under rough conditions to make certain that the table works as planned.

For use in port the gimballing needs stopping by having bolts or locks, one at each end, to make the table rigid. If there is no such locking system what happens is that the ship's cook prepares a vast meal and loads the table with every kind of delicacy, as well as with uncorked bottles and all the ship's plates

---

◁ *Fig. 22a Portable table*

The stiffening of the table top may be made from a box which also forms a locker, as shown in Section A–A, or alternatively there may be just two vertical stiffeners glued on with a solid end chock, as shown in Section B–B. The legs of the table are made of standard tube which may be of any metal available or even rugged plastic. The bottom of each tube is threaded and screws into a standard flange fitting. Some sizes of these are available from plumbers' merchants. Each flange is screwed into a hardwood chock which has a level top and each chock is copiously glassed into the bottom of the boat, or secured to strong floors. The top of each tube fits into holes in the table top stiffening. In Section A–A the tube passes up through a hole in the bottom of the locker and goes into a hole in the doubling piece on the underside of the table top. The alternative form has a hole drilled in the solid wood chock. To keep the tubes in place there is some form of locking device such as a small hardwood wedge, shown at the top of the page, or a pin as shown in the middle. A big ship-type fiddle is detailed; this consists of a rectangular framework which is fully portable and drops onto the table top where it lodges firmly. Almost the only disadvantage of this type of fiddle is that it takes up a lot of stowage space when lifted off the table.

A table on the bulkhead at the end of a settee is not as convenient as an ordinary table in the middle of the saloon, when it comes to eating meals. But it is an asset when cooking as it increases the 'put-down space'. Because it cannot be gimballed it should have higher fiddles than those in this picture, if it is to be used at sea. It is cheap and easy to make, being nothing more than a wide shelf well supported.

Standard table leg supports are available from wholesale chandlers. This flanged socket with T-handle threaded lock is shown on the underside of a wood table top. The same type of flanged socket can be used at the base of the tube.

and cutlery; someone comes down into the cabin and puts an incautious hand down on the table and tips the lot off in a great crash. This should not happen at sea because everyone can see that the table is in the gimballed mode; and because no-one puts more than the bare essentials on the table when offshore; and because when out at sea crews are alert and cautious and sober . . . or should be.

Gimballing makes a table heavy and relatively bulky. It puts up the price and doubles the time needed for construction. It is only favoured in large racing boats involved in long-distance races such as the Round the World Race.

To be successful, gimballed tables tend to need about 100 lbs (50 kilos) of ballast which is usually lead, located about 20 inches (500 mm) below the pivot point, but lesser weights can be used by fixing a bottle rack low down so that the ship's liquor store helps the lead to keep the table stable. A lever length of less than 17 inches (425 mm) is not recommended. It is usual to have the lead in the form of a cast weight but it can be a box full of lead shot. These figures apply to a typical table for four or at the most six people. If there are to be plates and dishes for more people on the table, the weights must be increased proportionately. The lever arm length can seldom be increased because the weight must not be obtrusive and cannot normally be below the cabin sole.

A form of table which is popular is the dinette type. This is a table during the day and it forms part of a double bunk at night. It is fairly cheap to make and fit but some of the low cost mass-produced types lack that strength which is needed if the table is still to be working well three years after the boat is launched.

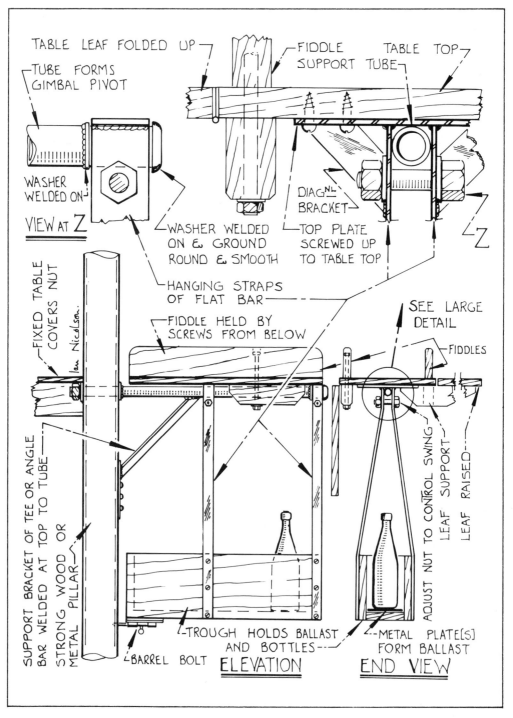

TABLE LEAF FOLDED UP

TUBE FORMS GIMBAL PIVOT

FIDDLE SUPPORT TUBE

TABLE TOP

WASHER WELDED ON

VIEW AT Z

WASHER WELDED ON & GROUND ROUND & SMOOTH

DIAG^NL BRACKET

TOP PLATE SCREWED UP TO TABLE TOP

Ian Nicolson.

FIXED TABLE COVERS NUT

HANGING STRAPS OF FLAT BAR

FIDDLE HELD BY SCREWS FROM BELOW

SEE LARGE DETAIL

FIDDLES

SUPPORT BRACKET OF TEE OR ANGLE BAR WELDED AT TOP TO TUBE

STRONG WOOD OR METAL PILLAR

ADJUST NUT TO CONTROL SWING

LEAF SUPPORT

LEAF RAISED

TROUGH HOLDS BALLAST AND BOTTLES

BARREL BOLT

ELEVATION

METAL PLATE[S] FORM BALLAST

END VIEW

Some dinettes have legs which fold up on the under side, then the table is set on ledges level with the adjacent U-shaped settee to form a bunk. Sometimes one end of the table in the lowered position rests on a ledge on a bulkhead and the other on a lip on the settee front. It is best if the table can be supported on three sides when in use for sleeping because when getting into bed people tend to kneel or sit on one corner or in the middle of one side. All the weight is then in one small area and if there is any shortage of local strength, splintering starts.

A table supported from above is seldom a good idea. If there is a real shortage of leg-room, a table hung on four rods, with some diagonal bracing athwartships as well as fore and aft might be considered. Using chain or Terylene rope to hang a table is not a good idea. However, if a table is very well secured along one edge and designed to hinge up out of the way when not in use, the free side may be supported by a pair of ropes or chains. But even here it is always best to arrange some sort of rigid support from above or below.

It is possible to buy, from the major wholesale chandlers who advertise in the boating magazines, various types of standard table legs. Some of these socket down into the cabin sole; some sit on top; some have gas-filled tubes so that the table height is varied simply by twisting the locking handle and pushing the table lightly up or down, the weight being supported by the gas pressure in the tube. They are all designed to take a top made by a shipwright to his own design and style. Their main disadvantage is that they are costly but the professional will find they often save him money.

Before making a table a drawing should be prepared. Even if this is a rough sketch on the back of an envelope, this stage in the construction should not be omitted because it will show up a dozen potential snags. Next, it is worth making a rough mock-up, even if this is nothing more than a few pieces of cardboard box held together by staples and sellotape. Put the model in position and get the crew to:

◁   *Fig. 22b   Gimballed table*

This very simple gimballed table is based on those old-fashioned inn signs which are hung on horizontal rods. There is only a single support which may be the mast pillar, or a pillar up the forward bulkhead of the saloon. Through this pillar there passes a tube which is threaded, with a nut to lock the tube on to the pillar. To support the tube there is a diagonal bracket, bottom left. Pairs of flat metal straps are welded to flat top bars, the latter being screwed up to the underside of the wood table top. The straps extend downwards and taper apart to embrace a trough which may be made of wood or metal. In the bottom of the trough there are lead or steel plates which form the basic ballast, supplemented by bottles or other heavy stores. To prevent the table from swinging when in harbour a barrel bolt on the bottom of the trough engages in the pillar.

To check excessive swinging the bolts at the top of the metal straps are tightened just slightly, trial and error being needed to get the correct clamping effect.

All sorts of variations can be worked out, for instance the end of the tube which is at present free can be secured to a semi-portable pillar. This will give the support bar a lot of extra strength and a much bigger and heavier table can then be carried.

1 Sit round as in harbour.
2 Scramble round as at sea when going through the cabin.
3 Test for foot-room, knee-room, elbow-room etc.
4 Mark the corners and edges which will need rounding off.

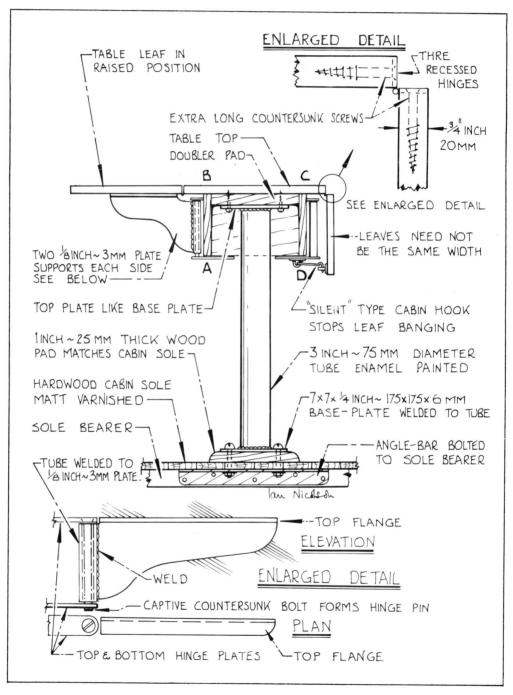

At the planning stage, the sizes of small women and large men have to be remembered, in case the current crew all happen to be a standard size. For usual table heights, widths etc consult *Boat Data Book*.

Almost always tables are made of wood, and usually a hardwood. Sometimes they have tubular metal legs and occasionally metal frames. Often they have Formica or a similar hard plastic top surface to make them easy to maintain and keep clean. But wood is the dominant material. Fibreglass is virtually unknown as a table material though it does not have many disadvantages for this job. The main reasons it is not used are its cost and weight.

The wood used is teak, or mahogany or one of its variations, or afrormosia (which is sometimes called African teak though this is thoroughly misleading), or peroba from Brazil, or very occasionally oak. There are plenty of relatively rare hardwoods which can be used provided that they can be bought in suitable qualities, so it is best to go to a wood mill which specialises in fine timbers and see what is available. An amateur should insist that the wood is easy to work, if necessary taking a sample home for testing.

Parts of a table which do not show can be of softwood, but whatever is used, it should hold fastenings well and be good for gluing. The table top will often be of ply, preferably marine grade but never less than exterior grade. Offcuts from bulkheads and doorway cut-outs can sometimes be used to save money. A common ply thickness is ½ inch (12 mm) because this is used so widely for bulkheads and other structural parts. However this is too thin without a stiffening rim all round and screws must go through this thickness of ply into another component. It is impossible to put screws through a component then into ½ inch (12 mm) ply and achieve a strong join. So if this thickness is used and if there are hinged leaves on the table, the hinges must be bolted. In practice it is much better to bolt on table hinges in every circumstance but suitable bolts with the right style and finish of head are not easy to find.

When making a table for any boat over about 35 feet (11 metres) it is in fact better to use ¾ inch (18 mm) ply and even here it may be necessary to glue on doublers in way of fastenings. Whatever ply is used, no edge should show. Not only is the appearance unacceptable but the edge is also too vulnerable and it cannot be satisfactorily bevelled or radiused.

When metal tube is used, square or rectangular section is a good choice because this is easy to bolt onto, easier to secure to the top panel, and easier to

◁   *Fig. 23   Strong table*

This sketch is based on the Camper & Nicholson table used in yachts like their 35 footer. The basis is a tough tube with identical flanges welded at each end. Screwed onto the top is a rigid box structure formed by the table top and its doubler pad (to take the long upward-reaching screws), two vertical side members and two vertical end pieces, all well glued together. The limits of this strong structure are shown by the letters A, B, C, & D. The hinged leaves need not be the same width and this can be a great help, for instance when there is a dinette on one side and an ordinary settee on the other. The leaves are supported by flanged, aluminium brackets with full length strong hinges made from standard countersunk bolts and standard aluminium tube.

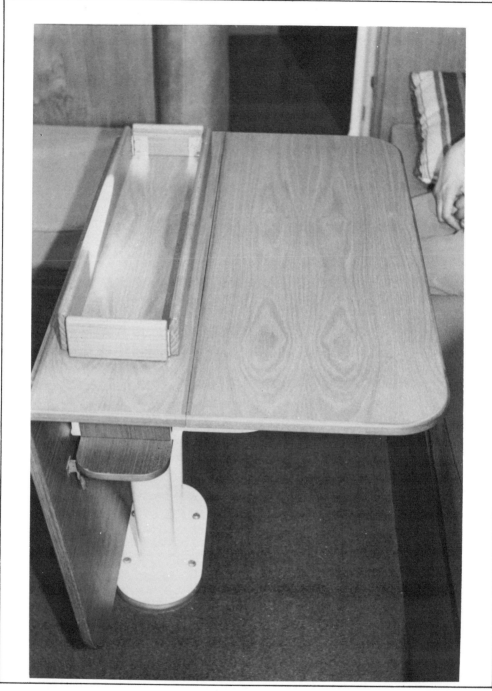

A popular type of table has no fiddles on the wide leaves, which are used in port, but at sea the narrow central part is fitted with high portable fiddles joined at the corners by hinges. When stowed the fiddles fold flat. They have metal pegs at the bottom which lodge in bushed holes in the table top.

weld together. Amateurs, who cannot weld, can make up all the parts and take them to a welding firm for assembly, or bolt the components together. For lightness aluminium alloy is best; for cheapness go for steel even though it has to be galvanised after assembly or rust will soon show, and for a modern appearance stainless steel looks good. Anyone who wants a traditional look should use brass or bronze and keep it polished, but work out the cost before starting the design!

To make a simple table:

1 A piece of ply about the right size for the top is found. It is taken aboard and the design stages mentioned above are gone through. The ply is cut to the right size for the table, but the length and width are reduced by the thickness of the edge pieces. A 'tray' is made up of the ply with hardwood edge pieces all round. Where the edge pieces meet at the corners they should be mitred or joined neatly by halving or a similar technique.

2 If the table is wanted for chart work, the top is turned so that the edge pieces are on the *under* side and this gives a flush surface. But for a normal onboard table fiddles are needed, so the top is used like a tray with the edges standing up all round. If the table is to be covered with Formica or a similar plastic material, this is fitted before the edging, and is glued down using a proprietary brand of adhesive. These glues have instructions for use on the containers; while the glue is sticking, use numerous weights on the Formica to hold it down.

3 The wood is given its finishing, which will be polish, varnish or lacquer to match the rest of the surrounding furniture. Other table components, such as hinge chocks, legs and supports, are made up and given their finish at the same time. Final finishing is done once the table is installed.

4 The table top is put on board and if it is designed to be attached to the boat, it is now hinged to a bulkhead or settee backrest, or engine casing side. To support it, use a hinged leg or, much better, a pair of legs, or rods hung from the deckhead. Because the hinges are bound to show, they should be decorative. The single tail type, as supplied by Simpson-Lawrence Ltd, catalogue numbers 195504, 195506 and 195508, are good because each flap has holes for four fastenings so they are well secured. The different numbers stand for the 6, 8 and 10 inch (150, 200 and 250 mm) sizes.

For a table which stands in the middle of the cabin, the table top is made as already described. A long, narrow box is secured under the table top to strengthen the whole table and give a good join between the legs and the top. This box will typically be $\frac{7}{8}$'s as long as the top and about 8×8 inches (200×200 mm) in section for boats between 25 and 45 feet (7.5 and 14 metres) long. As the box edges will show it is important to use plain wood, not ply, here. The sides or ends can be cut away to form a locker, or the ends cut out to take drawers.

The legs will typically be two $8 \times \frac{3}{4}$ inch (200×20 mm) solid wood

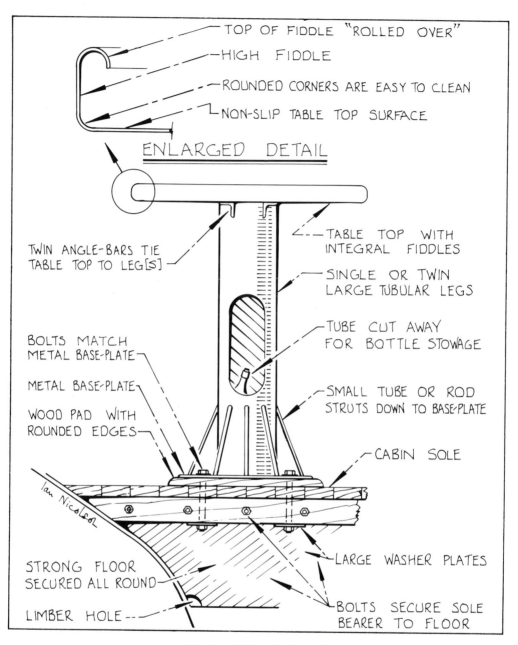

TOP OF FIDDLE "ROLLED OVER"

HIGH FIDDLE

ROUNDED CORNERS ARE EASY TO CLEAN

NON-SLIP TABLE TOP SURFACE

ENLARGED DETAIL

TWIN ANGLE-BARS TIE TABLE TOP TO LEG[S]

TABLE TOP WITH INTEGRAL FIDDLES

SINGLE OR TWIN LARGE TUBULAR LEGS

TUBE CUT AWAY FOR BOTTLE STOWAGE

BOLTS MATCH METAL BASE-PLATE

METAL BASE-PLATE

WOOD PAD WITH ROUNDED EDGES

SMALL TUBE OR ROD STRUTS DOWN TO BASE-PLATE

CABIN SOLE

Ian Nicolson

LARGE WASHER PLATES

STRONG FLOOR SECURED ALL ROUND

LIMBER HOLE

BOLTS SECURE SOLE BEARER TO FLOOR

Fig. 24 Cabin table of metal

Some people prefer to work in metal rather than wood and this table design suits them. The material may be aluminium, stainless steel, or bronze. For the single or twin main legs of the table, scrap lengths of aluminium mast section might be used. Those small struts at the bottom may not be needed, but they do give character and massive extra strength to the table. The same technique could be used at the top instead of the twin angle bars which are shown slotted in the tubular leg. Interesting and practical fiddles are not easy to work out for a metal table and the one shown in unusual, as well as giving the table top great strength.

This whole design could be adapted for fibreglass construction or even a combination of fibreglass and wood. The method of securing the table very strongly at the bottom can be used, regardless of what material is used for the table construction.

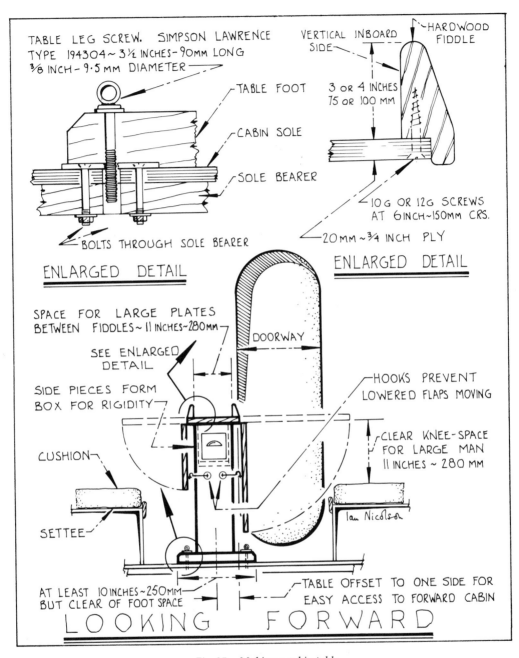

TABLE LEG SCREW. SIMPSON LAWRENCE
TYPE 194304 ~ 3½ INCHES ~ 90MM LONG
⅜ INCH ~ 9·5 MM DIAMETER

TABLE FOOT

CABIN SOLE

SOLE BEARER

BOLTS THROUGH SOLE BEARER

ENLARGED DETAIL

VERTICAL INBOARD
SIDE

HARDWOOD
FIDDLE

3 OR 4 INCHES
75 OR 100 MM

10 G OR 12G SCREWS
AT 6 INCH ~ 150MM CRS.

20 MM ~ ¾ INCH PLY

ENLARGED DETAIL

SPACE FOR LARGE PLATES
BETWEEN FIDDLES ~ 11 INCHES ~ 280MM

SEE ENLARGED
DETAIL

DOORWAY

SIDE PIECES FORM
BOX FOR RIGIDITY

HOOKS PREVENT
LOWERED FLAPS MOVING

CLEAR KNEE-SPACE
FOR LARGE MAN
11 INCHES ~ 280 MM

CUSHION

Ian Nicolson

SETTEE

AT LEAST 10 INCHES ~ 250MM
BUT CLEAR OF FOOT SPACE

TABLE OFFSET TO ONE SIDE FOR
EASY ACCESS TO FORWARD CABIN

LOOKING FORWARD

Fig. 25 Making a cabin table

In bad weather the crew will grab hold of the cabin table as they walk through the saloon so construction of this piece of furniture must be rugged. The top left-hand sketch shows one of the four leg screws, and there must be four, which are secured into really strong sole bearers. It may be necessary to glue doublers on to the sole bearers to make them large enough, both in depth and fore and aft thickness, to take the threaded plate for the table leg screws.

The detail top right shows the type of fiddle which will not splinter when a heavy man grabs hold of it. The main drawing at the bottom shows how the table is kept clear of the passage-way through the saloon. The hinged leaves must be designed to clear the settees and need strong hooks to prevent them banging when the boat rolls.

105

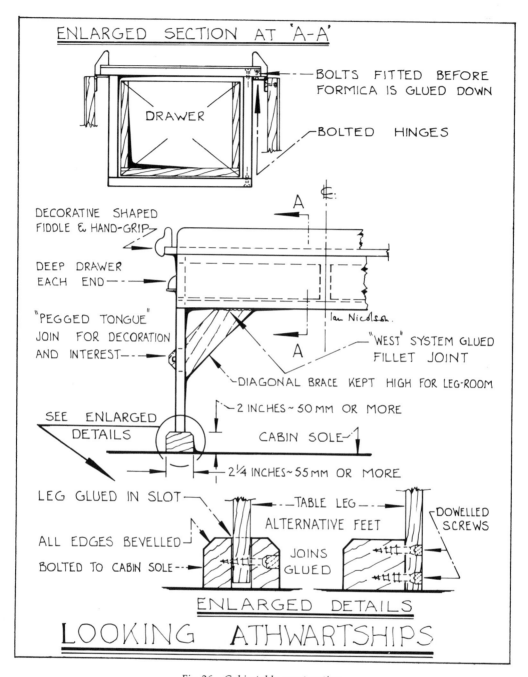

ENLARGED SECTION AT 'A-A'

BOLTS FITTED BEFORE
FORMICA IS GLUED DOWN

DRAWER

BOLTED HINGES

DECORATIVE SHAPED
FIDDLE & HAND-GRIP

DEEP DRAWER
EACH END

"PEGGED TONGUE"
JOIN FOR DECORATION
AND INTEREST

Ian Nicolson.

"WEST" SYSTEM GLUED
FILLET JOINT

DIAGONAL BRACE KEPT HIGH FOR LEG-ROOM

2 INCHES ~ 50 MM OR MORE

SEE ENLARGED
DETAILS

CABIN SOLE

2¼ INCHES ~ 55 MM OR MORE

LEG GLUED IN SLOT

TABLE LEG

ALTERNATIVE FEET

DOWELLED
SCREWS

ALL EDGES BEVELLED

JOINS
GLUED

BOLTED TO CABIN SOLE

ENLARGED DETAILS

LOOKING ATHWARTSHIPS

Fig. 26 Cabin table construction

If the top of a cabin table is made in the form of a box, it has strength and rigidity. This design of table has its leaves folded down at sea, so that just the middle part is used. In harbour the leaves fold up to give ample table-top area.

The middle sketch shows a side view of the table with the leaves taken away so that more details can be shown. The bottom sketches show the legs which must be strongly secured to feet well bolted not simply to the cabin sole but to a strong structure beneath the sole. All exposed wood edges are bevelled or rounded, not only for appearance but to prevent serious bruising of the crew in rough weather.

pieces, with feet of 2¼ × 2¼ inch (55 × 55 mm) hardwood about 15 inches (375 mm) long, glued athwartships across the bottom to take the holding down bolts. During fabrication all the exposed edges are 'broken', that is, either rounded or bevelled.

5   To make a table large enough for the whole crew, yet small when not in use, it is usual to have folding leaves on the table. Sometimes a single leaf is fitted and though this looks slightly unbalanced, it works well in practice because the whole table has to be tough enough to stand up to an offset load.

Leaves can be a nuisance. They put up the cost of the table and they pinch fingers. They work loose even with bolted hinges unless they are slightly massive and secured with at least three ¼ inch (6 mm) bolts in each flap of each hinge, with locked nuts. To stop a leaf clacking back and forth at sea it needs a barrel bolt to secure it or at least a 'silent' type of cabin hook each end. The feature of these hooks which makes them rigid and free from clicking back and forth is the tapered end of the hook which is received into a matching tapered hole in the gudgeon (metal eye on a flange plate).

If a leaf *is* needed, it is best to keep it less than 18 inches (450 mm) from hinge line to outer edge. The hinges must be a sea-going type, that is, all bronze, or stainless steel.

16 Tables for cockpit and wheelhouse

In the cockpit or wheelhouse a table is exposed to the weather and it has often to be fully portable. In contrast a saloon table is very much a piece of fine furniture, being permanently in full view and perhaps the most prominent feature below decks. It may well be beautifully finished, perhaps with a little inlay work or carving, even on a practical hard-working boat. It is likely to be highly polished, with concealed fastenings and a slick design. It will have as much elegance as the boatbuilder and his client can afford.

The cockpit table is different. Occasionally it will get wet from rain or spray. It will get bashed as it is put away in a hurry and scratched as it is slid into its cunning but cramped stowage in a cockpit locker or over the quarter berth, or adjacent to the spare anchor in the fo'c's'le.

To stand up to the weather it would normally be painted rather than varnished, and certainly not polished. However, well varnished furniture does have that 'Je ne sais quoi' which is (almost) French for 'I cannot say how lovely this is', so it is not unusual to see cockpit tables which are varnished, or at least have varnished edges and fiddles.

This brings up the point about whether a cockpit table needs fiddles. These fences certainly get in the way when eating a relaxed meal on moorings, which is a principal use of a cockpit table. When writing in the cockpit, or doing some pre-voyage chart work, the last thing anyone wants is an awkward ridge along each side of the table.

But even on moorings boats roll, especially when some idiot goes past in a large vessel at a fast speed. So it is necessary either to compromise or try to have the best of both worlds. The table may be fitted with fiddles on one surface and not on the other, with reversible fastenings so that the table is secured whichever way up suits the occasion. Or the fiddles can be made removable, or

---

Fig. 27 Chart table serves as cockpit table　　　　　　　　　　▷

It is always a problem to know where to stow a cockpit table, particularly on a small boat. The Belgian builders ETAP have worked out this ingenious idea which can be altered and adapted to different circumstances. The chart table top has no hinges and rests on ledges round the chart locker so that it can be lifted out. The table top is suitably stiffened and on the underside it has a flanged socket. To set the table up in the cockpit it is only necessary to drop the 3 inch (75 mm) diameter aluminium tube into the special socket in the bottom of the cockpit and then drop the table on top of the tube. For strength on a large boat one might have more tubes.

The chart locker must be deep enough, not only to hold charts but also to take the table top stiffener and the flange socket on the underside. The cockpit well socket for the tube must be deep enough to give a good grip and this will probably mean glassing in on the underside of the cockpit well a wood block or metal socket about 6 inches (150 mm) deep.

left off and the table top covered with those sticky rubber mats which stop things from sliding off . . . most of the time.

Everything said about cockpit tables applies to a greater or lesser degree to

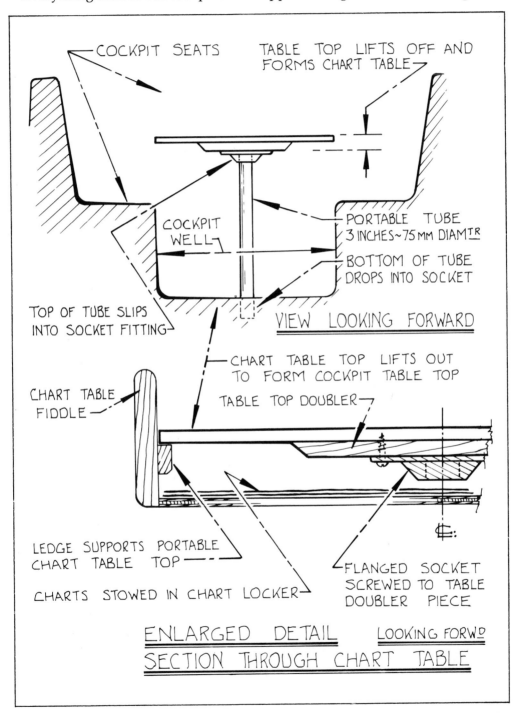

COCKPIT SEATS   TABLE TOP LIFTS OFF AND FORMS CHART TABLE

COCKPIT WELL

PORTABLE TUBE 3 INCHES ~ 75 MM DIAM^{TR}

BOTTOM OF TUBE DROPS INTO SOCKET

TOP OF TUBE SLIPS INTO SOCKET FITTING

VIEW LOOKING FORWARD

CHART TABLE TOP LIFTS OUT TO FORM COCKPIT TABLE TOP

TABLE TOP DOUBLER

CHART TABLE FIDDLE

LEDGE SUPPORTS PORTABLE CHART TABLE TOP

CHARTS STOWED IN CHART LOCKER

FLANGED SOCKET SCREWED TO TABLE DOUBLER PIECE

ENLARGED DETAIL   LOOKING FORW^D

SECTION THROUGH CHART TABLE

tables fitted in a wheelhouse, which may be fully or partly enclosed. The cockpit or wheelhouse on a boat is the main working area when the boat is under way. Furniture must be unobtrusive and strictly practical. It must stand up to the severest weather and be multi-purpose. All this means that if the table is not fully portable, it must fold away so as to give ample room to work the ship. Edges must be well rounded, or even padded. Whatever holds the table in place might have to stand the weight of three fat people all falling against one edge at once.

The classic cockpit table extends down the middle of the well so that the crew

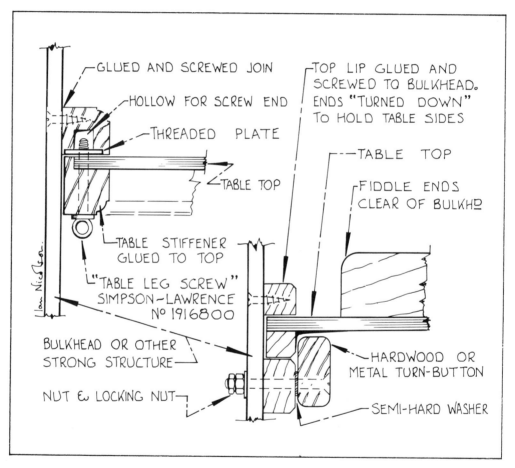

Fig. 28 Securing tables and other semi-portable fittings

The left-hand sketch shows one way of fixing a table, or work bench, or engine casing. This type of fitting can be used in the cabin, in the cockpit – indeed just about anywhere. At least two 'Table Leg Screws' should be used and if the furniture is large or likely to be heavily stressed, it is a good idea to have three. The lightweight table top is made rigid by the strong rebated edge moulding which extends all around the bottom.

The right-hand sketch shows another way of fixing a piece of furniture. Here again at least two and, better still, three securing devices should be used. A turn-button can be bought from the chandlers, or one can be made up as shown in this sketch. Notice how the wood button has all its corners well rounded.

sit either side, on the cockpit seats. The forward end may reach to the bridge deck, on which the cook sits, so that when the first course of the meal is finished he is close to the cabin entrance and can easily nip below for the next lot of food. But having the table extend so far forward does make access into and out of the cabin awkward for everyone else and a shorter table which leaves standing space in the cockpit well at the fore end is usually best.

The table legs have to be unobtrusive and should be inboard of the well sides, otherwise no one can slide fore and aft along the cockpit seats. This means that table legs which socket into the cockpit drains are not popular. If there is a binnacle in the cockpit it makes an ideal securing point for one end of the table. The other end may have a single leg which is fixed to the table with a couple of strong brackets to triangulate the join. On the bottom of the leg there may be a piece of wood which extends right across the well making a snug fit. To stop this foot piece from moving fore and aft, there may be a pair of barrel bolts on the cockpit well sides, or lashings to the eyebolts which take the crew's personal harnesses in bad weather.

The table will generally be made of wood because:

1   Few boats come with cockpit tables as a standard part of the gear, so the table has to be specially made, perhaps by an amateur.
2   Wood is cheap, widely available, easily worked and repaired, is light for its strength, floats if blown overboard, looks and feels good . . . what more can one say except that its Inventor did a good job and no one has come up with a better all-round material.
3   After the table has been used for a season or two, it may need modifying as improvements are thought up. This is particularly easy in wood.
4   The standard fittings which are widely available and cheap for fixing a table in place, are easily secured to wood.

Rival materials such as fibreglass and seawater-resistant aluminium alloys do not have all the virtues of wood. However they might be selected by a boatyard or amateur who is more used to these materials than to working wood.

When making up a cockpit table it is an excellent idea to make a mock-up first. It can be of cardboard or pieces of wood held together temporarily with sellotape or clamps. The mock-up is tried in place to confirm it will carry the requisite number of plates and glasses, or take a half-folded chart, or is adequate for the whole crew to sit around at once. The bolts, clips, or other fittings to fix the table may be tried out in their planned positions, temporarily held by plasticine or sellotape, to check that they are not going to be obtrusive even when the table is stowed away. Nothing tears oilskins and flesh like metal projections in a cockpit. If the fittings cannot be recessed, they should be secured to the table so that they are stowed away with it, leaving nothing except holes for barrel bolts, or slots for clips or Velcro strips in the cockpit.

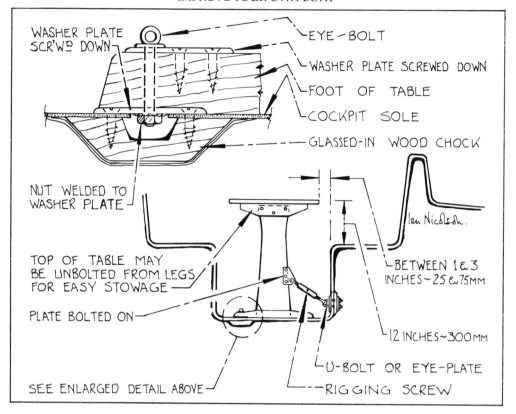

WASHER PLATE
SCR'WᴰᴰDOWN

NUT WELDED TO
WASHER PLATE

TOP OF TABLE MAY
BE UNBOLTED FROM LEGS
FOR EASY STOWAGE

PLATE BOLTED ON

SEE ENLARGED DETAIL ABOVE

EYE-BOLT

WASHER PLATE SCREWED DOWN

FOOT OF TABLE

COCKPIT SOLE

GLASSED-IN WOOD CHOCK

Ian Nicolson.

BETWEEN 1 & 3
INCHES ~ 25 & 75MM

12 INCHES ~ 300MM

U-BOLT OR EYE-PLATE

RIGGING SCREW

Fig. 29   Securing down a cockpit table

Two techniques are shown in this sketch. On the right-hand side the table has a metal bracket bolted to each leg and each bracket is linked to a 'U' bolt or eyeplate by a rigging screw. Incidentally the same 'U' bolt will serve to take the clip on the crew's personal lifelines in bad weather.

Top left: the table foot is held down on to a washer plate secured to the bottom of the cockpit. This plate has a hole in it with a nut welded on the underside and an eyebolt is put through the foot of the table into the nut on the washer plate. So that the eyebolt does not crush the wood of the table foot, there is a washer plate under the head of the bolt.

Table tops are often made from a single piece of marine ply, usually ½ inch (12 mm) thick. As this is available in 8 × 4 feet (2.44 × 1.22 metres) sheets, it needs no joins. If there is one dimension more than 2 feet 6 inches (750 mm) for ½ inch (12 mm) ply, or more than 2 feet (600 mm) for 5/16 inch (8 mm) ply, there must be stiffeners, but in practice the fiddles are often strong enough to keep the table top flat and sufficiently rigid.

For a long, narrow table, such as one extending athwartships from cockpit coaming to coaming, a piece of solid wood has advantages. The edges are easily bevelled or rounded to give a good finish, whereas with ply the edges have to be covered by moulding which will need gluing on and then the moulding has to have its edges faired off. Solid wood is easy enough to obtain to about 8 inches (200 mm) wide, but beyond that the choice tends to be much more limited. Edge joining wood planks is easy enough with epoxy resins, but not every amateur feels he has the skill and clamping facilities for this work. So for tables wider than the breadth of locally available solid wood, ply is usually the logical choice. Large dining plates are about 10½ inches (270 mm) in diameter and soup plates usually about 8 inches (200 mm) across, so narrow tables are not satisfactory for conventional eating, as opposed to picnicing.

When it comes to fixing the table down, it is necessary to have at least three widely spaced securing devices, firmly fixed to rigid parts of the boat's structure. A simple arrangement consists of common bolts through the base or legs of the table and through the bottom or sides of the cockpit well. Butterfly nuts are desirable as they can be put on and off by hand. When the table is

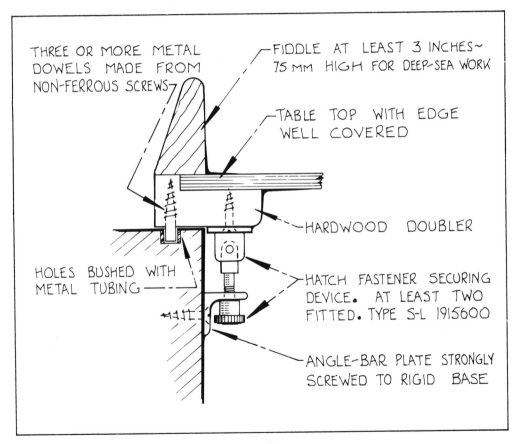

Fig. 30   Fixing portable furniture
If a table has to be mounted and taken down quite often, the arrangements for holding it in place need to be simple and easy to use. Hatch fasteners, which must be used in pairs or in batches of three or even four, can be extremely useful because they are easy to secure to the furniture and only take a second to tighten up. As shown in this section through a portable table, hatch fasteners on their own are not enough since they only hold the unit down. To prevent the table top moving athwartships or fore and aft there are metal dowels which drop into holes in a strong adjacent structure.

stowed away, the bolts are left in the holes to prevent water from going through into the bilge. Each bolt will have a semi-soft washer under a hard one, to prevent crushing the wood when the table is up and to make a watertight seal when it has been taken down. The bolts, nuts and metal washers are not those dreadful thinly plated steel fastenings which rust within hours, but they can be cheap brass, provided the bolt diameter is $\frac{5}{16}$ inch (8 mm) or larger. To look up-to-date they should be of stainless steel, though butterfly nuts in this material are not widely available, so they may have to be made specially by welding wings onto standard nuts. Alternatively, brass bolts can be chromium plated, though this never exactly matches the stainless steel which is now the common material for most deck fittings.

Other devices are hatch fasteners, such as the Simpson-Lawrence clamps, catalogue No. 1915600, or toggle fasteners such as the Simpson-Lawrence catalogue No. 1916001 for the horizontal type and No. 1916003 for the vertical type. These are seen on small deck locker lids and they work by having a metal hook on a pivot which, having engaged over a metal loop, is pulling down 'over top dead centre' so that it comes free only by pulling the hook handle up. Like all small metal fittings, they should be bolted in place and, like the hatch clamps, should be used in twos, or threes, or fours.

In practice, it is often impossible to have all the clips, hooks and assorted metalware fitted in such a way that no one jags themselves and their clothing. The problem is minimised by having tapered, rounded chocks each side of each fitting. This double-chocking arrangement can be used in dozens of places all over any boat and is much to be commended; it is about one tenth as effective as recessing a fitting, but we cannot have everything perfect all the time.

=17 *Low cost deck fittings*=

Apart from the cost of buying or making a fitting, there is the time and expenditure on bolts and bedding needed to fix it down. It is therefore logical to reduce the total number of fittings by combining two into one, or better still, seven into one. The stemhead fitting often includes the forestay tang and the roller for the anchor chain. It can also include a pair of fairleads, a mooring bollard or cleat, the forward two feet of the pulpit, a chock for an anchor, perhaps a water tank filler or chain pipe and maybe a fitting to hold the forward end of the spinnaker boom. Once this fitting has been secured in place, the foredeck is almost fully equipped.

One of the most successful combined fittings is the bollard-vent. I invented this in 1947 and it has been used, copied, altered, gone out of fashion and come back again several times since that date. There are versions which can be closed down in very severe conditions and others which stay open all the time and only let in water if the deck is immersed for a long spell. For plans of the bollard-vent (and lots of other gear and gadgets) see my previous books, *Designer's Notebook*, *Marinize Your Boat* and *Yacht Designer's Sketchbook*.

The chances of combining two fittings into one is limited but a wander round a boat show or marina will show what other people's ingenuity has done. An aft pulpit can have its foot flanges made extra strong to serve as bases for permanent backstays, or its side feet may have very strong base plates designed to take spinnaker sheet lead blocks, or the aft end of a jackstay wire for personal lifelines.

At the foot of the mast a water-box for a Dorade vent may also serve as a locker for winch handles and perhaps even as the base for a winch, because halliard winches often need raising up to make the lead from the foot of the mast fair, since the rope has to lead slightly upwards to the winch drum, otherwise the rope will over-ride and jam.

The next technique for cost cutting is to do without some fittings. Instead of a group of halliard winches, it may be possible to fit just one or two winches plus halliard stoppers, or substitute a tackle for a halliard which does not need the power of a winch. On a boat used for estuary cruising and racing it is possible to do without a pulpit at bow and stern, provided that the owner and crew are fit, not too old or too young, and are constantly aware that the deck is not fenced all round. A few purists, who do not race, will even do without stanchions and guardrails on the principle that these things were not put on small yachts before 1920 and boats look all the neater without them . . . and besides, people took trouble to hang on and hardly ever fell overboard.

A compromise between doing without and using conventional fittings is to substitute cheap components for expensive ones. I remember one boat which had on her foredeck a big eye-plate strongly bolted down with a good hard-wood pad under it and another below deck. The forestay rigging screw was attached to the eye-plate. One end of the anchor was lashed down to the eye, the headsails had their tacks secured to short lengths of line on the same eye

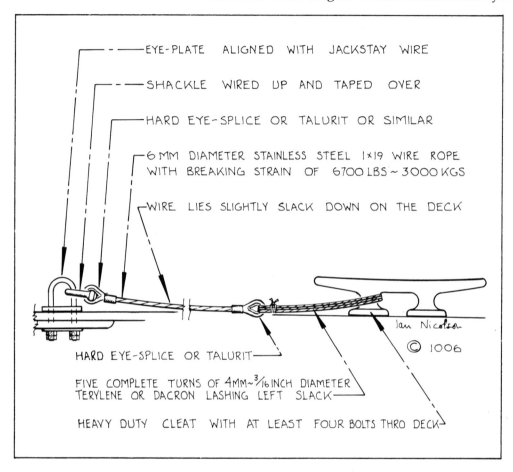

EYE-PLATE ALIGNED WITH JACKSTAY WIRE

SHACKLE WIRED UP AND TAPED OVER

HARD EYE-SPLICE OR TALURIT OR SIMILAR

6 MM DIAMETER STAINLESS STEEL 1×19 WIRE ROPE WITH BREAKING STRAIN OF 6700 LBS ~ 3000 KGS

WIRE LIES SLIGHTLY SLACK DOWN ON THE DECK

HARD EYE-SPLICE OR TALURIT

FIVE COMPLETE TURNS OF 4MM~3/16 INCH DIAMETER TERYLENE OR DACRON LASHING LEFT SLACK

HEAVY DUTY CLEAT WITH AT LEAST FOUR BOLTS THRO DECK

Ian Nicolson
© 1006

Fig. 31   Jackstays for personal lifelines

A jackstay should not be rigged along the deck tightly; otherwise it will tend to trip the crew. It is usual to make up a jackstay wire with a hard eye at each end and shackle one eye to a strong point such as the toerail or an eyeplate. The other end is lashed to another strong point such as a mooring cleat. The lashing is not pulled up tight and must be as strong as the jackstay wire itself. By using a mooring cleat, the expense of fitting a second U-bolt is saved.

Fig. 32   Improved Samson Post   ▷

This Samson Post starts off like many others, being made of hardwood. It stands well up from the deck and extends down to a strong point inside the hull. The unusual feature is the slot down the centre to take the anchor chain. This slot (and its metal back plate) must be made to fit the boat's chain.

   As the chain is hauled in, the crew lean back, gain a few feet and then drop the chain into the slot. In this way the mooring post acts almost as efficiently as a pawl on the chain roller at the stemhead, but it has the advantage that there are no moving parts. This device has been called a 'poor man's anchor winch' because it saves the cost of a winch – but only on a small boat.

and, when the mooring was hauled aboard, it too was lashed to this eye-plate.

A substitution which must be viewed with mixed feelings is the use of a single forward stanchion instead of a pulpit. This only works well if the

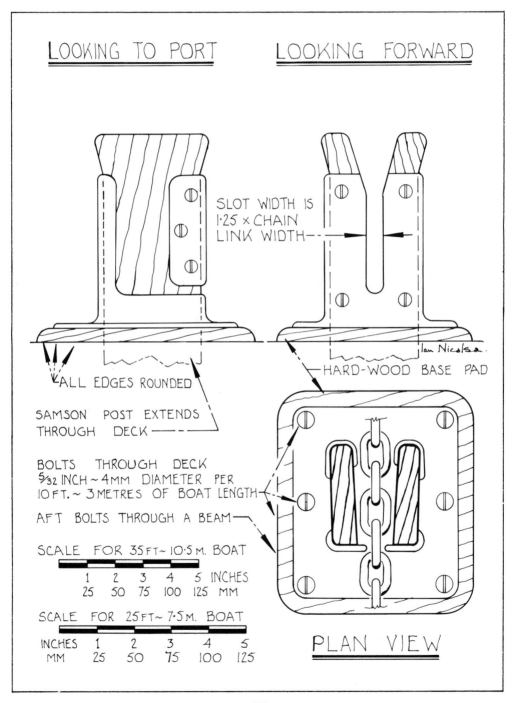

LOOKING TO PORT   LOOKING FORWARD

SLOT WIDTH IS
1·25 × CHAIN
LINK WIDTH

Ian Nicolson.

ALL EDGES ROUNDED

HARD-WOOD BASE PAD

SAMSON POST EXTENDS
THROUGH DECK

BOLTS THROUGH DECK
5/32 INCH ~ 4MM DIAMETER PER
10 FT. ~ 3 METRES OF BOAT LENGTH

AFT BOLTS THROUGH A BEAM

SCALE FOR 35 FT ~ 10·5 M. BOAT

| 1 | 2 | 3 | 4 | 5 INCHES |
| 25 | 50 | 75 | 100 | 125 MM |

SCALE FOR 25 FT ~ 7·5 M. BOAT

| INCHES | 1 | 2 | 3 | 4 | 5 |
| MM | 25 | 50 | 75 | 100 | 125 |

PLAN VIEW

117

forestay comes down to the deck aft of the stemhead. Even then, it is usually necessary to have the bow and forward pair of side stanchions angled outboard to give working room. The use of stanchions aft instead of a pushpit (i.e. aft pulpit) is fairly common. The stanchions set at each side of the transom need triangulating legs extending forward along the sheer and inboard across the top of the transom to prevent the stanchions bending inwards.

It is satisfying, as well as economical, to make up deck fittings and it gives the builder a chance to use his skills, as well as giving the boat some personality. In a world of mass-produced articles, something which has obviously been specially designed and made with loving care attracts

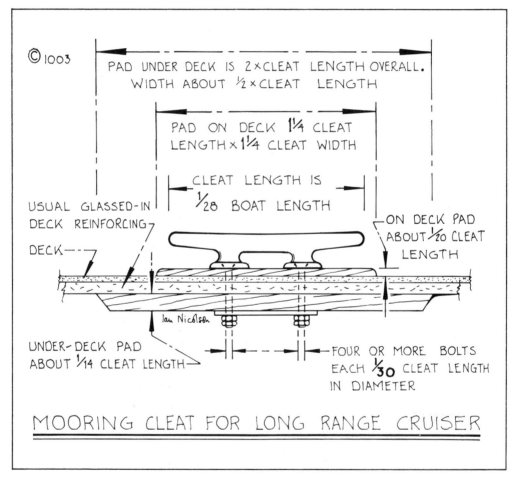

© 1003

PAD UNDER DECK IS 2×CLEAT LENGTH OVERALL. WIDTH ABOUT ½×CLEAT LENGTH

PAD ON DECK 1¼ CLEAT LENGTH × 1¼ CLEAT WIDTH

CLEAT LENGTH IS ½₈ BOAT LENGTH

USUAL GLASSED-IN DECK REINFORCING

DECK

ON DECK PAD ABOUT ½₀ CLEAT LENGTH

Ian Nicolson

UNDER-DECK PAD ABOUT ¼₄ CLEAT LENGTH

FOUR OR MORE BOLTS EACH ½₀ CLEAT LENGTH IN DIAMETER

MOORING CLEAT FOR LONG RANGE CRUISER

Fig. 33 Heavy duty mooring cleat

A boat going on a long range cruise needs extra strong deck gear, like this cleat. Ideally there should be two of these cleats forward, two amidships and two aft. They must be secured to a section of the deck which is extra strong, and stiffened with beams, stringers or a bulkhead. The size of the cleat is based on the boat's overall length. The sizes of the wood pads and holding down bolts are dependent on the cleat length. All these proportions give equipment which looks massive and inspires confidence when the weather turns dangerous.

favourable attention in every port. For a mooring strong point, for example, it is cheaper to make up a hardwood cleat instead of buying a bollard. The cleat may have to be much bigger than usual and it will need three or four or even six bolts through but it will be a pleasant change to see an elegant piece of woodwork with well rounded edges, perhaps with the boat's name carved along the top and a coat of glistening varnish, instead of a standard fitting.

Several skills are necessary to make up fittings. The first is the ability to decide when to buy a stock fitting and when it is better to fabricate a special one. It seldom pays to make up anything used on dinghies, because these parts are mass-produced in such numbers that they are cheap and well developed. Poor quality products seldom last long in this critical, competitive market. The same applies to blocks. Winches, too, in the smaller sizes are not worth making unless the builder has his own source of basic castings and loves to work on a lathe. Things which are worth considering include hatches, ventilators, cleats and bollards, stanchions perhaps (especially if they are wanted extra high or stronger than the usual relatively flimsy products sold by so many chandlers), and all those things which are not found on the great majority of boats. These include hatchway hoods, boom gallows, deck lockers, helmsman's seats as well as chocks for dinghies and liferafts.

Before making deck fittings, experienced boatbuilders browse through a selection of chandlers' catalogues. For a professional it is usually worth going to a lot of trouble to buy standard fittings, maybe modifying them here and there, rather than spending time making special deck fittings. For an amateur, who does not cost his own time, there are many reasons for making up fittings, quite apart from saving money. As so many of us use standard hulls, it is tempting (and it is worth succumbing) to give our boats individuality by having rare and special parts adorning the deck. It gives us a chance to invent new shapes and improve current designs. It is a great opportunity to do some carving, to embellish, to get one up on the rest of the fleet and to make a boat more valuable when the time comes to sell. But the fittings have to be well made; they should look as if they are professionally designed and finished; and they must be free from sharp edges, visible weld marks, uneven surfaces and unrounded corners.

A well known method of saving money is to buy fittings of a different material, for example galvanised fittings rather than stainless steel or bronze ones. When making fittings it is often worth considering the cheaper alternative of mild steel galvanised provided precautions are taken. The galvanising must be hot-dipped, never sprayed on or deposited electrolytically. Hot-dip galvanising is cheap because the charge is by weight and few owners can muster even 100 lbs (50 kg) of fittings, so they never have to pay much for this tough, long-lasting finish. Since there is often a minimum charge, it is good sense to assemble all the fittings from several boats and have them all galvanised together.

Producing home-made fittings needs a collection of skills but if one person

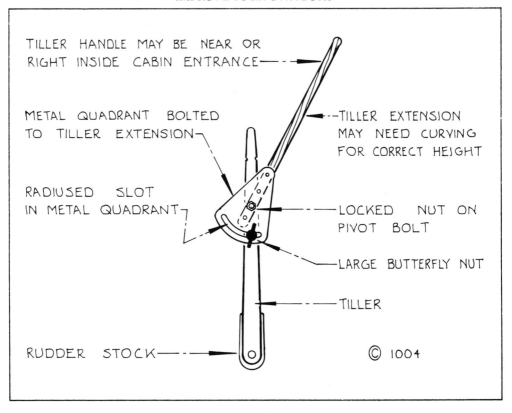

TILLER HANDLE MAY BE NEAR OR
RIGHT INSIDE CABIN ENTRANCE———·——➤

METAL QUADRANT BOLTED
TO TILLER EXTENSION⌐

➤——·—TILLER EXTENSION
MAY NEED CURVING
FOR CORRECT HEIGHT

RADIUSED SLOT
IN METAL QUADRANT⌐

——·——LOCKED NUT ON
PIVOT BOLT

——LARGE BUTTERFLY NUT

——·——TILLER

RUDDER STOCK———·——➤

© 1004

Fig. 34   Rigid tiller extension

When sailing single-handed or short-handed it is useful to have an extension to the tiller which makes it possible to steer without leaving the cabin. The extension must be rigidly secured to the tiller, and adjustable to different angles so that the boat's natural weather helm is no disadvantage. If the tiller end is normally say 12 inches to windward, the extension is angled so that its fore end is 12 inches down-wind, and so right on the centre-line. That way the extension is just inside or just outside the cabin entrance and normally on the boat's centre-line. The helmsman can cook or navigate with one hand, and steer with the other. A compass just inside the cabin is needed for this type of sailing, and some skill too.

If the forward end of the cockpit is sheltered by a hood, this type of tiller extension ensures that the helmsman can huddle in the shelter and stay dry while in the cockpit. This device is far cheaper than any sort of self-steering gear but is almost as useful in many circumstances.

Fig. 35   Securing personal lifelines   ▷

If there are eye-plates just outside the cabin entrance, the crew can hook their personal lifelines on while working in the galley or at the chart-table and they are safe during that dangerous time when they are coming on deck when plenty of people have been pitched overboard. The same strong point will allow a crew member to go aft to steer or to adjust the self-steering gear.

For working on deck a jackstay wire running the major length of the boat is a help, as the carbine clip need not be released while its owner moves from aft to the fore-deck and back again. The ends of the wire should not be too far aft or forward, as the lifeline length will give the wearer sufficient scope to reach the bow and stern.

A short jackstay near the mast is handy especially when there are two people working on deck. Both jackstays have to be kept clear of other rigging. The presence of jackstays does not mean that hand-rails are unnecessary . . . on the contrary, there are never too many hand-grips.

does not have them, a complete crew or family or drinking partnership usually does . . . or thinks it does . . . and confidence is what is needed as much as anything. The first move is to sketch and re-sketch the fitting until everyone concerned is pleased with it. At this stage decisions have to be made about materials, fastenings and finish. If a fitting is to be of bronze, the material

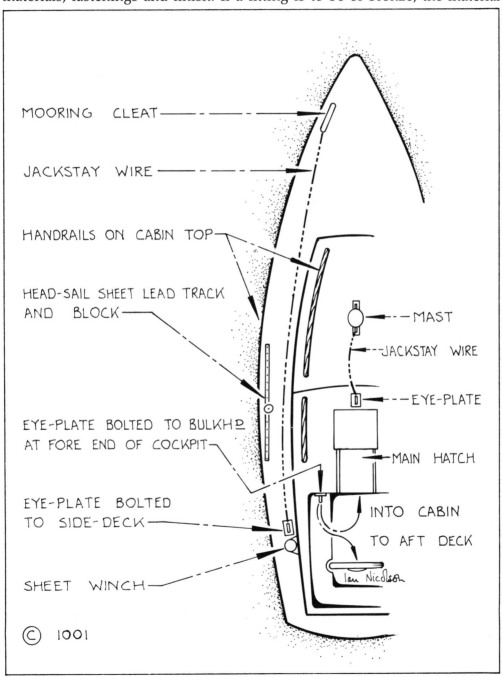

MOORING CLEAT

JACKSTAY WIRE

HANDRAILS ON CABIN TOP

HEAD-SAIL SHEET LEAD TRACK AND BLOCK

MAST

JACKSTAY WIRE

EYE-PLATE

EYE-PLATE BOLTED TO BULKHᴰ AT FORE END OF COCKPIT

MAIN HATCH

EYE-PLATE BOLTED TO SIDE-DECK

INTO CABIN

TO AFT DECK

SHEET WINCH

Ian Nicolson

© 1001

stockist has to be telephoned or, better still, visited to see what the standard sizes of bar, tube and plate are. If the fitting is to be super-cheap, then the home workshop and friends' scrap bins have to be examined to see what is available.

A high cowl vent is a good thing for an amateur or professional builder to make because few chandlers can supply these and this is much the best type for hot-weather sailing. Before going far with the sketch it is important to find out what diameter of thin-wall tubing is available at a reasonable price. Bronze would be best but it is hilariously expensive. Brass is not much cheaper; aluminium tends to corrode so it has to be carefully painted inside and out unless it is of a sea-water resistant type; stainless steel is fashionable but tubing is not widely available; mild steel is cheap and easy to work but the tube wall thicknesses available tend to be either too thick, being common gas or water pipe, or too thin, being ventilation trunking. Fibreglass tubing could be the answer but it is not sold in high street shops and may be hard to find. Maybe the best plan would be to make up a fibreglass tube; the wall thicknesses can be laid up to suit and any piece of metal tube of the right diameter can be used as a forming jig.

The best material that can be afforded is the only one to select because it will cut down maintenance and increase the pride of ownership. It will also add to the boat's safety and reliability. In addition it will be a work of art, and one which will certainly be more beautiful than any modern sculpture.

Once the sketches have been adjusted until they are right, a set of drawings to scale is made showing side, top and end views. When possible, they should be full size but if they are going to be too big, it is best to go for ¼ or ⅕ size. Avoid half-size because this scale is misleading; the eye and brain cannot grasp that the drawing is not full size. Even experienced draughtsmen find it hard to visualise final products when viewing half-size drawings.

If the boat is to race, the drawings have to be scanned to see how weight can be saved. The overall size is kept down and inessential parts are cut away. For instance, a base flange may be reduced to half its width, except in way of the fastenings. Lightening holes may be drilled in thick parts and, on items like cleats, the ends may be tapered almost to a rounded point. On cruising boats the factors of safety should be kept up. Items like our tall cowl ventilator, if made of metal, should not have base flanges only ⅛ inch (3 mm) thick, because in practice this is too weak. A thickness of 3/16 inch (4.5 mm) suits a wide variety of fittings on boats up to about 40 feet (12 m).

Many people, who are not used to plans, find it hard to imagine a solid object when looking at a drawing, so it pays to make up a full size model, which may be the pattern if the final fitting is to be made up in fibreglass. A cardboard model may be made if the fitting is to be of metal. It is set on deck in the right place, then everyone concerned can suggest modifications. Maybe the fitting will limit the helmsman's vision, or it might be in line to catch sheets, or trip crew going forward at night.

This is the time to ask if the fitting will stand up to a breaking wave or a

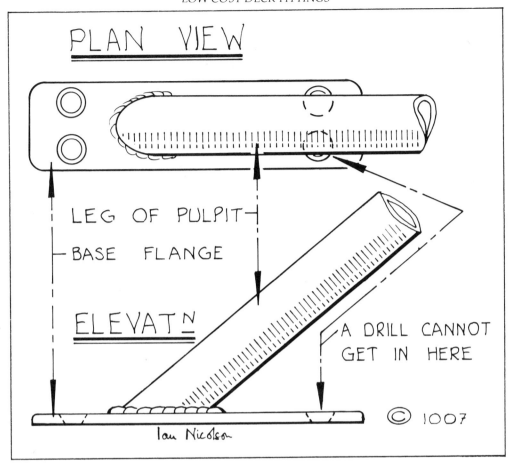

PLAN VIEW

LEG OF PULPIT
BASE FLANGE

ELEVAT^N

A DRILL CANNOT
GET IN HERE

© 1007

Ian Nicolson

Fig. 36 Badly designed fitting

When bolting down a fitting, the base flange is normally used as a jig for making the holes in the deck. However the access to each hole must be good otherwise a drill cannot be put into position. This sketch of a sloping leg of a pulpit is a good example of a badly designed fitting; the flange is too narrow and so the forward holes are underneath the leg of the pulpit. The only way to fit these bolts is to put the pulpit in position, pencil in the holes at the forward end, take the fitting away and then drill through the deck. Even then the bolts will only go through if they are shorter than the distance from the flange to the leg of the pulpit vertically above.

stumbling crew, those two ever-present bulldozers which crash about on every boat. Will it be easy to fasten down? Most fittings actually need more fastenings than is common . . . two bolts are seldom enough and ventilators which have to be waterproof need at least six fastenings around the base flange. Full vertical access to a flange from above is needed, otherwise bolt holes cannot be drilled.

It is obvious even at the sketch stage that our ventilator presents lots of construction problems. The cowl shape at the top is a complex bunch of curves and the height, which is essential, makes it vulnerable. One approach would

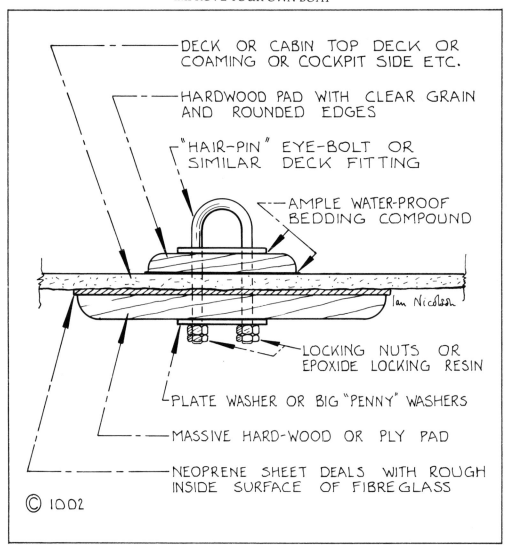

DECK OR CABIN TOP DECK OR COAMING OR COCKPIT SIDE ETC.

HARDWOOD PAD WITH CLEAR GRAIN AND ROUNDED EDGES

"HAIR-PIN" EYE-BOLT OR SIMILAR DECK FITTING

AMPLE WATER-PROOF BEDDING COMPOUND

Ian Nicolson

LOCKING NUTS OR EPOXIDE LOCKING RESIN

PLATE WASHER OR BIG "PENNY" WASHERS

MASSIVE HARD-WOOD OR PLY PAD

NEOPRENE SHEET DEALS WITH ROUGH INSIDE SURFACE OF FIBREGLASS

© 1002

Fig. 37 Fitting an eye-plate
For personal lifelines or for securing a spinnaker pole end, for spinnaker sheet lead blocks and many other purposes, a strongly secured eye-plate is needed. This sort of fitting must be above suspicion and able to stand up to high loadings without letting even a dribble of water through into the cabin. Waterproof bedding is essential under the flange plate and under the wood pads. The neoprene sheet acts partly as a water seal and partly as a bedding material to take up the roughnesses of the unfinished inside of the fibreglass.

be to use a standard mass-produced plastic cowl, easily available in chandlers, and set this up on a piece of standard piping. To give the fitting strength it may be made part of another fitting such as permanent boom gallows, or one of those pulpits sometimes called 'granny rails' which are set either side of the mast to help the crew work in bad weather.

Before starting to make a fitting a further attempt is made to bring down its cost. It is usually cheaper to make a batch of fittings rather than just one, so in the case of the high cowl vent all the air intakes on the boat are made the same. Going one stage further, there may be other builders who will order some of these new super-vents. This spreading of the cost is particularly advantageous if the fitting is to be welded up, or machined, or otherwise treated by a professional in any trade. Amateurs will save money by doing the maximum amount of work like cutting and marking themselves, leaving perhaps just the assembly welding to a professional. And after the welding the amateur will take the fitting home and do the grinding and filing of the welds until all joins show just smooth, rounded metal that looks good and holds paint well. Polishing and painting and other finishing jobs are often best done by the owner, who is going to live with the fitting, so that he has the maximum incentive to aim for in perfection.

=18 *Anchor handling gear*=

Since every boat's anchor chain or warp has to run out over the bow, it is usual to fit a roller on the stemhead fitting. To save money some builders have, instead of a roller, a curved stainless steel plate, something like a rounded chute. It works quite well provided that the curve is gentle, the tension on the chain or warp is not too severe, and the crew are tough or armed with a good anchor winch. It only suits boats under 36 feet (11 metres) and a roller is to be preferred even here.

To be long-lasting a roller has to be of hard metal like phosphor bronze, aluminium bronze or stainless steel. Some people use galvanised mild steel but it rusts quickly and always looks sad thereafter. Brass wears quickly and aluminium is too soft. The modern roller used by production builders is made of plastic, so that in a matter of months it is worn oval and makes it hard work to recover the anchor.

The roller can be bushed with a self-lubricating plastic like Tufnol. Common nylon is no good as the load on it makes it go oval, then the roller will not rotate easily. To make it run well and reduce the load, when the warp or chain is being hauled in, the roller should be much bigger than usual. It is impossible for a roller to be too big and occasionally one sees superb jobs about 1 foot (300 mm) in diameter on some big boats. A good working diameter is about 2½ inches (65 mm) for every 20 feet (6.5 m) of boat's length. The athwartships dimension needs to be around twice the width of the chain. Those side ears, or guards, which stop the chain coming off, should extend above the top of the roller by about 2½ times the chain width. This gives room for rags to be wrapped round a rope anchor warp to prevent chafing. Near the top of the side ears there is a horizontal pin to prevent the mooring line from jumping off if the boat is anchored in an exposed place or sheering about in a tideway. This pin should be tough and it should have a device to keep it in place like a drop-nose pin, which should be 5⁄16 inch (8 mm) thick for every 20 feet (6.5 m) of boat's length. These figures (and a good many more in this book) are well above current practice in boat factories but then these establishments are mainly interested in cutting everything to the bone to save pennies and weight.

Two medium-sized rollers, one above and behind the other, are better than one large roller, because then the anchor chain comes in over two 45° angles instead of over one at 90°. This reduces the effort of heaving such laden link over the roller. It also helps if each roller axle is large, ideally about half the diameter of the roller, with a grease nipple to supply lubrication. To save weight the roller can be drilled with horizontal lightening holes and the axle can be hollow.

Boats used for extended cruising need port and starboard rollers and they sometimes have permanent straps over the top of one or both, so that, if the boat has to be towed, the line will not pull off the roller. Other craft have special, enclosed, circular fairleads forward and these are to be recommended for use in canals where the bow warp has to be hauled in as water surges and boils in locks. Since the lead to the lock bollards is often almost straight up, the warp will not stay in place at all if it is not trapped inside a totally enclosed fairlead.

An addition to a standard roller, which helps the crew a lot in heavy conditions, is a pawl, which operates on the same principle as a ratchet. It is made of the same sort of hard, reliable metal as the roller and it hangs down at about 70° to the horizontal facing aft, with its bottom end touching the top of the roller. As the chain comes in, the crew can take frequent rests with the certain knowledge that every link they pull in is held in the pawl. Because the crew do not have to keep snatching a turn of chain around a bollard, their work is much easier. Nevertheless the pawl has a fearsome job in rough conditions so it has to be very strong. Even then the boat should never be left permanently with the chain held just by the pawl. On the contrary, when mooring, the pawl is flicked 'over the top' or reversed, so that it is taking no load. It needs to be on a pivot bolt about ½ inch (12 mm) thick for every 20 feet (6.5 m) length of boat, with plenty of clearance so that the pawl never has the least tendency to bind or seize. The bolt needs a locked nut and very good support. It is not adequate, for instance, for the bolt to go through just one side plate of the roller; it should be through at least two plates separated by a distance at least equal to the roller's width.

Pawls cannot be used on warps as they will just chop through the rope. However, with a rope there should not be much load to haul in – at least until the anchor is coming off the bottom. Whatever is being recovered, whether it is rope or chain or a combination, the boat should be sailed or motored up to the point where the anchor is directly below the bow. For a single-hander it is a great convenience to have a set of engine controls on the foredeck, or at least a method of putting the engine in and out of gear. When there is searoom and the boat is good tempered, the mainsail can be set and the boat left to sail herself up to the anchor. The warp pulls the bow round on to the opposite tack when the craft gets off abeam of the anchor.

Once the anchor is out of the water, there are handling problems unless it is so light that the crew can grab it and heave it inboard. The best plan for a big anchor is to have it on a chain leading up inside a hawse-pipe which extends from the topsides up through the deck, so the anchor self-stows inside this pipe. The chain is pulled in until the anchor is snug up inside the pipe. Of course, nothing in the realm of boats is straightforward. For instance, on any boat that is not made of steel, a hawse-pipe needs ample protection all round its lower end, otherwise the chain and anchor will do extensive damage to the hull. Once right up, the anchor has to be rigidly secured to prevent it flopping about and doing more damage. In heavy weather water spurts up hawse-pipes unless they have good covers which slide into position along the deck once the anchor is secured. Hawse-pipes offend many people because they are obtrusive and, except on metal boats, they tend to leak. But above all they are expensive. If there is only one, the second anchor has to be manhandled overboard and may be hard, perhaps almost impossible, to get back on board without equipment such as a cat davit and tackles (see below) so the boat must have these as well.

A solution that is becoming very popular is an arrangement whereby the anchor is hauled home over a bow roller and left lying there. The roller has to be large, or there have to be two of them, one ahead and lower than the other. Whichever arrangement is used, it should be specially designed to fit the anchor accurately. The best sort of anchors for this sort of stowage are either a Bruce or plough anchor. When hoisted home, the anchor is held firmly in place by the tension on the chain, but for added security a lashing or two is a good idea. To ensure that the anchor does not damage the hull as it comes in, the rollers are often set on the end of a flat-topped extension to the stem called a plank bowsprit. This is described fully in Chapter 20. This may have a pulpit round it and it is sometimes made retractable, partly to save length and so cut down the cost of a marina berth, partly to make the boat less vulnerable when offshore in severe conditions, and partly to make the boat easier to manage in canal locks and cramped marinas. The bowsprit may also carry the lower end of the outer forestay and it is a great place to laze when the boat is thrusting along in pleasant conditions.

On boats that cannot have this sort of bowsprit the anchor may be lifted inboard using tackles hung from the pulpit which will need to be stronger. Occasionally the anchor can be hauled up tight to the top of the pulpit and stowed there, although this does mean that there is weight and windage high up, which offends anyone in a hurry. A standard pulpit is likely to need reinforcing, perhaps with extra legs or diagonal struts. To secure the lifting tackle to the anchor an anchor hook may be needed. This is a device used when a cat davit is carried, and is described below.

Cat davits

Cat davits are simply miniature cranes, often made of piping, set on a pivot on the deck forward and reaching outboard to hoist the anchors in. Sometimes the socket is located on the centreline so that the davit can hoist in the anchor port or starboard. Alternatively, there is a socket on each side and the davit is put in whichever one is required. When not in use it is usual to have the davit lying flat on deck stowed in chocks with lashings, just like the anchors.

A cat davit needs plenty of reserve strength since it may have to lift an anchor which is thick with heavy mud, as well as a loop of anchor chain, and all this with the boat rolling and snatching in frightening conditions. So the davit is designed to support say four times the anchor's weight and to do this it must have a strong socket which may extend 1 or 2 feet (300 or 600 mm) below deck or be raised on deck with diagonal supports. In addition the davit may have stays or a bracket on to the top of the bulwark. The outreach of the derrick must be about the same as the anchor's width but even so, there will be times when the anchor swings towards the hull. To prevent damage a flat fender like a thick mat, made of strong canvas with a semi-soft padding is hung over the side by two lines.

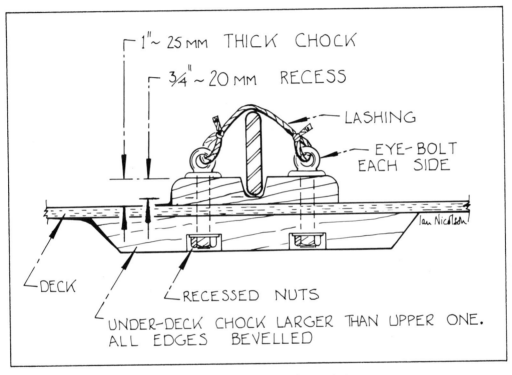

Fig. 37a   Securing an anchor on deck

Three recessed chocks are used to hold an anchor on deck. If there are eyebolts to hold these chocks down, the eyes can be used for the anchor lashings. Teak is the best wood for these chocks, and afrormosia or a similar hard-wood which weathers well a second choice.

If the under-deck chock is not recessed the nuts on the eyebolts may scalp the crew. This lower chock must be large if the deck is light and the anchor heavy. Both chocks should be bedded on a material like Farocaulk, to prevent drips through the deck.

To prevent the davit from swinging about out of control a rope leading forward and another aft are made fast to the end of the outreaching arm and led to convenient cleats. As the anchor comes to the waterline, the crew reach down and hook the cat davit tackle's bottom block to a metal eye on the anchor. In theory the hook could go through the chain's shackle on the anchor but this would mean lifting the anchor inboard hanging downwards. On craft big enough to need a cat davit the anchors are too big for bringing aboard this way, so each anchor has a 'lifting eye' at its centre of gravity. The lower block is hooked into this and, using the anchor chain to steady the anchor in a nicely horizontal position, the crew swing the weight inboard over the bulwark or guardrails and down on to the anchor chocks, which are exactly below the davit's arm when it is swung inboard.

There is one trouble: when the anchor breaks surface it is often too far down for the crew to get the lower block of the tackle hooked into the lifting eye. To solve the problem an anchor hook is used. This is a rigid bar or tube with a hook at the bottom end and an eye at the top. The crew hold this tool like a boat-hook and engage the hook end on to the anchor; they secure the bottom block of the cat davit onto the top ring of the anchor hook. The rest is easy except that the anchor hook prevents the tackle from lifting the anchor high and there is always the possibility that it will be difficult to clear the top of the bulwark or guardrails. One way to overcome this is to have a portable section in the bulwark or guardrails which is taken out to swing the anchor inboard. Having them portable means that it is easier to reach down to the anchor for clipping on the anchor hook. Another is to have a second tackle on the cat davit: when the first has hauled the anchor hook up chock-a-block, the second tackle is slipped on and this raises the anchor right up to the arm of the davit.

So far, so good. But what about getting the anchor over the side when it has to go down? It is no good hooking the lower block of the cat davit tackle on to the lifting band of the anchor, as there is no way of getting the anchor to drop off, unless the weight is taken on the anchor chain and then the block hook wriggled out at long range, perhaps with the help of a boathook. What is needed is a quick release shackle between the lower block and the anchor eye with a light line leading up to the crew on deck. When the anchor is to be let go, the crew snatch at the release line and the anchor drops, pulling its chain after it. Or does it? Those of us who have sweated and sworn and struggled to get quick-release shackles to let go of spinnaker tacks have become cynical after the number of broken nails and heart-snatches we have suffered. These quick-release shackles sometimes do not know their job in life. They hang on with infuriating tenacity. So a crude alternative, which goes back several hundred years, is sometimes used instead; this consists of a few turns of light line lashed between the lower block and the anchor. When the anchor has to be let go, a swift slash with a sharp knife slices through the line . . . a most satisfying operation.

=======19 *Cockpit hood*=======

(Sometimes called a 'pram' hood, sometimes a main hatch cover and other names in different localities.)

The open cockpit of any boat is at times wet, spray-blasted and windy. Yachting is uncomfortable much of the time, but it reaches grim depths if the crew have no protection from the worst of the weather. One of the best ways of keeping unpleasantness at bay is to have a folding hood over the hatch at the fore end of the cockpit, something like the one fitted on a child's pram. When the weather relents, the hood is folded down till it has to be raised again to fend off sunstroke.

If the hood is made the full width of the forward end of the cockpit and extended well back, the spray and rain will be kept off almost totally. However, such a hood is costly, fairly vulnerable to very severe seas and it offers a lot of windage. So some owners prefer a hood which fits neatly over the hatch but does not protrude each side, or any distance aft. This allows the hatch to be

This view, looking forward through the three windows of a hood, shows how much protection there is over the open main hatch. The instruments are protected from the weather, but in this arrangement there is not much space to spread out a chart under the hood. The reefing lines are led through holes in the break-water which forms the base of the hood.

131

kept open in the rain but gives much less weather protection to the crew in the cockpit. It costs maybe half as much. As usual each person has to make his choice according to the circumstances, available cash and past experience.

It is not easy to buy a standard hood, though a few builders and even fewer

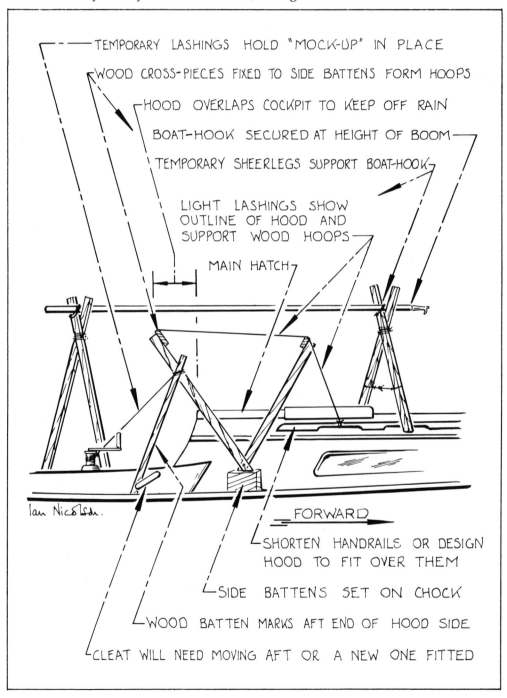

TEMPORARY LASHINGS HOLD "MOCK-UP" IN PLACE

WOOD CROSS-PIECES FIXED TO SIDE BATTENS FORM HOOPS

HOOD OVERLAPS COCKPIT TO KEEP OFF RAIN

BOAT-HOOK SECURED AT HEIGHT OF BOOM

TEMPORARY SHEERLEGS SUPPORT BOAT-HOOK

LIGHT LASHINGS SHOW OUTLINE OF HOOD AND SUPPORT WOOD HOOPS

MAIN HATCH

Ian Nicolson.

FORWARD

SHORTEN HANDRAILS OR DESIGN HOOD TO FIT OVER THEM

SIDE BATTENS SET ON CHOCK

WOOD BATTEN MARKS AFT END OF HOOD SIDE

CLEAT WILL NEED MOVING AFT OR A NEW ONE FITTED

chandlers have them. However, it is a certain bet that a stock hood will not suit many owners, being too big for some, too small or low, or weak, or shoddily made, or the wrong colour, for others.

To fit a hood, first draw out a detailed plan. Even a rough sketch is better than nothing, but for the best results it is well worth having an accurate plan, even if a draughtsman has to be commissioned to draw it up. If there are proper drawings of the boat, his work will be halved, as it will not be necessary to take measurements off the deck and cabin top. Once the cockpit area has been drawn in plan, elevation and from ahead and astern, the proposed hood is sketched in, modified, enlarged, given more tumble-home each side and so on, till it looks as if it is part of the boat and not an ugly late addition.

The outline of the hood is transferred to the boat. Coloured chalk can be used to mark the base and a few sticks of wood or metal battens are tied together to form a mock-up of the hoops. At this stage the crew can make sure they have a good view forward, check that the sheet winch handles are not obstructed, see there is enough space to spread out a standard chart on the cabin top beside the hatch, confirm that the boom is not going to shatter the hood every time there is a dramatic gybe, and so on.

The hoops and base fittings are next made and bolted down. With lengths of string the hoops are secured at the correct angle, just the way they will be when the hood is complete. Now a local sailmaker or hoodmaker is called in to take his measurements. When he has completed the hood cover and fitted it, a shipwright puts the lashing eyeplate or hooks round the bottom of the coamings to accord with the metal eyes on the bottom seam of the hood, or the press-studs are fitted on the coamings to match their opposite halves on the bottom seam of the hood.

At this stage it is best to take a long thoughtful look at the hood and make sure it does not need some modifications. These things are not like other creations of man – they are awkward, angular, knobbly and unco-operative. It is not unusual to find that a tuck is needed to tighten the cover and prevent sagging. A fore-and-aft or athwartships batten, or even three of them, may be

◁   *Fig. 38 Making a mock-up*

Though this sketch shows a mock-up for a hood to go over a main hatch, the techniques apply to mock-ups of all sorts, on deck and in the cabin. So as to be sure that the hood is not too high, a couple of sheerlegs are rigged up, one on the cabin top and one in the cockpit, with a boathook or similar piece of wood laid between them to indicate the main boom in its lowest position. Wooden hoops are made up of side battens and cross pieces screwed together to form the hoops of the hood, with bolts at each bottom corner to represent the pivots for the hoops. The pivot must be at the correct height so wooden boxes or chocks are laid on deck to support the side battens at the correct height. Pieces of string are used to lash the battens at exactly the right angle and, if there are no convenient fittings for securing the ends of the strings, lengths of electrician's tape stuck on the topsides, the deck and the cabin top will hold the strings where required.

The wooden 'goal-posts' can be used by the framemaker, and the sailmaker can take his initial dimensions off the mock-up. Before he does this the whole crew should stand in the cockpit and in the cabin entrance, so they can visualise exactly what it will be like with the hood up and they can check the view forward from the cockpit.

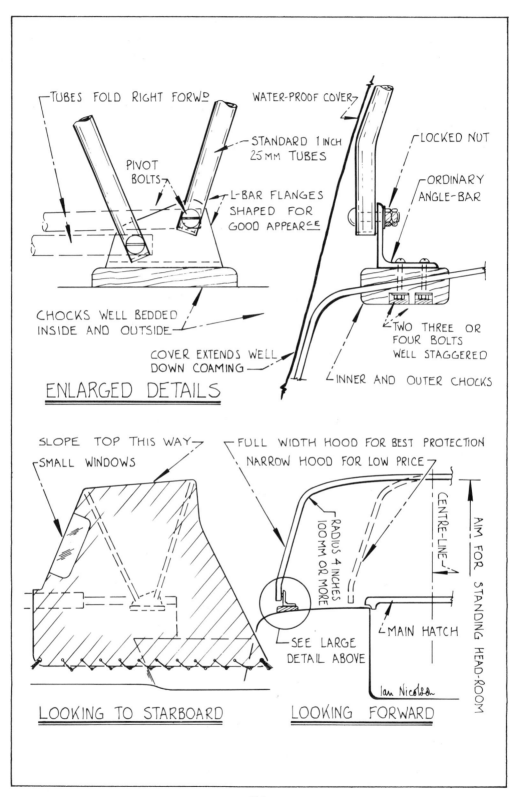

TUBES FOLD RIGHT FORWᴰ

PIVOT BOLTS

STANDARD 1 INCH 25 MM TUBES

L-BAR FLANGES SHAPED FOR GOOD APPEARᶜᴱ

WATER-PROOF COVER

LOCKED NUT

ORDINARY ANGLE-BAR

CHOCKS WELL BEDDED INSIDE AND OUTSIDE

COVER EXTENDS WELL DOWN COAMING

TWO THREE OR FOUR BOLTS WELL STAGGERED

INNER AND OUTER CHOCKS

ENLARGED DETAILS

SLOPE TOP THIS WAY

SMALL WINDOWS

FULL WIDTH HOOD FOR BEST PROTECTION

NARROW HOOD FOR LOW PRICE

RADIUS 4 INCHES 100 MM OR MORE

CENTRE-LINE

AIM FOR STANDING HEAD-ROOM

SEE LARGE DETAIL ABOVE

MAIN HATCH

Ian Nicolson

LOOKING TO STARBOARD

LOOKING FORWARD

134

needed in the hood to give it a good shape and prevent the upper parts from drooping. Battens may be of wood or fibreglass fitted in pockets like sail battens. It may be found that there is space to sew in a pouch or two each side, inside the hood for keeping a torch, some line and maybe a tide table, handy for anyone in the cockpit but out of the wet.

Hoods are made of any strong stitchable flexible waterproof or water-resistant material such as PVC, proofed nylon, very occasionally rot-proofed canvas, man-made canvas and sometimes even a cheap canvas type material treated with a waterproofing compound. All the edges are strongly seamed,

Windows in a hood should be on the forward face and on the sides so that the crew can keep a good look-out all round. This hood is supplemented by a cockpit cover rigged forward on a stainless steel hoop and aft onto the twin main backstays: spanned by stainless 'beams' bent to form an attractive rain-shedding shape so the crew are protected from rain and sun.

◁   *Fig. 39   Main hatch hood or 'pram' hood*

The first decision which has to be made relates to the width of the hood. Most people prefer a hood which extends right across the cabin top and cockpit because this gives good protection. However, this type of hood is expensive and relatively heavy. A little hood just over the main hatch keeps out a great deal of water (bottom right), and the hatch can be kept open in all but the worst weather.

A hood which is as wide as the cabin top can extend well down the coamings so that water breaking on board has less chance of getting up underneath the side of the hood (bottom left).

An inexpensive type of hood support bracket is shown at the top. It is made from common angle bar bevelled and cut with radii at the corners to improve the appearance and reduce weight. The horizontal flange needs a packing chock to cope with the slope of the deck and the sketch top right shows how a rectangular chock is cut at the correct angle to form the inner and outer blocks of wood. Bolts, not screws, must be used for holding the brackets down.

partly for strength, partly to take the wear and strains, partly for the edge lashing eyes or Prestadots, or other fastenings. The cloth is doubled in way of the hoops to strengthen the cover and absorb the wear.

Hoods are expensive, typically about half the cost of a good quality inflatable dinghy if one includes the fitting costs. The price can be brought down a little by using galvanised steel tube instead of the more popular and smarter stainless steel. To save every penny, the tube can be bought galvanised and the cut ends painted to prevent rusting, but if mild steel is being used, the best technique is to make the hoops and their bases complete, drill the holes in the base flanges about ⅛ inch (3 mm) oversize, round off all edges and corners, then have the whole affair hot-dip galvanised. After this the metalwork should be de-greased and fully painted. This treatment will hold off rust for a long time.

Whatever type of tube is used, 1 inch (25 mm) diameter is usually selected, though the next size down may be chosen on a light boat or to save weight. For deep sea use 1¼ inch (30 mm) tube or even bigger is needed. Occasionally aluminium alloy or brass tube is used for the hoops and very occasionally, laminated wood is chosen.

The sides of the hood have at each bottom aft corner a strong eye which has a lashing pulled back to an eyeplate to hold the hood up. Sometimes these eyes pull out long before the hood is worn out, so to avoid this it is best to have hydraulically pressed eyes, or the old-fashioned sailmaker's ring-and-turnover stitched in by hand. This aftwards pull to keep the hoops up is not always easy to achieve; for instance, there may be sheet winches in the way. Instead, an arrangement of port and starboard lashings down from the top of the aft hoop to the deck will be almost as effective, especially if the aft hoop lies back at a steep angle from its pivots.

When not in use, the whole hood should fold forward clear of the hatch and lie snugly on deck. Occasionally hoods are made with hoops which plug into the deck fittings so that apart from the deck plates, the whole affair can be taken off and stowed away each winter.

The same type of hood can be used over a forehatch to allow air to circulate through the open hatch in all but the worst weather. It is also an idea to fit a hood over the helmsman at the aft end of a long cockpit. Yet another place for

---

Fig. 40   Main hatch hood   ▷

The hood can cover a chart table for use by the crew in the cockpit. Naturally the wider the hood, the more space there is for charts, but the sides of the hood should lean in to give triangulation strength and a good appearance. A grab rail sewn to the hood cover on each side may not be the strongest on the boat but it can be extremely useful.

Bottom left, two alternative hood designs are shown using one main extra strong tube and either one or two lighter tubes pivoted on it. This arrangement can be most useful if the deck pivots have to be positioned in a small space, or at an awkward location.

A strong form of hoop end is shown in the enlarged detail bottom right. It is most important that the tubing is kept clear of the base bracket in such a way that the tubes can be folded right down flat when the hood is not wanted.

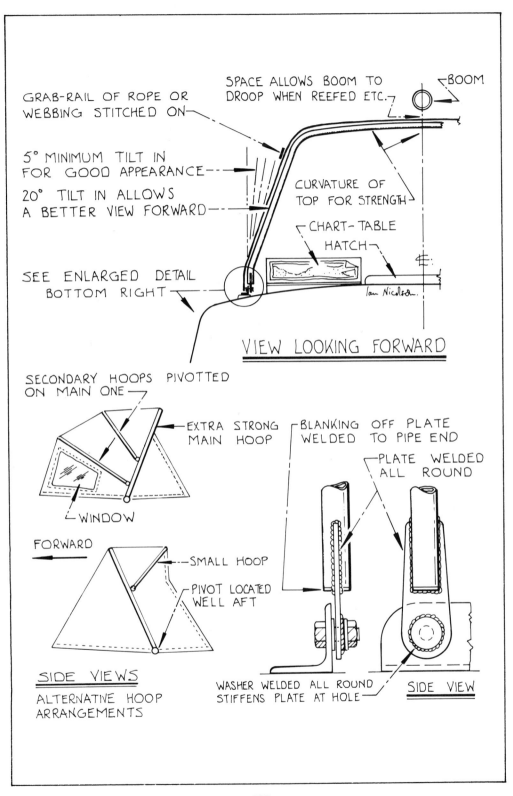

GRAB-RAIL OF ROPE OR
WEBBING STITCHED ON

SPACE ALLOWS BOOM TO
DROOP WHEN REEFED ETC.

BOOM

5° MINIMUM TILT IN
FOR GOOD APPEARANCE

20° TILT IN ALLOWS
A BETTER VIEW FORWARD

CURVATURE OF
TOP FOR STRENGTH

CHART-TABLE
HATCH

SEE ENLARGED DETAIL
BOTTOM RIGHT

Ian Nicolson.

VIEW LOOKING FORWARD

SECONDARY HOOPS PIVOTTED
ON MAIN ONE

EXTRA STRONG
MAIN HOOP

BLANKING OFF PLATE
WELDED TO PIPE END

PLATE WELDED
ALL ROUND

WINDOW

FORWARD

SMALL HOOP

PIVOT LOCATED
WELL AFT

SIDE VIEWS
ALTERNATIVE HOOP
ARRANGEMENTS

WASHER WELDED ALL ROUND
STIFFENS PLATE AT HOLE

SIDE VIEW

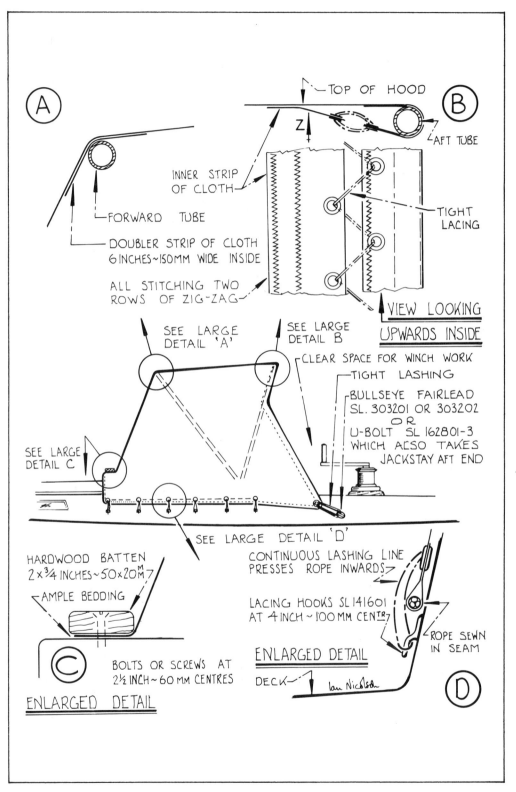

(A)

(B)

TOP OF HOOD

Z

AFT TUBE

INNER STRIP
OF CLOTH

TIGHT
LACING

FORWARD TUBE

DOUBLER STRIP OF CLOTH
6 INCHES ~ 150 MM WIDE INSIDE

ALL STITCHING TWO
ROWS OF ZIG-ZAG

VIEW LOOKING
UPWARDS INSIDE

SEE LARGE
DETAIL 'A'

SEE LARGE
DETAIL B

CLEAR SPACE FOR WINCH WORK

TIGHT LASHING

BULLSEYE FAIRLEAD
SL. 303201 OR 303202
OR
U-BOLT SL 162801-3
WHICH ALSO TAKES
JACKSTAY AFT END

SEE LARGE
DETAIL C

SEE LARGE DETAIL 'D'

HARDWOOD BATTEN
2 x ¾ INCHES ~ 50 x 20 ^{M} 7

AMPLE BEDDING

(C)

BOLTS OR SCREWS AT
2½ INCH ~ 60 MM CENTRES

ENLARGED DETAIL

CONTINUOUS LASHING LINE
PRESSES ROPE INWARDS

LACING HOOKS SL 141601
AT 4 INCH ~ 100 MM CEN^{TR}7

ENLARGED DETAIL

DECK

ROPE SEWN
IN SEAM

Ian Nicolson

(D)

138

one of these hoods is over the hatch into an aft cabin of a centre cockpit boat. To be really useful this hood should be designed so that it can protect the entrance from spray coming from forward or aft.

Hoods over the forward end of a cockpit should have windows partly to let in light but most important, to let the crew see what they are about to hit. Though the material from which hood windows are made is far tougher than it was ten years ago, this is still the weakest point of any hood. To reduce the risk of damage, windows should not be made more than about 8 inches (200 mm) wide, though they can extend almost half the full length of the panel. They should never go over a metal hoop and should be carefully folded when the hood is lowered or taken off.

Before ordering a hood, it is worth inspecting one from the same source. When the owner is not looking, lean heavily on it to make sure it has the ruggedness which is essential in anything on any boat. Check that the stitching has not started to rot because the maker has saved a few pence using common cotton in his sewing machine. Sit behind it and see how well you can view that unlit buoy lurking just ahead. Snuggle inside the hood and make certain that the rain will not drip on you. Walk down the cabin steps and check the head-room. Swing the boom across and confirm it clears the hood. Like a lot of things on boats, hoods need thought and planning.

◁   *Fig. 41   Main hatch hood*

A hood is made of waterproof material such as PVC. It needs ample strengthening, as shown at A. The top right-hand detail B, shows a good way of securing the aft edge of the hood to its framework. As the hood weathers and stretches the lacing is tightened and this avoids ugly sags and creases.

The sketch at C shows one way of securing the edge of a hood in such a way that it is truly watertight, while the sketch at D suggests one method of lacing down the sides of the hood. When the lacing is pulled tight the rope sewn into the bottom seam is pressed hard against the coaming and this stops water getting in. Notice how the rope is looped over each hook but passes straight back up inside the hood from eye to eye, these details being seen in the middle drawing and at D.

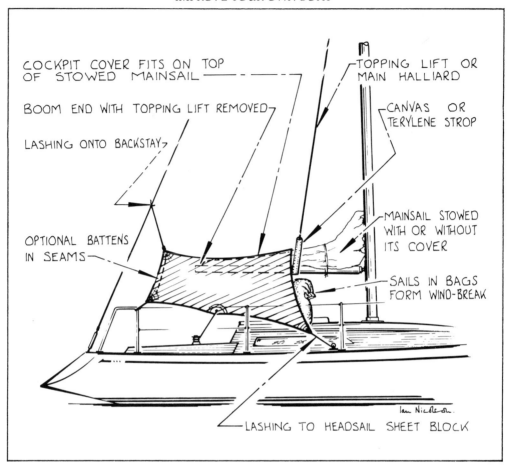

COCKPIT COVER FITS ON TOP
OF STOWED MAINSAIL

BOOM END WITH TOPPING LIFT REMOVED

LASHING ONTO BACKSTAY

OPTIONAL BATTENS
IN SEAMS

TOPPING LIFT OR
MAIN HALLIARD

CANVAS OR
TERYLENE STROP

MAINSAIL STOWED
WITH OR WITHOUT
ITS COVER

SAILS IN BAGS
FORM WIND-BREAK

LASHING TO HEADSAIL SHEET BLOCK

Fig. 42 Cockpit cover

This type of cover keeps off both the sun and the rain. Modern boats have short booms, so the cover has to be made to extend well beyond it with a lashing onto the backstay and possibly lashings onto the runners. The aft end is often cut up higher and made narrower so that the crew can get into the cockpit more easily. The forward end is generally secured up against the cabin top to make access fore and aft along the side decks easy. If the distance from the forward end of the main hatch to the mast is very small, the main halliard may not be able to support the boom properly and it may be necessary to have some sort of boom crutch or boom gallows to support the boom. A single boom crutch which can also double as a boat hook, saves weight and stowage space.

This cover is cheaper and easier to make than a hood over the main hatch only and gives more protection, but it can only be used in port or when under way using the engine in calm conditions.

20 Fitting a bowsprit . . .
a new trend

It's just a bit disconcerting, this current interest in bowsprits. After all, not so many years ago owners, designers, builders, writers, everyone was saying what a good thing it was that bowsprits were going right out of fashion.

Now they are back. Boats which never had bowsprits and boats which had them but discarded them 20 and 40 years ago, are sporting them. It's all surprising, but quite logical.

Here are just some of the reasons why boats are being fitted or refitted with bowsprits. In some cases several of these reasons apply, sometimes one reason alone is enough.

1 To reduce weather helm.
2 Because the boat used to have one.
3 Because she looks better with one.
4 Because it makes a handy anchor handling platform.
5 And a very handy anchor stowage device.
6 It is a good way to increase the sail area and hence the boat's speed, especially in light airs.
7 For the fun of having a good platform for taking interesting photos.
8 For spearing fish, even if the chances of success are 0.0000002 to 1.
9 For the pleasure of lying in the bowsprit net while the boat is sailing or anchored.
10 For the sake of tradition.
11 Because so many boats look alike and it is enjoyable being different.

Bowsprits come in a range of types, including:

(a) Traditional tapered solid spar, made of Oregon pine or spruce, varnished and glossy.
(b) Like (a) but made hollow to save weight.
(c) Like (a) or (b) but with a walk-way fixed along the top to make it easy to get to the fore end.
(d) Made of a wood plank, parallel sided.
(e) Like (d) but tapered towards the outer end and therefore more elegant and a better spar from the point of view of good engineering.
(f) Like (e) or (f) but hollow, that is in the form of a flat box, with solid sides and perhaps a ply-wood top and bottom.

(g) Made of metal in the form of a straight, tubular spar, tapered or untapered and akin to (b).

(h) Of metal tubing, bent in the form of an old-fashioned hairpin when viewed from above, so that each end is fixed to the topsides, well back from the stem. The tube runs from the port topsides forward and diagonally in towards the centreline, round a radius at the outer end and back to the starboard topsides.

There are other variations, but this list gives an idea of the alternatives which can be chosen. Each type has its assets and problems. For instance, if the bowsprit is in the form of a flat plank, especially if it is wide at the inboard end, it will need no shrouds. These wires are just like the shrouds of a mast, being side stays secured at the outer end of the bowsprit and led back to the hull very roughly the same distance aft of the stem that the bowsprit extends forward of it. Sometimes, though rarely nowadays, and very rarely on a boat under 50 feet (15 metres) overall length, there are whiskers which are like spreaders, except that they extend outboard from the deck edge and push the bowsprit shrouds out to a greater angle at the forward and aft ends.

A bowsprit should be tilted up at the forward end so that its top runs on at the same angle as the forward part of the sheer. If the bowsprit is tapered, the under side is tapered up to the top and great care should be taken to keep the top face running with the sheer line. If necessary, have the bowsprit fitted temporarily, then stand back and make sure it looks right from forward, from aft and from abeam. If in doubt, cock the forward end up a lot – almost outrageously. This will give added advantages such as keeping the headsails out of the water and the crew will get less wet when they go out to the end when sailing offshore.

When it comes to judging how long a bowsprit should be, there are several rules which can be followed, but nothing can beat copying the great designers. If dealing with a weather helm problem the way to get the right length is to work out where the sail centres should be and design the bowsprit accordingly. Another trick is to copy similar yachts. Another is to draw something which you and all your friends reckon looks right. Another is to make the bowsprit only 2 foot 6 inches (760 mm) outboard because then the average crew will be able to reach the forestay without leaving the main deck.

Yet another scheme is to make the bowsprit extend forward of the bow between 8% and 18% of the boat's length beyond the bow. For offshore work or if the crew is small, go for the lower limit. And if the local harbours are crowded, or if you are worried about high stresses, go for the shorter length. But if you want elegance, or if you want to impress your neighbours and frighten the other people who keep their boats near yours, go for the longer length. It's like most things in yachting . . . suit yourself without being excessive.

Just as important as the length of the bowsprit is the way it is finished. If it is of wood it should be varnished unless all the other spars are painted, in which case it should match them. If it is of metal it often looks good painted, but if of aluminium then anodising to match the other spars is smart. If it is of steel it should be galvanised, then painted to accord with the rest of the boat. A metal tubular bowsprit often has a wood walkway and probably this has toerails of timber. All this wood looks good if varnished, but the wood should all match.

Whatever material is used, and regardless of the shape and size, a bowsprit has to be easy to fit, to take off and to mend. Few things are more vulnerable so it is tempting fate to secure a bowsprit like a keel which is fixed for most of eternity and damn hard to get off even with good equipment and bright shipwrights.

Some people go further. They make their bowsprits reefable, so that when coming into a crowded harbour or anchorage, they bring in the proboscis. This means the ship's overall length is less, so there is less chance of an accident, and the boatyard storage and hauling out fees are less because these are almost universally calculated on total overall length. A bowsprit which slides inboard, partly or wholly, can be taken off easily in winter, or it may be designed to tilt up to a vertical position to support a winter cover.

All this suggests that a bowsprit should be bolted, not welded, to a steel or aluminium boat. On a wood or fibreglass boat it should be secured by well greased bolts rather than screws. Its fittings should be designed to help this reefing or shortening, or carrying ashore in the winter. And a portable or semi-movable one is going to be easier to get mended when an accident does happen. Years ago some bowsprits were fitted so as to slide smoothly inboard, with a tackle to hold them out. When the boat got out of control and approached a danger head-on, one of the crew would dash forward and slacken off the tackle end, then he would ease off the rope at just the right speed at the moment of impact. This allowed the bowsprit to act like a shock absorber, provided the crew were skilful and the momentum not too great! Learning the trick must have been an expensive and splintering pastime.

There are no formulae for calculating the size of a bowsprit because the requirements vary from boat to boat. On one the bowsprit will just carry a light headsail in gentle conditions. On another the 'sprit will have to stand up to hammering in harbours and hurricanes at sea. As a rough guide a plank bowsprit might be as tabulated below.

It cannot be over-emphasised that this is a starting guide and that it is based on a dense high strength timber free from all faults.

Boat overall length	*Bowsprit width at inner end*	*Thickness*
25 ft (7.5 metres)	10 inches (250 mm)	1¼ inches (30 mm)
35 ft (10.5 metres)	20 inches (500 mm)	2 inches (70 mm)
45 ft (13.5 metres)	30 inches (750 mm)	2¾ inches (70 mm)

For a steel tubular bowsprit of the 'hairpin' type, bent round into a U-shape and secured well aft of the stem, with ample spread to cope with the side forces, a rough guide as to size is as follows:

Boat overall length	Tube diameter
25 ft (7.5 metres)	1¼ inches (30 mm)
35 ft (10.5 metres)	2½ inches (65 mm)
45 ft (13.5 metres)	4 inches (100 mm)

When designing a bowsprit, it is worth starting with the breaking load of the forestay and assume this is the maximum load applied. This will give the load on the bobstay and the compression loading on the bowsprit. In practice, a breakage is most likely to occur when there is a combined compression load *and* sideways force, a very 'unfair' situation and one hard to predict since who is to say what the side load is? Will it be a thump from a breaking sea into a full headsail or a collision with a quay wall?

Designing the fittings for a bowsprit calls for a bit of cunning. The best ploy is to make each fitting about twice the strength of the wire onto it, for a racing boat, four times for a cruiser and six times for a long-range cruiser. It is logical to use long lasting metals which can stand wear because this will occur. Where a conventional bowsprit goes through the cranse iron there is subtle movement due to the varying end loads; the anchor chain chafes on the bobstay and applies severe side loads; a flogging headsail on the outer forestay will cause the fore end of the bowsprit to vibrate . . . and so on.

Stainless steel of a true seawater resistant type is acceptable, though not for the bobstay bottom end fitting which is in or near the sea.

The traditional round section bowsprit spar has a 'four-eye' band at the outer end, the upper eye being for the forestay and headsail tack securing device, the lower one for the bobstay and the side ones for the shrouds.

A plank bowsprit can have the same sort of arrangement, only instead of a circular band with four metal eyes, there will be a flat bar bent right round the end of the 'sprit, like a rectangular collar. Incidentally this type of fitting also prevents the plank splitting. Alternatively, standard eyeplates bought from a

---

Fig. 43   A tapered plank bowsprit   ▷

If a bowsprit is being added to a boat which did not formerly have one, the original stem-head fitting is usually a great nuisance. Getting a fitting off may be very difficult and even when it is off, there may be an up-standing stem which prevents the plank bowsprit lying flat on deck. This bowsprit has a rectangular hole cut out of it to fit over the old fitting (which may still be used for an inner forestay). To compensate for the lost strength a doubler piece of wood is glued on top of the bowsprit.

The bobstay fitting is fitted above the waterline to reduce corrosion, but the angle between the bobstay and the bowsprit should be as big as possible and not less than about 16°. All sorts of outer end fittings can be used, but the one shown is made up from two eye-plates and a U-bolt, all of which can be bought at a chandlery. One final detail: the anchor winch is offset to line up with the starboard chain roller.

chandler can be bolted on top and bottom, possibly sharing bolts. Another alternative is to have a typical stemhead fitting just like on the top of a bow, mounted on the end of the plank, fully bolted down with a tang over the fore end of the plank bend aft to take the bobstay.

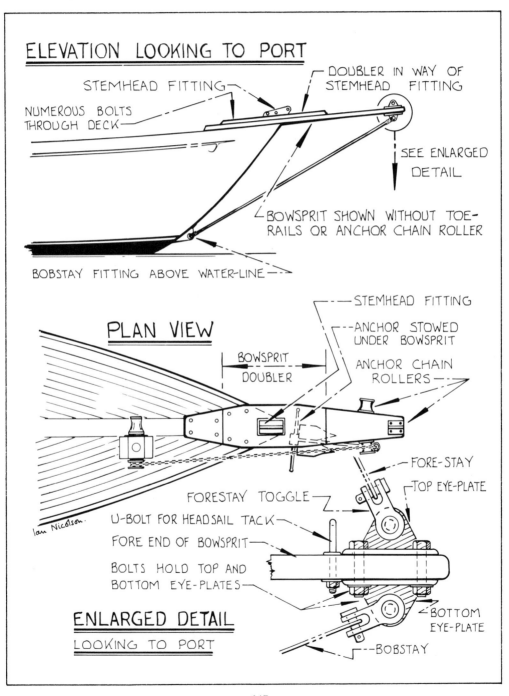

ELEVATION LOOKING TO PORT

STEMHEAD FITTING

DOUBLER IN WAY OF
STEMHEAD FITTING

NUMEROUS BOLTS
THROUGH DECK

SEE ENLARGED
DETAIL

BOWSPRIT SHOWN WITHOUT TOE-
RAILS OR ANCHOR CHAIN ROLLER

BOBSTAY FITTING ABOVE WATER-LINE

PLAN VIEW

STEMHEAD FITTING

ANCHOR STOWED
UNDER BOWSPRIT

BOWSPRIT
DOUBLER

ANCHOR CHAIN
ROLLERS

FORE-STAY

TOP EYE-PLATE

FORESTAY TOGGLE

U-BOLT FOR HEADSAIL TACK

FORE END OF BOWSPRIT

BOLTS HOLD TOP AND
BOTTOM EYE-PLATES

Ian Nicolson.

ENLARGED DETAIL

LOOKING TO PORT

BOTTOM
EYE-PLATE

BOBSTAY

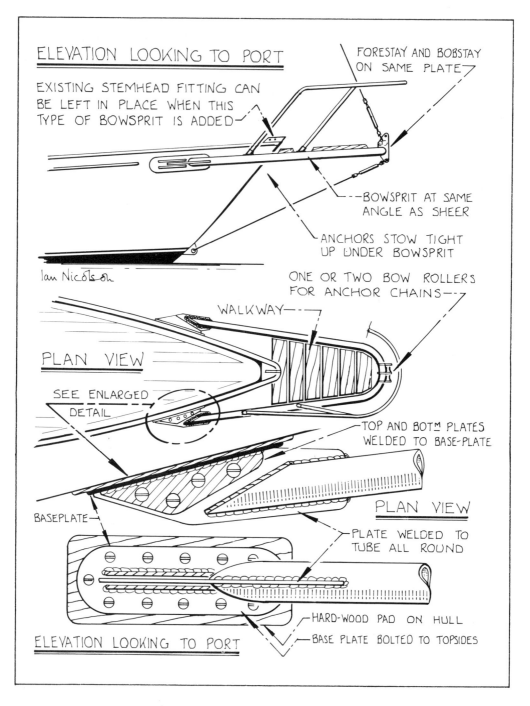

ELEVATION LOOKING TO PORT

EXISTING STEMHEAD FITTING CAN
BE LEFT IN PLACE WHEN THIS
TYPE OF BOWSPRIT IS ADDED

FORESTAY AND BOBSTAY
ON SAME PLATE

BOWSPRIT AT SAME
ANGLE AS SHEER

ANCHORS STOW TIGHT
UP UNDER BOWSPRIT

Ian Nicolson

ONE OR TWO BOW ROLLERS
FOR ANCHOR CHAINS

WALKWAY

PLAN VIEW

SEE ENLARGED
DETAIL

TOP AND BOTᴹ PLATES
WELDED TO BASE-PLATE

PLAN VIEW

BASEPLATE

PLATE WELDED TO
TUBE ALL ROUND

HARD-WOOD PAD ON HULL

BASE PLATE BOLTED TO TOPSIDES

ELEVATION LOOKING TO PORT

Fig. 44   Tubular bowsprit

This type of bowsprit is modern, strong, and it stands up to a lot of abuse. To make it easy to fit, to remove and to repair it is bolted to base-plates which in turn are bolted to the topsides. Each end of the tube is cut at a steep angle, and a plate welded over, then a fork plate welded to the tube. This gives a very strong end fitting, and by sealing the tube ends, prevents internal corrosion.

The rigging screw on the bobstay is at the top end, to keep it clear of the sea and so minimise corrosion. At the aft end of the walk-way there is a gap which is handy for hauling the anchor up once it is clear of the sea, and it can then be lashed to the tube.

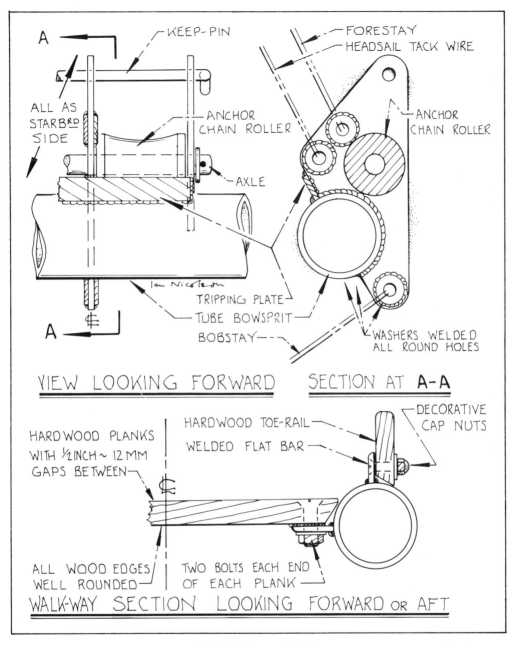

Fig. 45 *Bowsprit details*

Though this sketch shows parts of the tubular bowsprit opposite, the top fittings can be used on different types of bowsprit. Where the rigging is attached the plates are strengthened by welding washers round the holes. There may be a single washer on one side of the hole, or a pair provided they do not make the plate too thick for the rigging end fitting.

To prevent the vertical plates from being twisted sideways there is a tripping plate welded across the aft end. The artist might have shown another tripping plate below the anchor chain roller, set aft of the front of the roller so as not to foul the chain as it is hauled in.

The outboard plates only have to support the rollers so they are stopped level with the middle of the bowsprit tube, whereas the middle plate extends down to take the bobstay.

On the bottom sketch the bolts through the toerail have their nuts on the outside otherwise they might catch the toes of anyone walking forward.

At the outer end of a tubular bowsprit there must be a vertical plate to take the outer forestay and the same fitting should take the bobstay. If this flange is aligned fore and aft it can act as one side of a stemhead roller support, perhaps with a matching stemhead roller on the other side. The plate may be big enough to include a hole for the sail tack shackle or pennant, or there may be a piece of steel rod bent into a loop and welded each end to take the tack fitting.

Most modern bowsprits are guarded by a pulpit and if the extension is more than about 2 feet (600 mm) long, the forward feet of the pulpit will rest on the out-reaching spar. This is one good reason for having a plank or U-shaped tubular 'sprit rather than a traditional round spar type.

The inner end of a plank bowsprit is bolted through the deck with an outsize pad below the deck and very probably another pad between the deck and the bowsprit. There will be six or eight or twelve bolts in a staggered pattern, with big washers under their heads and nuts, also plenty of lanolin on the bolt threads so that it is easy to extract the bolts. Careful owners remove parts like varnished bowsprits each year and take them home for re-varnishing in the warm, dry conditions of the family home. Wives seldom object more than four times monthly.

A hairpin type bowsprit is secured outboard on the topsides. There may be a welded flange on each end of the tube which is through-bolted with a wood pad between the metal plate and the hull with a plate washer inboard and nuts locked on. Because bowsprits are vulnerable, some designs separate the bowsprit from the flanged fittings bolted to the hull. In this case the aft ends of the tube have welded horizontal plates which in turn are bolted to plates welded to flanges bolted to the topsides. The thinking here is that:

(a) It is easy to get the bowsprit off for winter storage or repairs or alterations.
(b) If the bowsprit is damaged, it takes a few minutes to get the 'sprit off and repairs or total renewal is reasonably quick and uncomplicated.
(c) The initial fitting is easier if the hull plates are secured first and the bowsprit made to accord with the lugs extending from the boat. Even if the boat is new and carefully built, it is a bit of a miracle if everything made solely off drawings and the mould loft fits perfectly. Most builders will want to check the angles on the boat and many will lift all the angles and sizes from the boat.

A tubular bowsprit is held by a circular strap on the stemhead and a fitting over or behind the inboard end of the spar. This inner fitting can be in the form of a goalpost astride the spar, with an athwartships bolt through both uprights of the goalpost and the bowsprit. When the bolt is extracted, the bowsprit can be run inboard or pulled forward and taken off the ship. Extra holes may be arranged along the length of the spar so that the bowsprit can be reefed half or one-quarter inboard. This is handy in crowded harbours or when there are rapacious marina rent-gatherers about, demanding money based on the total overall length of the boat.

To prevent the bowsprit from being torn upwards, there has to be a bobstay from the spar and down to the stem near the waterline. Plenty of draughtsmen have gone through stressing calculations and tried in vain to design bowsprits with no bobstays, to save weight and money, but above all to avoid the chafe between the bobstay and the mooring. When anchored or on a permanent mooring, there is an almost constant battle between two opposing pieces of chain or wire. They damage each other and grind together all night so that only the very drunk can get any sleep on board. However, bobstays are essential, as the simplest calculation will show.

The bobstay can be of wire or chain, with a tackle at the top end so that on moorings the whole affair is slackened right off and hauled up tight under the bowsprit. In this way there is no chafe between the bobstay and anchor chain, but the tackle has to be tough and therefore bulky to be strong enough. Another technique is to make the bobstay of solid rod on the principle that this can stand up to a lot of chafe. It tends to get bent instead and the fork ends are vulnerable to the side forces when the boat swings wildly sideways in a wind-over-tide mêlée.

What makes modern bowsprits better than the traditional type is the walkway along the top. If the spar is round, it may have a flat surface planed along the top, but this is narrow and seldom satisfactory even on a very big boat. A better arrangement is to have a catwalk complete with toerails each side secured on top of the spar.

Plank bowsprits need no walkway . . . the whole spar makes a good path out to the forestay. This is one reason why they are so popular. The 'hairpin' type has slats laid athwartships or fore and aft between the side tubes, the wood being strong enough to support a heavy man or two. Wood about 4 inches × ¾ inches (100 mm × 20 mm) and not over 12 inches (300 mm) between supports works well. Gaps about ½ inch (12 mm) between the planks ensure prompt drainage and slightly reduce the slamming effect when the bowsprit thrashes down onto the sea as the boat plunges bows under.

The toerails may have holes at intervals of say 10 inches (250 mm) for lashings to secure a headsail when it has been hauled down, or before it is set. The only snag about this is that in vicious weather the sail may get torn off its lashings, taking bits of woodwork with it.

21 Fitting an inner
════════forestay════════

There are varieties of reasons why anyone might want to fit an inner forestay. Some examples follow:

1 Sometimes a mast needs extra support.
2 The mast may need pulling forward to achieve the correct bend.
3 An inner forestay allows the crew to set a staysail.
4 This stay is the ideal place for a heavy weather headsail.
5 An inner stay is a great asset on an ocean cruiser and some boats have a pair of these stays.
6 It is a valuable hand-hold for the crew on an otherwise barren foredeck.
7 It stops headsail sheets from fouling winches and cleats on the mast, though it does need a roller or tube on the stay to ease jib sheets across.

Most of these reasons are self-explanatory, but until the advantages of an inner stay for setting sails has been experienced, it is difficult to appreciate the gains.

For instance, during a headsail change many boats have nothing set forward of the mast for many minutes, so during this time the boat makes little progress. When racing this is disastrous, and when cruising it can be dangerous off a lee shore. Even a small staysail is far better than no headsail. If the speed were 6 knots with main and jib, it might well drop to below 3 if the headsail were lowered, but if there is just a small staysail set, a speed of perhaps 4½ knots can often be maintained. On big boats these speeds will be proportionately greater.

In bad weather it can take an age to wrestle the storm jib up from below, stagger along the side deck, totter across the sea-swept fore deck and struggle to hank on the sail. A much better plan is to hank the sail onto the inner forestay before putting to sea and secure it down on deck under a specially made PVC or canvas cover. The halliard and sheets are put on, all ready for bad weather. When things get rugged, the storm jib is quite easily and quickly hoisted, then the big headsail is lowered and lashed on deck or, better still, taken off its stay – all with comparatively little effort and no loss of time.

For ocean cruising, a few boats have two stays set apart by about a foot or even more at the deck, and at the top a wood chock keeps them well separated. On one is a fair weather staysail of light cloth, and on the other a storm jib as described above. The light sail will extend well aft of the mast, whereas the bad

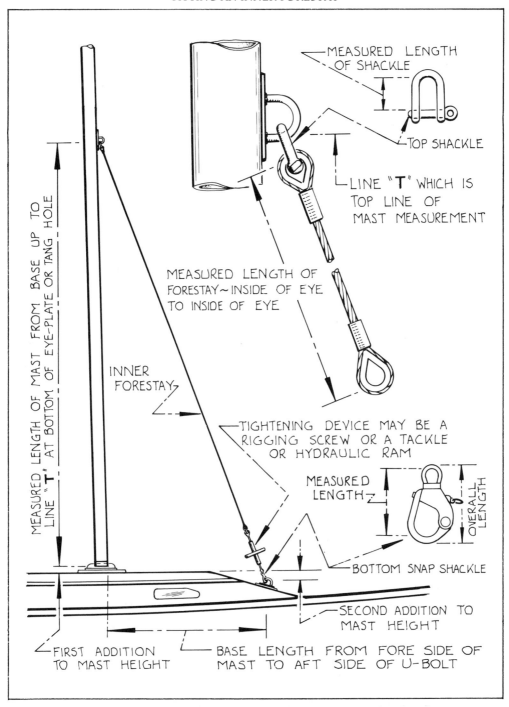

Fig. 46   Measurements needed when making up a new forestay

The lengths of shackles and snap hooks are taken 'from inside to inside' as that is the effective length which these items add to the forestay length. This diagram shows how other rigging lengths can be worked out when the mast is not stepped.

weather sail will be cut so that it clears the shrouds, to minimise chafe. The light sail will be long and low-footed to prevent the wind from getting below it, but the other will be cut high to prevent seas from breaking into it dangerously.

The diameter and type of wire for an inner forestay will be the same as for lower shrouds. If in doubt, *Boat Data Book* has tables of rigging sizes. The top end of the inner forestay is normally secured near the spreaders, or if there are two sets of spreaders, near the upper ones. With specialist racing rigs there may be three sets of spreaders and the inner forestay may be at any one of them, depending on such factors as the required mast bend, the location of other rigging, and so on.

If the mast fitting which holds the spreaders has a tang or lug for a forestay, this is good luck and there is no doubt where the stay is attached. If there is no attachment point on the fitting, a new fitting has to be secured to the mast. It should typically be within 4% of the mast length of the spreaders, but mast makers often say it is better not to have the new fitting too close to the one already riveted to the mast so as to avoid a concentration of fastenings close together.

If for any reason the inner forestay is well clear of the point where the lower shrouds are secured to the mast, it is probably going to be necessary to fit new aft lower shrouds or runners to match the pull of the inner forestay. Mast bend is all very well, but it must not be allowed to get out of control, or it becomes mast over-bend and that causes breakages.

At the bottom of the stay there must be a device for applying tension. When the stay is permanently set up, like a shroud, a rigging screw or hydraulic tensioner will be used. If the inner stay is semi-portable, the extreme bottom end will normally have a tough snap shackle and above this there may be a tackle, or a hydraulic tensioner, or one of those special rigging screws which have a horizontal wheel for quick tightening and loosening.

Where a tackle is used, the end of the rope is led to a winch which may well be near the cockpit, so that without going forward the crew can vary the forestay tension and thus change the mast bend. When the mast 'pumps' as the boat lurches over lumpy seas, the load on the tackle will be measured in tonnes, not kilos, so the rope must be thick enough to avoid serious stretch. Typically the tackle will be a three or four part one, so the rope strength must be one-third or one-quarter the wire strength, and preferably rather better than this.

The one annoying attribute of an inner forestay is that it makes tacking more difficult. This is why some of these stays have snap shackles at the bottom. When the weather is light and provided the mast and the rest of the rigging are adequate, the inner forestay is unclipped and lightly secured at the bottom of the mast, sometimes with a length of light line, sometimes by the end snap shackle with an arrangement to keep the wire tight, such as a piece of shock-cord.

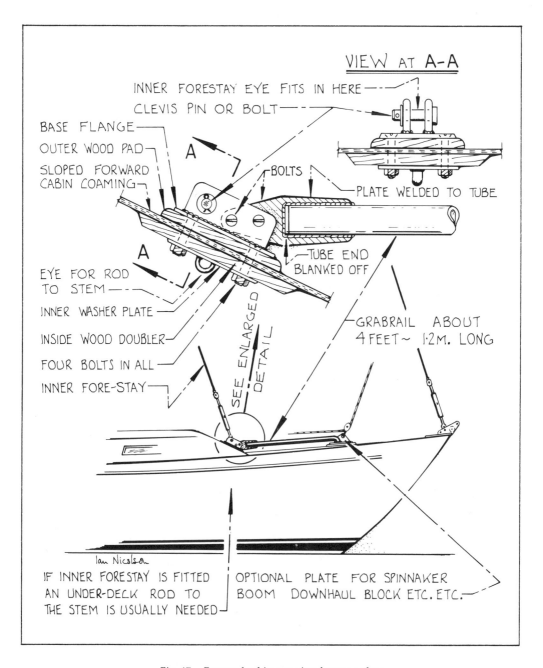

VIEW AT **A-A**

INNER FORESTAY EYE FITS IN HERE —·—
CLEVIS PIN OR BOLT——·—

BASE FLANGE———
OUTER WOOD PAD—
SLOPED FORWARD
CABIN COAMING—

BOLTS

PLATE WELDED TO TUBE

TUBE END
BLANKED OFF

EYE FOR ROD
TO STEM—·—
INNER WASHER PLATE—
INSIDE WOOD DOUBLER—
FOUR BOLTS IN ALL—
INNER FORE-STAY—

SEE ENLARGED DETAIL

GRABRAIL ABOUT
4 FEET~ 1·2M. LONG

Ian Nicolson

IF INNER FORESTAY IS FITTED
AN UNDER-DECK ROD TO
THE STEM IS USUALLY NEEDED⌐

OPTIONAL PLATE FOR SPINNAKER
BOOM DOWNHAUL BLOCK ETC. ETC.

Fig. 47   Forward cabin coaming forestay plate

Very often the inner forestay has to come down onto the steeply sloped forward coaming of the cabin top. Unless it can be guaranteed that there will never be a strong load on the inner forestay, or unless there is a strong beam nearby, a rod or rigging wire is usually needed to take the load down to the inside of the stem where there will be another eyeplate, or a glassed-in U-bolt or similar termination.

The eyeplate drawn here is unusual in that it has a grabrail attached at the forward end. This also acts as a footrail, and headsails can be lashed to it too. It should not be more than about 4 feet (1.2 metres) long without additional mid-length supports, otherwise the 1 inch tube is liable to bend under load.

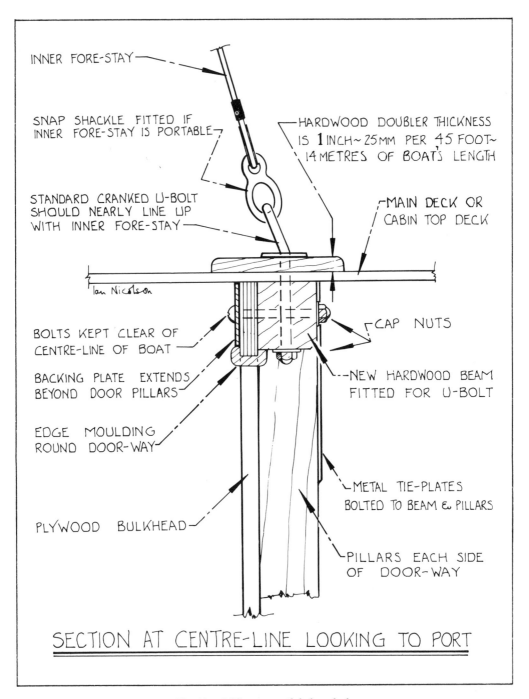

INNER FORE-STAY

SNAP SHACKLE FITTED IF
INNER FORE-STAY IS PORTABLE

STANDARD CRANKED U-BOLT
SHOULD NEARLY LINE UP
WITH INNER FORE-STAY

HARDWOOD DOUBLER THICKNESS
IS 1 INCH ~ 25MM PER 45 FOOT ~
14 METRES OF BOAT'S LENGTH

MAIN DECK OR
CABIN TOP DECK

Ian Nicolson

BOLTS KEPT CLEAR OF
CENTRE-LINE OF BOAT

CAP NUTS

BACKING PLATE EXTENDS
BEYOND DOOR PILLARS

NEW HARDWOOD BEAM
FITTED FOR U-BOLT

EDGE MOULDING
ROUND DOOR-WAY

METAL TIE-PLATES
BOLTED TO BEAM & PILLARS

PLYWOOD BULKHEAD

PILLARS EACH SIDE
OF DOOR-WAY

SECTION AT CENTRE-LINE LOOKING TO PORT

Fig. 48   Adding strength below deck

Because the upward pull on the deck fitting which holds a forestay is so strong there must be plenty of reliable structure to take the load. It is easy to make even a flimsy bulkhead rugged, by adding a beam, and perhaps door-way pillar stiffeners and so on.

If no bulkhead is located conveniently, it may pay to fit one, or put in a beam and pair of pillars down the inside of the cabin top. Whatever the arrangement, there should be a well bedded hard-wood pad on top of the deck to prevent leaking.

A wood or Tufnol or plastic roller on the inner forestay helps tacking when the wire is in position. Such a roller makes it difficult or impossible to hank on a headsail unless provision is made for this. The roller can be in two longitudinal halves and held together by plastic electrician's tape at top and bottom, so that to remove the roller takes only a minute with a knife. Or the roller can be in short lengths so that the jib hanks are clipped on between the pieces of roller. Another ploy is to use shackles instead of jib hanks, so that these will slide over even a largish diameter tube. If the headsail is secured more or less permanently onto the forestay, the time taken to put the shackles on is not important. However the top of the tube must be within reach of the deck so that when the sail is lowered each shackle can be passed down over the top of the tube.

If a spinnaker is to be used, it might be thought that the inner forestay simply *had* to be portable, to allow for easy gybing of the spinnaker boom. In practice, plenty of boats have permanent inner forestays and they manage the neatest, quickest gybes. Practice and skill make light of the obstruction caused by the wire growing up out of the middle of the foredeck.

=22 *Headsail luff groove*=

Genoas and jibs have for many years been secured to the forestay by jib hanks, those bronze or stainless steel hooks with spring-loaded closures. To change headsails, as the wind increases or dies away, the sail is lowered and another sail is hanked onto the forestay. Next the halliard is changed onto the new sail and then the sheets. After four or fourteen or even thirty-four minutes, depending on the size of the boat and also the crew's energy and skill, not to mention the stress of weather, the new headsail is set and drawing.

It is well known that races galore are lost by slow headsail changes and this is a main reason why there is such a demand for headsail luff groove units, sometimes called headsail foils and sometimes called headsail slides. This device, normally made of aluminium and occasionally of plastic, is nothing more than a very special shape of tubing which fits round the forestay. Instead of the headsail being clipped onto the forestay wire, the sail is slid into the groove, just the way a dinghy or racing boat's mainsail slides into the mast groove. Once the sail has been entered into the groove, it can be hoisted as fast as the halliard can be hauled down.

There are various makes of headsail luff groove unit. The one described here is the Hood Gemini because it is widely available, well tried, easy to fit, and simple to use. It has two side-by-side grooves, so that a second sail can be set before the first one is taken down.

Before fitting one of these luff groove units it is a good idea to think about the disadvantages they have. First they cost more than an ordinary forestay. Also, existing headsails have to have their jib hanks removed and the correct size of luff tape to fit the groove sewn on instead. This is not a job for amateur sailmakers. Perhaps more important for the yacht which is handled by in-experienced people or by a cruising crew, when the sail comes down and out of the groove, it is no longer attached to the forestay, so it can blow overboard. For this reason many boats have light Terylene lines worked diagonally up and down between the deck or toerail and the lower guardrail. Sometimes this cat's-cradle of thin line goes to the upper guardrail, forming a very open weave netting which prevents the headsail from falling overboard when the sail is on deck.

Some cheap luff groove units may not be able to cope with the very high wind strengths if the boat is caught in ferocious conditions and the grooves may open so the sail blows free. Or it may be impossible to coax the storm jib into the groove because of the way the wind forces the sail to leeward. The smallest headsail should therefore have ordinary jib hanks and clip onto an inner forestay (which may be portable). Alternatively there may be eyelets up the luff of the storm jib which are used with lengths of lacing or light line to secure the luff of the sail to the forestay which is encased in the luff groove unit.

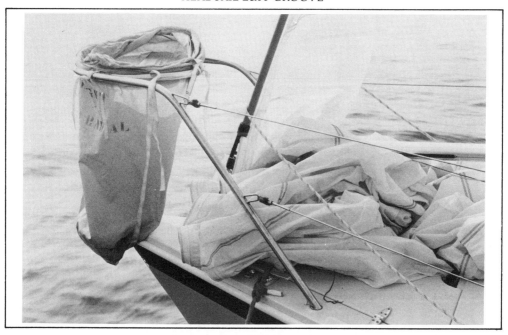

The spinnaker has just been hoisted from the bag which fits snugly in a special ring in the top of the pulpit, and the genoa has been lowered. As the headsail comes out of the forestay groove it lies unsecured on the deck, and this boat needs light lines or a broad mesh net between the top guardrail and the deck to prevent the sail going overboard.

However, handling lacing on a plunging foredeck in half a hurricane is no fun and old-fashioned jib hanks (which incidentally should be extra big and kept well greased) onto an inner wire forestay suit most people best. Alternatively the hanks can be clipped onto a wire jib halliard which is secured at the bottom to a foredeck cleat or eyeplate and made up very tight, so as to act like an inner forestay.

Fitting a luff groove unit like the Hood Gemini is a job best done by two people. Ideally the boat should be in a marina, or ashore. The mast must be up and fully rigged complete with forestay. If the boat is on a mooring, choose a quiet day, preferably one free from rain, snow and hail. The unit arrives in the form of 6 foot (1.8 metres) lengths of alloy tubing made up of forward and aft halves which slide together so that they can easily be taken apart, but only by slipping the front unit up or down the back one. They cannot be pulled apart at right angles to their length.

If the forestay is of galvanised wire and it is rusting, it should be renewed before the job is started. If the wire is stainless steel and more than 8 years old, or it has broken strands, it should be renewed to be safe. Incidentally if a new forestay is being made, the whole luff groove unit can be fitted by sliding the wire through it and only the clamp piece remains to be put on when the final length of the forestay is known.

To start the job the front and aft halves of the alloy tubing are separated and laid either on the dock adjacent or on the side deck where they will not slide overboard. The tools needed are laid out on the foredeck at the bow and consist of a Mole grip (sometimes called a vice-grip), or two of these, a pair of pliers, a hacksaw which can be the miniature type, though the full size type is much to be preferred, a flat file and a round file (sometimes called a rat-tail file), some emery cloth (i.e. sandpaper of the type used by engineers) in a medium and fairly fine grade, and a set of Allen keys (called Allen wrenches in America). The Allen key diameter is to suit the size of Gemini and for the smallest one this is ³⁄₃₂ inches. Finally some electricians' plastic tape is required.

When the sections have been separated, the two forward *half* lengths and the luff feeder section (which takes the head of the sail when it is being put up) are put apart from the others.

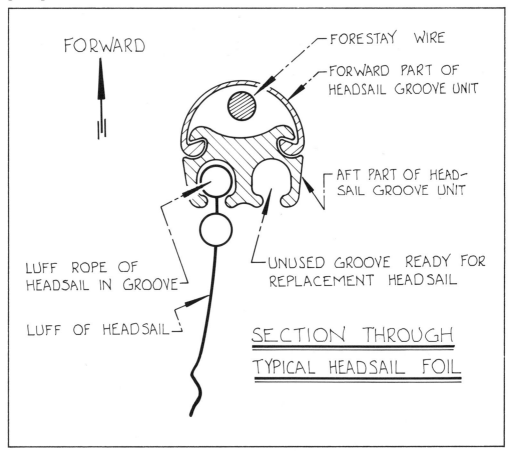

FORWARD

FORESTAY WIRE

FORWARD PART OF HEADSAIL GROOVE UNIT

AFT PART OF HEADSAIL GROOVE UNIT

LUFF ROPE OF HEADSAIL IN GROOVE

UNUSED GROOVE READY FOR REPLACEMENT HEADSAIL

LUFF OF HEADSAIL

SECTION THROUGH TYPICAL HEADSAIL FOIL

Fig. 49 Section through Hood headsail foil
This foil is formed by two aluminium extrusions which clip together around the forestay. Two headsails can be set at once, either for changing sail or for going down wind with one sail boomed out on each side. This sketch shows how important it is to have the correct luff rope stitched to each headsail so that it fits snugly in its groove without any risk of pulling out (if it is too small) or jamming inside the groove (if it is too big).

Put on the forestay a split stainless steel washer followed by a plastic washer. On some versions only a stainless steel washer goes on and no plastic washers are supplied in the kit. The metal washers must be flattened with pliers after fitting. Next the spiral spring is put onto the forestay using a Mole grip (vice-grip) and perhaps a screwdriver to open the end of the spring. Once the spring has been entered onto the forestay it can be rotated so that it is wound onto it. The final part may need some extra force to get it onto the forestay and this is where a second Mole grip or a big pair of pliers is needed.

When the spring is on, another washer is fitted onto the wire. Now the main part of the luff groove unit, the alloy tubing, is put on. First a front piece half length is held in place on the front of the forestay; a full length aft part is slid up the front part; a full length front part is slid up the aft part already on . . . and so on. As each piece of alloy tubing goes on the assembled part is pushed up the forestay. This may sound complicated but once the parts are being handled it is easy.

If the forestay is secured at the bottom well aft of the bow, there may be difficulty getting each alloy section to start sliding into the existing part of the tube on the forestay, because the new part going on fouls the deck and its bottom end has to be held over the side of the boat. Get over this problem by standing on a wooden box or stool and pushing the assembled parts of the tube higher up the forestay. Try not to fall off the stool and overboard when a motor boat hastens past.

When the first (half length) front section and the first aft part have been slid together they are taped together at the top to hold them in place. As each new part of the alloy tube is slid into place, a check is made to ensure it goes hard up against the part above it.

The final piece of the aft extrusions is put on upside down, with the rounded ends of the luff slots at the top. This is made certain by having the tape with the word 'FEED' at the top. Push all the alloy tubing which has been assembled hard up till it will not go further, and mark with a line with a pencil about 30 inches (750 mm) from the deck. This mark needs only to be accurate to the nearest 2 inches (50 mm).

The bottom two parts of the alloy tube, one front, one back, are now taken off the forestay, and the forward section removed is cut off at the pencil mark, the cut being as near to a right angle to the tube length as can be judged by eye. The aft section is cut through $4\frac{5}{8}$ inches (116 mm) above the pencil mark, again taking care not to tilt the hacksaw. The $4\frac{5}{8}$ inch reduction is to allow the feeder and spacer piece to go on aft of the forestay.

After the cutting it is important to smooth off all edges and rough metal chips using files, then emery paper or a de-burring tool, or a combination of these. This job should not be rushed because the luff tape wears even when conditions are ideal and if there is any slight roughness in the tubing it will soon chafe the sails seriously. As a primitive check, make sure this smoothing process takes quite 10 minutes.

The bottom parts of the alloy tubing are reassembled, only this time the feeder mouths on the aft part are on the bottom. The feeder piece, which is stainless steel, is slipped in place, followed by the spacer piece. A stainless washer is forced onto the wire and flattened. Take the clamp, which is of light alloy and in two halves, and separate these two parts. Put the clamp round the wire loosely and see if the wire fits tightly in the vertical hole down the centre of the assembled clamp. It may be necessary to reamer out this hole slightly, but obviously not too much or the clamp will not grip immovably on the wire. Tighten the clamp round the wire after the alloy tubing has been forced as far up the wire as it will go, then lower it ¾ inch (20 mm). This has the effect of getting the spring tension just right. Once the Allen screws on the clamp have been tightened, it is easy to see if it is at the correct point on the wire; just slide the alloy tubing up the wire by pulling upwards hard and there should be a ¾ inch (20 mm) gap between the top of the clamp and the bottom of the alloy tube.

The pre-feeders, which are C-shaped metal plates for guiding the sails towards the groove, are now tied onto the forestay wire so that they are about 8 inches (200 mm) below the feeder piece when lifted to the full extent of their retaining lines. The Allen screws should have a water-resisting grease pushed into their sockets and smeared over their heads, then the whole lot should be taped over to defy the worst the weather can do.

This protective care should be taken with every type of forestay groove and on all those small important parts which hold the equipment together. Just as important, the insides of the grooves should be lubricated with the special spray lubricant sold by Hoods.

Before doing all this work it is worth going on board a yacht which already has a luff groove. Five minutes inspecting the gear and perhaps taking photos of the equipment, will make the fitting work quick and easy.

When hoisting sail, it is best to set the sail in the lee side groove, then when a different headsail is wanted it is hoisted on the weather groove. At this stage it may be hard to get the unwanted sail down in a breeze as it will be behind the windward sail and possibly jammed against the pulpit too. To clear the problem the boat is tacked and the new weather sail dropped at the same time.

If the boat is on a long tack and she cannot be put about to get the sail down, then it is best to arrange things so that the second sail to go up is on the lee side, because getting a sail up there is generally easier than getting one down.

=23 *On-deck ventilators* =

The number, type and size of ventilators on a boat depends on where she operates. In hot climates there should be two large high-standing vents for each cabin in the boat. For moderately warm conditions the same standards should be set, but the vents can be located so that minor compartments are ventilated indirectly from major ones. This means the total number of vents through the deck is reduced. Ducting, slots in bulkheads, as well as secondary vents like grilles in the weather-boards at the main and secondary hatches, all ensure air circulation. Other minor vents can be used like sealable slots in the sides of the cockpit well, low profile cowl vents, slots in deck boxes round the mast base and so on.

For chilly climates there is no final solution to the ventilation problem because, if enough are fitted, there will be draughts which make the cabins miserable at times and, if inadequate arrangements are made, there will be mildew growth and condensation through the boat.

Production boatbuilders generally fit the minimum number of ventilators they hope will satisfy the majority of their potential customers. These builders work on the principle that most boats are raced or cruised in temperate climates, so the ventilators need not cope with hot, airless conditions.

To be effective in all conditions, a ventilator has to stand well above the deck and it must have some form of scoop which can be directed into or away from the breeze, to act as inlet or outlet as the situation demands. To suit these requirements there is wide agreement that an ordinary cowl vent about 18 inches (450 mm) high deals with most conditions, provided it is protected from errant ropes and has a large water-box to filter out spray or solid water and feed only fresh air into the boat. This is shown in Fig. 51. So much for the ideal. At sea, conditions are at times so difficult that ventilators do not survive unscathed, even though extensive precautions are taken. Cowls made of metal get dented or even bent right over, plastic ones get whipped off by flaying sheets, even when there are guard bars over them. As usual afloat, a compromise has to be worked out and it will be a different one for each boat.

The standard plastic cowl vent which is widely used and is sold in most chandleries, is often only 6 or at best 8 inches (150 or 200 mm) high. To get it up above the deck into a clear air-flow it must be set on a water-box which will prevent spray and worse getting into the cabin. The water-box itself may be mounted on the cabin top, or on top of a deck box, or an extension of a deep fore hatch. Alternatively, the cowl can be set on a tube which has a flange at the bottom and this flange will be bolted to the top of the water-box, though this arrangement is unusual. High cowl vents are very hard to find in a standard form and they tend to be costly, due to small production runs. This in part explains the many and varied alternatives and special vents which are illustrated in such books as *Yacht Designers Sketch-book* and *Marinize Your Boat*.

To fit a ventilator to the deck, decide with care exactly where it is to be located, by selecting a place in the cabin where the inevitable splashes from above will cause the least discomfort. In the saloon the vents should be over the sole, not over the settees or chart table. Drips over the galley are a nuisance, but much less of a menace than over a berth. In the toilet compartment the vent should be over the shower or even the basin – not the WC.

To transfer the location from inside the cabin up on to the deck, measure the

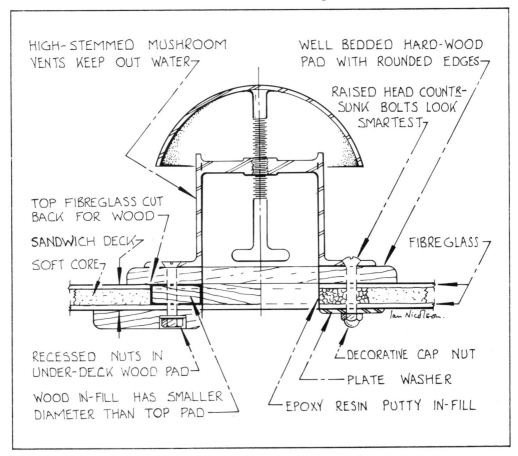

Fig. 50 Mushroom vent on sandwich deck

Two separate methods of fixing down a vent, or indeed any fitting, on a fibreglass deck with soft core are shown here. On the left, the top layer of fibreglass is cut away more than the bottom layer and a large wooden filling piece set down on top of the bottom fibreglass with ample bedding. The hard wood pad on top of the deck overlaps the join of the new piece of wood with the fibreglass deck and prevents water from getting in here.

On the right hand side, the hole for the vent is cut and then the soft core routed out all round and replaced with an epoxy putty which extends well back into the deck core, beyond the holding down bolts. A ring plate washer is shown underneath the deck, which tends to be more expensive than the wood pad as shown on the left-hand side.

distance from the point on the under side of the deck forward or aft to a convenient window. Now go out on deck and measure from the window along the deck the same amount. To get the distance athwartships, measure inside the cabin to the centreline of the cabin top. Go out on deck and measure off the same distance from the centreline to the centre of the vent. Put the vent in place and draw around it. Pause for thought. Re-check the dimension. Double check by measuring from the aft (or forward) side of the mast to the vent inside the cabin and outside. If you think this is being over cautious, just look at all those grey hairs on the foreman shipwright next time you visit your favourite boatyard. Each grey strand is the result of a botched measurement.

Take a ⅛ inch (3 mm) drill bit and drill a pilot hole right through the cabin top deck (or main deck if that is where the vent is). Now go below and check that the hole in the deckhead *is* centred exactly where it is wanted. If you are an inch or two adrift this does not matter at this stage as the cut-out can be adjusted for position round this hole. This pilot hole is just a double check to get the location exactly right.

Enlarge the pilot hole so that it will take the blade of the electric saw or hand pad-saw, then cut out the piece of deck needed to fit the vent. If the deck is made of two layers of fibreglass with a core of balsa or foam plastic, two important jobs must now be done: the first is to prevent the core being crushed when the vent is bolted down, the second is to seal the exposed edges of the core.

Just how these objectives are achieved depends on the skill, cunning, experience and determination of the shipwright. One technique is to rout out the soft core for say 2 inches (50 mm) all round and pack in a putty of epoxy resin made thick with one of the standard fillers. Another trick is to rout out the core and slide in segments of wood which must each be small enough to pass vertically down the vent hole before being slid sideways into the gap made by removing the core locally. Another technique is to cut out a bigger circle of the top fibreglass than the bottom, but not so much that the vent flange will not cover the cut-away part. Another trick is to use short spacer tubes at each vent fastening and use epoxy resin to seal the core edge. Ingenious boat builders invent new tricks for this problem every month.

If the deck is only one thickness of fibreglass, it is essential to fit a doubler pad in way of the vent. Even with a double thickness deck, a pad should be fitted and the best builders tend to have a pad on deck and another under, ideally both made of teak or a dense hardwood.

The vent flange has to be bedded down so that when the bolts are tightened the waterproof sealing material oozes out all round. It must also ooze continuously round the edge of the wood pad(s), showing that there is no chance of water seeping in when the boat is being punched into a wicked head sea and taking green water over the bow every few seconds. The wood pad under deck should be recessed so that the nuts do not protrude down below it and plough furrows in scalps.

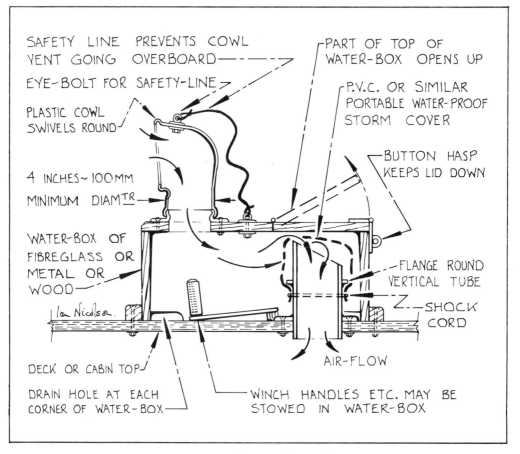

SAFETY LINE PREVENTS COWL
VENT GOING OVERBOARD

PART OF TOP OF
WATER-BOX OPENS UP

EYE-BOLT FOR SAFETY-LINE

P.V.C. OR SIMILAR
PORTABLE WATER-PROOF
STORM COVER

PLASTIC COWL
SWIVELS ROUND

BUTTON HASP
KEEPS LID DOWN

4 INCHES ~ 100 MM
MINIMUM DIAM^{TR}

WATER-BOX OF
FIBREGLASS OR
METAL OR
WOOD

FLANGE ROUND
VERTICAL TUBE

SHOCK
CORD

Ian Nicolson.

DECK OR CABIN TOP

AIR-FLOW

DRAIN HOLE AT EACH
CORNER OF WATER-BOX

WINCH HANDLES ETC. MAY BE
STOWED IN WATER-BOX

Fig. 51   Cowl vent with water-box

Cowl vents must be high otherwise they do not scoop in air all the time. A water box helps to raise them well up and is needed to prevent water from getting into the cabin. In very severe conditions, the downpipe through the deck needs sealing off and on a yacht this is almost always done from above. Ideally, all ventilators should have closures which can be worked from inside the cabin but these are seldom seen and are almost always very expensive.

A large water-box is much more likely to give a good air flow and keep water from getting below, so it makes sense to design the box to double as a deck stowage locker for minor items. Plastic cowls which rotate on a flange are liable to be knocked off and so need safety lines which need to be 4 mm Terylene, well secured at each end. Sometimes the water-box is built with two alternative positions for the cowl, one giving an indirect airflow as shown here, and another giving a direct airflow. Whichever position is not in use is sealed off by a lid which screws down onto the circular flanged opening at the base of the cowl. In this drawing, the direct airflow position would be on the section of the water-box which opens up.

Once the vents have been fitted, interesting tests can be tried to make sure that the draughts do indeed blow through the boat even when there is not much of a breeze over the deck. Smoking candles or a pipe smoker are used to trace the air flow, which will normally be from the main cabin entrance forwards. The area from the steps aft may have a flow of air forwards or aft, but in practice there is usually no flow because the vents are too few and too small.

It is a general truth that vents of less than 4 inches (100 mm) internal diameter do not work except in fresh breezes and these occur only a small proportion of the time in most latitudes. Besides, during the off-season many boats are laid up under cover or in a sheltered boatyard, perhaps with a tarpaulin over; under these conditions ventilation is as important as when the boat is in use, but the inlets and outlets will seldom work if they are less than this critical size of 4 inches (100 mm). For boats over 50 feet (15 metres), internal diameter vents of 6 inches (150 mm) are needed, certainly for hot weather.

'Soup plate' vents have their nickname because they look like upturned deep plates. They are unobtrusive and can be walked over; they virtually never catch ropes or get damaged by the hurly-burly of sail changing. They suit boats used inshore, but they do not seem to be able to stand up to a wave galloping over the deck. When they are covered by deep water they let in too much, even though they have internal baffles.

Some of these vents have deadlights in the top to let daylight through and some have built-in electric fans. It is now fashionable to arrange for the fans to be driven by sunlight so that there is no drain on the ship's electrical power. All this is ingenious and much in keeping with current thinking, which is often angled at clever gadgetry, but when one asks the critical question 'How does it stand up to conditions offshore in a lively gale?' too often experience replies with a sad and saturated sigh 'Not so well as some older well tried equipment'.

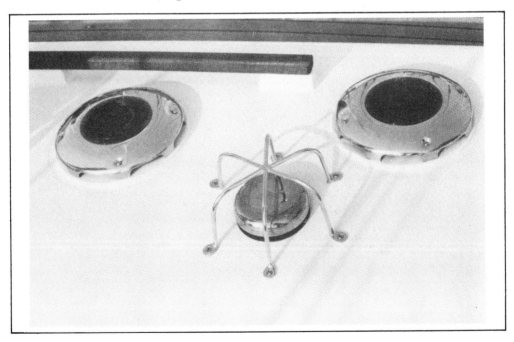

Stainless steel bars form a guard over the mushroom vent in the middle, but it would be better if the vertical legs of the guard were angled at 45° to steer ropes smoothly over the top. On each side are 'soup-plate' vents with transparent centre pieces to let light into the cabin.

There is a type of metal grating vent which suits inshore boats but again is not recommended for offshore use. This is the 'Hit-and-miss' type which is sometimes circular and sometimes rectangular. It is fitted in cabin doors or weather boards, or in external bulkheads, and it has inner and outer plates (one of which slides) with holes in both which can coincide or not so as to let air in or exclude it.

One maddening failure of these sliding closures is that they seize up. The idea behind them is that they are kept open until the weather gets bad, then they are slid closed. However, the seal formed by the inner metal plate sliding over the slots in the outer plate will not keep out torrential rain, let alone solid thundering water curling aboard with a deep foaming crest. Just as serious, the slots tend to be too small to let a slow air-flow filter through, so these vents are seldom effective.

=24 *Ventilation below decks*=

Plenty of boats have some form of ventilation *through* the deck, though very few have half enough. Below decks, only a tiny minority of craft have adequate passages for the free flow of air. As a result most boats have puddles in their lower lockers and musty smells in enclosed spaces. Also mildew is often found in hidden corners and equipment which needs to be kept dry has to be carefully wrapped in polythene bags. Only on a few boats can charts be left lying about without getting at least slightly soft as a result of soaking up

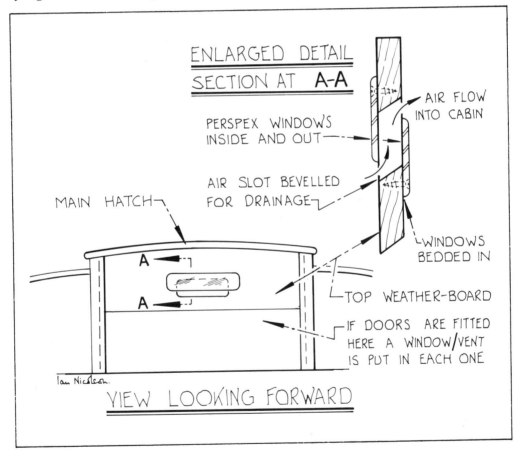

ENLARGED DETAIL
SECTION AT A-A

AIR FLOW
INTO CABIN

PERSPEX WINDOWS
INSIDE AND OUT

AIR SLOT BEVELLED
FOR DRAINAGE

MAIN HATCH

WINDOWS
BEDDED IN

A

A

TOP WEATHER-BOARD

IF DOORS ARE FITTED
HERE A WINDOW/VENT
IS PUT IN EACH ONE

Ian Nicolson.

VIEW LOOKING FORWARD

Fig. 52   Low price ventilator

If a slot is cut in the upper weatherboard, or in each door at the cabin entrance, this forms a good inlet for ventilation. To prevent rain and spray from driving in, a pair of transparent baffles are screwed over the slot so that the outer perspex extends over the top of the slot and the inner one over the bottom, as shown in the enlarged detail. The perspex needs no maintenance and it lets in light. This type of ventilator can also be fitted on the aft cabin coaming at the forward end of the cockpit.

moisture. Toilet paper becomes at least partly ineffective, tins of food rust, cushions become clammy, cookers corrode, polished wood loses its pleasant sheen, condensation accumulates, curtains actually drip, shoes left on board grow green beards – the consequences of poor ventilation range from the inconvenient to the dangerous.

The cure is usually simple and cheap, though it does take time, patience and thought. What each boat needs is a gentle but continuous flow of dry air through each enclosed compartment. To get this there must be at least two holes in each space, one to let the air in, one to let it out. These holes should be about the same area, but if one is very long and thin, it needs a greater area than one more nearly square, because air does not easily flow through confined gaps. This is proved by anyone who takes the trouble to hold a smoking candle at vent slots in different locations throughout a boat.

The first lesson which will be learned is that the traditional row of 1 inch (25 mm) diameter holes drilled in engine casings and across locker doors does not work. Only when the wind is blowing strongly will this size of hole let a draft through. The aim of the ventilating engineer is to get the air to waft gently from stern to bow (in that direction) all the time. When the wind over the deck is gentle, it is more likely to be dry and that is when it will do most good inside a vessel.

An effective way of making air holes is with a 'hole cutter', a sort of super-drill which cuts large round holes through wood or plastic. It works in an electric drill, but can be used in a hand drill too, provided there is enough determination and effort available. Ideally, two holes are drilled and these are joined up with a jig-saw or hand-held pad-saw, forming a slot hole with nicely rounded ends. Holes should not be cut nearer than 3 inches (75 mm) from the edge of a bulkhead, and 6 inches (150 mm) is a much better minimum. Where there is glassing in, or where the bulkhead supports a major load like a mast the larger dimensions must be taken as a minimum. In cheap boats the slot is left as cut but careful craftsmen finish off the job neatly, using at least two grades of glass-paper to smooth the edges.

To be sure – well fairly sure – that air will flow, each compartment needs two holes about 6×2 inches (150 mm × 50 mm) minimum unimpeded area. If a ventilator or grille or other check of free flow is fitted, the size of the hole needs to be much bigger. In practice the boats which have the best ventilation often have slatted doors, soles, lining, settee fronts, sail bins, clothes lockers and chart lockers. The gaps between the slats are more than ¼ inch (6 mm) but not much more, otherwise things start to fall out of lockers. For the fronts of sail lockers the gaps are likely to be 3 inches (75 mm) or even more, because sails are stowed wet.

For cabin soles, the best solution is to have sections of grating. They are smart and a grating at the bottom of the companionway steps will not only let air flow under the sole, but will also collect dirt from shoes. If a tray is set a few inches below the grating it will help keep dirt out of the bilge and when the cabin sole is swept, the dust can be pushed through the grating and the tray emptied overboard.

Another grating under the forehatch helps to deal with drips through the hatch and the wetness coming off the sails as they are stuffed below, besides forming the second air aperture for the space below the sole.

To get the best flow through lockers, one hole should be low down forward, the other high up aft. Two holes high up or low down are not truly effective, because the air current dashes from one hole to the other ignoring the main bulk of the locker. As gear is more likely to fall out of holes set low, it may be necessary to have some sort of grid over them. But the traditional style of vent grating is not a great success, being designed more to look good than to be effective – a curse applicable to plenty of yacht fittings. What is needed is something which has the maximum unblocked area and the minimum material in the grid. A good example is netting, which works well in places where it is not seen. I know of one boat which had the lockers under the settees lined with common galvanised chicken netting. It looked odd but it worked well and as it was only in view when the settee bases were lifted, the appearance was scarcely important. The ventilation was admirable, which is exactly what the designer intended.

Many owners prefer the ventilation facilities to be concealed so they make the slots in the ends of the lockers. One will be under the chart table, the next into the clothes locker, the next into the back of the sail locker, and so on, all fore and aft. Where a slot opens into a space like a sail locker it may be best to fit a cowl or sloping cover over the hole; otherwise the adjacent sail bag will jam up against the air slot and block it.

Another way to conceal the ventilation holes is to locate them at the back of a bookcase, or behind the mast if it extends down into the cabin, or even stand a picture slightly off a bulkhead and have a hole behind it, so that air gets all round the picture and through the vent slot.

An attractive trick is to make the locker doors and fronts with panels of plaited straw, such as is seen on the seats of some fine chairs. Admittedly this is rather liable to damage by clumsy crews in bad weather. Another ploy is to use furnishing materials not only for the doors but also for locker ends, carefully selecting a cloth with many open interstices. Yet another approach is to make the locker doors, and even the full size cabin doors, with slots along the top and bottom.

If all else fails, there is always the traditional vent which normally looks dated but can be modernised. It used to be the shape of an anchor, a flower, a dolphin or a prancing horse cut out of the front panel with a fret-saw. By careful design this idea can be made to look smart, contemporary and amusing. For instance, the boat's name may be machined out of port and starboard locker doors in the saloon, or a row of breaking waves cut out, especially if the boat has a name like *Storm Tide* or *White Water*. Our boat is called *St. Margaret* and as she was a queen besides being the patron saint of Scotland, we have the choice of a thistle or a crown, not to mention the flower of the same name, and *Margaret* is also the name of a type of apple and a pear, so we have an embarrassment of choice.

=====25 *Burglar beating*=====

A boat may be made hard to break into, but if a burglar thinks the entrance is vulnerable, he will chip and chop away at the corners of doors and hatches, doing a lot of damage, even if he never does get in. So it is doubly sensible to make a boat *look* burglar-proof. The cabin doors should be very obviously tough and thick, therefore it is better to have them of solid wood rather than thin ply. If there is a steel bar, or better still three of them, across the outside of the door, with massive padlocks holding each bar, most thieves will move on to the next boat without making an attack on such a well-defended entrance.

A steel mesh grille over a doorway and another over the forehatch, both held by thick lugs, is the sort of discouraging sight which will urge a pilferer to look for easier pickings. Even a stout cockpit cover, with ample tight lacings all round, will add to the time and difficulty of getting into a boat's cabin, though it is important to make sure a thief cannot get under the cover and work away for ages, picking locks, without being seen.

Two contrasting, different locks (both of the burglar-proof type) is a good dissuader, because different tricks are likely to be needed for different locks. And just because one lock surrenders after a very few minutes does not mean that a different one will be as easy.

Even if a burglar succeeds in breaking in, if things can be properly hidden they can hardly be stolen. A boat is full of nooks and crannies which can be turned into secret hiding places. Under the batteries, behind drawers, under a secured cabin sole and up under the deck in the counter, are all places which are worth considering.

Some people go to a lot of trouble to make good hiding places, not of course to mislead the Customs. They have false water tanks, berth mattresses which are hollowed out at the foot end where the softness is not required, detachable panels of cabin lining and secret drawers with concealed locks. The latter are an interesting challenge to any enthusiastic joiner, whether amateur or professional.

Things which are hard to lock up or bolt down need to be copiously marked with the boat's name or the owner's, or both. The dinghy is the obvious example and a good defence is massive and repeated markings. A dinghy with the parent boat's name on both bows, on the transom, on all the floorboards, on the bottom port and starboard and carved into the main thwart, is going to be hard to hide unless some substantial work has been done on her by the thief.

It is worthwhile getting a stencil with the boat's name and another with the owner's name and using these on the dinghy, oars, boat-hook, portable boom gallows, anchors, loose fuel cans and so on and on. If the thief sees this sort of precaution being taken, he will burst into tears and take up betting instead of pilfering.

A rubber dinghy with the owner's name stencilled 20 times on it all over the inside and outside does not look odd and it would need 3 coats of paint all over

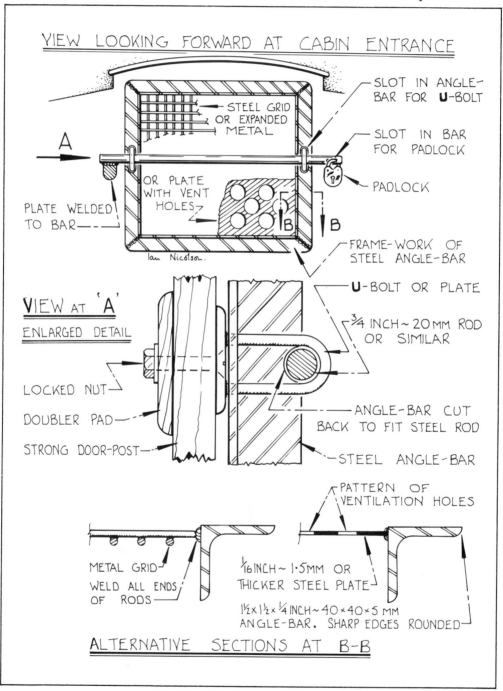

VIEW LOOKING FORWARD AT CABIN ENTRANCE

SLOT IN ANGLE-BAR FOR **U**-BOLT

SLOT IN BAR FOR PADLOCK

PADLOCK

STEEL GRID OR EXPANDED METAL

A

OR PLATE WITH VENT HOLES

PLATE WELDED TO BAR

Ian Nicolson.

B B

FRAME-WORK OF STEEL ANGLE-BAR

U-BOLT OR PLATE

¾ INCH ~ 20 MM ROD OR SIMILAR

VIEW AT 'A'
ENLARGED DETAIL

LOCKED NUT
DOUBLER PAD
STRONG DOOR-POST

ANGLE-BAR CUT BACK TO FIT STEEL ROD

STEEL ANGLE-BAR

PATTERN OF VENTILATION HOLES

METAL GRID
WELD ALL ENDS OF RODS

⅟₁₆ INCH ~ 1·5MM OR THICKER STEEL PLATE

1½ × 1½ × ¼ INCH ~ 40 × 40 × 5 MM ANGLE-BAR. SHARP EDGES ROUNDED

ALTERNATIVE SECTIONS AT B-B

inside and out to obliterate all this identification. Another worthwhile protection is a notice on the boat, or inside a window, listing the two or three different types of burglar alarm which have been fitted. Burglars are, by their nature, lazy and will prefer to break into a boat which is not labelled as dangerous.

If a burglar gets through the first line of defence, he can still be beaten. Inside the cabin a series of alarms will make him flee when they go off, provided they are loud enough. Some alarms work when anyone treads on the floorboard or carpet which has a pressure pad under it. These pads are nothing more than electric switches which activate an alarm siren and this type of anti-burglar system is now widely available from chandlers. It is best to get the sophisticated type which has both pressure alarms and door-operated switches. A bright burglar may avoid treading on the cabin sole by crawling over the settees, but if he wants to steal anything, he cannot avoid opening cupboard doors and that is when the secondary alarm switches work.

All good alarms are made so that when a thief tampers with the wiring, the siren blasts off. However, batteries can go flat, so it is best to have two systems wired to different batteries if the boat is a large valuable one in a dangerous area. Incidentally, the modern type of battery that never needs topping up is best for this job because it can be located somewhere very awkward to find, let alone touch, and it is then almost impossible to disconnect the terminal wires, except after a long delay.

Once inside the boat, a thief will look around for portable items which have value and are easy to sell. These things should either be taken home or well hidden by the owner. If they are left on board, they should be so well secured that it is hard to get them free. Bolts with locked nuts are better than screws and a good batch of screws better than a simple lashing. Good fastenings are, in any case, advantageous when the boat is at sea, as they keep everything secure. Gear which can be bolted in place includes clocks, barometers, radios, electronic equipment, and sextant boxes (so the thief will not easily get the box even if he takes the sextant, and that will make his life more difficult).

What cannot be bolted down can be locked up. It's astonishing how many boats have liquor in open lockers on board permanently, even when the boat is laid up ashore. Incidentally, this is very unfair to boatyard personnel who may be accused of stealing drink when the fault lies with someone not connected

---

◁   *Fig. 53   Security without destroying ventilation*
Maintenance nowadays includes preventing vandalism. A steel grid over the cabin entrance is a good way to keep out burglars whether the boat is ashore or afloat. If she is laid up under cover or with a tarpaulin over her a weather-board can be left out for ventilation, and the steel guard fitted over the opening. The appearance of this grid and the noise a thief must make if he tries to break it are good protection.

The U-bolts or plates each side are used at sea for securing the crew's personal lifelines. Being near the cabin entrance, the lifelines can be hooked on before the crew come on deck, and the navigator on some boats can remain hooked on while working at his table near the main hatch.

with the yard. A liquor locker with a thief-proof lock used to be fitted on many boats so that it could also be used for keeping drink 'in bond'.

When thinking about burglar-proofing a boat, it is important to remember the insurance policy. This will often not cover boat's gear which can come

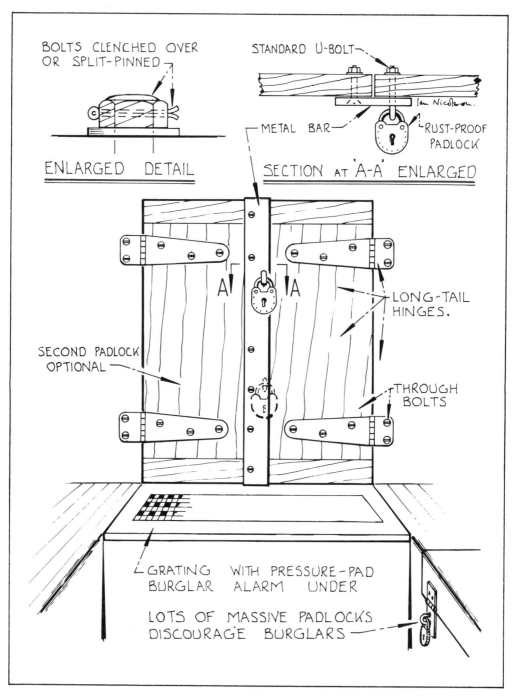

under the heading of personal equipment. Such items as binoculars, sextants, portable radios, navigation computers, sleeping bags, blankets, towels, books (apart from navigation tomes) and flashlights may be considered part of the owner's or crew's private possessions and so the insurance company will not pay up on just those items most likely to be taken by thieves. When filling in an insurance proposal form it is advisable to get the brokers' or underwriters' advice on this sort of equipment. It is often worth 5% of the value of the boat and maybe more. Most yacht insurance forms have provision for including personal possessions provided that their total value is stated.

Finally, if the boat is afloat ladders should not be left over the side. People with houses overlooking the anchorage or marina should be asked to keep an eye on the boat and should be given the owner's phone number, as well as the phone numbers of local water police, local boatyards with launches and other agencies who can help guard the area.

It pays to row round your boat or visit her in the marina occasionally after dark between weekends. Challenge anyone who is on *any* boat, just to make sure the word gets round the district that your boat and those near her are kept under observation.

◁ *Fig. 54 Burglar proofing*
A cabin entrance which looks difficult to break through is discouraging to any thief. Long-tailed hinges which extend right across solid wood doors with a stout metal strip down the centre gives the cabin entrance the appearance of a fortified castle, particularly if there are two big padlocks. Small padlocks are very easily broken, so it is best to use the kind which have rings ⅜ inch (10 mm) thick. Naturally the padlocks must be of the weather-proof kind.

To prevent anyone from unscrewing the bolts from the outside, all the nuts must be locked either with split pins or by peening over the ends of the bolts. This is done by cutting the bolts slightly too long and hammering the ends in such a way that there is a spread of metal over the nut top.

If there is a pressure pad type burglar alarm under the grating at the cabin entrance, there should be a second alarm inside the boat. The alarm outside should be of the type which goes off when anyone cuts its wire.

Long-tailed hinges are not easy to get, but they are sold by Simpson-Lawrence Ltd and the 6 inch (150 mm) type have the Catalogue No. SL 195504, the 8 inch (200 mm) type have the Catalogue No. SL 195506, while the longest type, 10 inch (250 mm) long have the Catalogue No. SL 195508.

26 *Stowing dinghies on* ==*board*==

Inflatable dinghies

One of the best ways to stow an inflatable dinghy is to deflate it and put it inside a deck locker. Putting it below decks in the cabin is unpopular because the dinghy is usually wet, so it dampens cushions, charts and anything it touches as it is manhandled below. Also, most main hatches are too small to swallow a collapsed dinghy easily. But once below, the dinghy is safe from vandals and rogue waves, from bright sunlight and friends who borrow it without asking. Any stowage below deck must be free from sharp edges of fibreglass or bolt ends, not to mention rough plywood edges and loose gear like anchors. Inflatables are vulnerable to anything hard, especially if it has sharp edges or corners.

Probably the best place to put an inflatable is in a cockpit locker. It may be necessary to make the lid extra large, or cut away part of the front of the locker and hinge it, to give easy access. Once in the locker, the dinghy is as safe as can be and its weight is nearly as low down in the boat as if it were tucked away below a quarter berth or in the fo'c's'le. To get a dinghy into a locker, deflating must be thorough. When all the valves have been opened, the boat is rolled up tight – a job hard to do single-handed. This rolling expels the air and makes the inflatable into a sausage shape which is fairly easy to manhandle especially if the painter is wrapped round and tied tightly. Some dinghy pumps have reversible actions so that the air can be extracted thoroughly without any gymnastics by the crew.

Dinghies with no floorboards and no wooden transom are by far the best for this type of stowage. The main disadvantage of total collapse for stowage is that it takes time to reinflate the dinghy, which might be wanted in a hurry. Some people have two pumps available, and Avon inflatables can be supplied with CO_2 cannisters which give virtually instant inflation.

On boats with a large cockpit, the deflated dinghy can be stowed in the well, or across the aft end of the seats. For ocean cruising this has advantages: it partly fills an over-large cockpit so that less water can get in when a big one breaks aboard; the dinghy is close to hand in a crisis; it is less obtrusive than on the cabin top, and therefore less likely to be washed overboard or stolen, and there is no windage.

There should be a tough PVC or canvas cover right over the dinghy, which may be deflated, partly inflated or fully blown up, according to the available space. This cover keeps off the sun, hides the dinghy from vandals – at least partly – and helps hold the dinghy in place if the yacht capsizes, and finally, it protects the rubber fabric from wear and tear.

The same sort of cover is useful over an inflatable stowed on deck. It can be bright orange for safety reasons and, if the crew have to abandon the yacht, the cover will act as a high-visibility tarpaulin over the crew, increasing the chances of rescue whilst keeping off the worst rigours of the weather. The yacht's name or number marked boldly on the cover is also useful for identification. Each corner of the cover and the middle of each edge has a strong eye worked in it to take the lashings down to deck. These eyes must be hydraulically pressed in, or be hand-worked sailmaker's eyes, in each case with ample cloth doubling, otherwise they will tear out. The cheap type of brass eye which is hammered in is totally inadequate for this job.

Just where the inflatable stows on deck depends on the available space, the need to have a clear view forward, the crew's tolerance to a cluttered foredeck, and so on. If there is plenty of room, the dinghy may be stowed fully inflated. On most boats under about 35 feet (10.5 metres) it is necessary to deflate one end of the dinghy and fold this part under. The resulting package is easy to lash down forward or aft of the mast, or on the aft deck, or over the fore hatch, as preferred.

A half inflated dinghy can be thrown into the sea and the crew can get aboard and paddle away from a sinking yacht, while the other half of the inflatable is pumped up. It is not easy in rough conditions but inflatables have so much buoyancy in their side tubes, they keep a crew afloat even when half inflated.

If an overall cover is not used to secure the dinghy down, two straps are needed and for serious offshore work, three or even four straps are best. Rope lashings over an inflatable are unacceptable because they chafe. Straps can be made of the same webbing used for dinghy toe-straps, or sewn up by a sailmaker from broad strips of Terylene (Dacron) cloth. At each end there is a tough eye made like a corner eye on a sail. An amateur who does not have the facilities for making a metal eye can turn each end of the strap up and stitch it into a loop, but these wear fairly quickly.

To hold the strap ends down some people use simple lashings which can be cut in an emergency; on other boats the technique is to have a lashing at one end and a well greased snap shackle at the other, in case a knife is not instantly to hand when trouble strikes. Very few boats are built with eyes on deck to take the lashings so it is common to use the handrails. This is poor practice because when the going gets super-tough, big seas will burst against the dinghy and rip it off the deck, taking lengths of handrail with it. Eye plates secured with 2 or 4 bolts through stout backing chocks are needed, though on a small boat used for coastal cruising it might be acceptable to use common eyebolts. The disadvantage of this type of fastening is that it cannot take sideways loads so it soon tilts, lets in drips, makes its hole slightly too big, which then leaks. Not entirely satisfactory.

Rubber dinghies should not be stowed the right way up, though there is a great temptation to do this because they make such handy stowage lockers for oars, fishing gear, fenders, side ladder, bailers, fresh vegetables, the kedge anchor, a genoa or two, buckets and the baby. In practice, a dinghy the right way up fills with water and becomes massively heavy, it gets lots of chafe, loose gear is blown overboard when the going gets lumpy – in short, the idea is a bad one. It does make sense to tie inside the oars, bailer and other essential gear because in a crisis the dinghy often proves as valuable as the liferaft. Also plenty of boats do not carry rafts, or if they do, the owners do not have them serviced annually so that they refuse to inflate when needed.

Solid or rigid dinghies

Any rigid dinghy has to be light, otherwise it is impossible to haul aboard easily, and lightness is only achieved by keeping the structure relatively thin and flimsy. This means that once aboard, it needs properly shaped chocks to support it on deck and keep it firmly in place. On most boats, especially those under 40 feet (12 metres) long, dinghies are carried upside down, so the chocks are simple deeply grooved pieces of wood to fit the dinghy gunwale. It is usual to fit only 4, but for real ocean-bashing, 6 or 8 give peace of mind and are much more likely to keep the dinghy in place when tumbling mountains of water come in over the decks.

If the dinghy is secured down the right way up, big boat style, the chocks have to fit the dinghy's underwater shape. Again, two chocks are usual, but three so much better, especially when someone forgets to leave the bung out and the dinghy fills with water. Incidentally, the bung must be well secured on a lanyard, with a spare bung or two kept in the boat, also tied on.

To make the chocks, cardboard or ply templates are cut to fit the dinghy's bottom, and hardwood pieces made up the same shape. The chocks are located about one-quarter of the boat's length from bow and stern, if there are 2 of them, and about one-fifth the length if there are 3, with one amidships. The ends of the chocks are made with eye-plates or holes to take the lashings and

---

Fig. 55   Securing a dinghy on deck   ▷
The chocks on which a dinghy rests should be very strongly bolted down and made to fit the dinghy accurately. The underdeck chock extends over a bigger area than the chock on deck, both fore and aft and athwartships and can, incidentally, be used as the base for grab rails inside the cabin (see bottom right).
Holes in the chocks are used for lashings, though some people prefer to have eyebolts or eyeplates because they are easier for threading the lashing through, though they will cost a little more. If a hole is drilled through each chock for the lashings, there should be a strong metal plate bolted over it to prevent the grain from splitting across in way of the hole.
When making chocks of this sort it is not a bad idea to incorporate extra features such as stowage for boathooks and deck mops (bottom left). Many of the details shown here can equally be used in a stowage plan for a liferaft.

the top face of each chock is padded with foam plastic covered with PVC or Terylene or some similar soft material to give a comfortable resting place which will not chafe the bottom of the dinghy.

A dinghy stowed the right way up needs an overall cover, lashed all round,

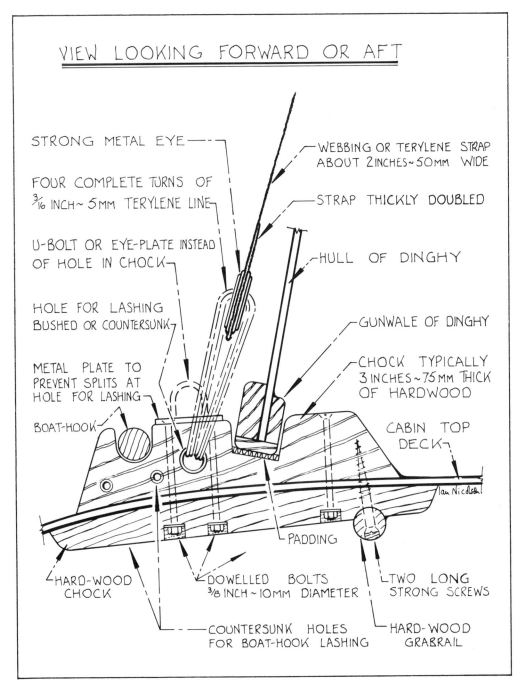

VIEW LOOKING FORWARD OR AFT

STRONG METAL EYE

FOUR COMPLETE TURNS OF $\frac{3}{16}$ INCH ~ 5MM TERYLENE LINE

U-BOLT OR EYE-PLATE INSTEAD OF HOLE IN CHOCK

HOLE FOR LASHING BUSHED OR COUNTERSUNK

METAL PLATE TO PREVENT SPLITS AT HOLE FOR LASHING

BOAT-HOOK

WEBBING OR TERYLENE STRAP ABOUT 2 INCHES ~ 50MM WIDE

STRAP THICKLY DOUBLED

HULL OF DINGHY

GUNWALE OF DINGHY

CHOCK TYPICALLY 3 INCHES ~ 75MM THICK OF HARDWOOD

CABIN TOP DECK

PADDING

HARD-WOOD CHOCK

DOWELLED BOLTS $\frac{3}{8}$ INCH ~ 10MM DIAMETER

TWO LONG STRONG SCREWS

COUNTERSUNK HOLES FOR BOAT-HOOK LASHING

HARD-WOOD GRABRAIL

to limit the amount of gear put in and to keep water out. There is no way of preventing the crew using this space for general stowage – it is too convenient. The cover will sag and fill with rainwater and in time burst unless there is a raised ridge pole from bow to stern, making the cover into a roof shape, sloped at least 20°, which easily sheds water.

Getting a solid dinghy on board needs a little cunning to supplement brute force. One trick is to thread plastic balls on the top guardrail so that they act as rollers. There are several types of ball available including 'stopper knobs' (supplied by chandlers like Holt-Allen, UK) and fishing floats. The bigger the balls the better they work, but the more inconvenient they are when anyone wants to grab onto the guardrail.

Another ploy is to have detachable guardrails and then the dinghy only has to be lifted to the level of the yacht's deck. If this method is used, it is important to have softly rounded metal or plastic rubbing strips with well countersunk screws on the toerail.

A wire or rope span is made fast to each end of the dinghy and clipped on to a halliard or topping lift for lifting aboard. This is better than hoisting the dinghy from one end only, as water will tend to fill the stern if the bow only is hoisted, or vice versa. The painters at bow and stern can be used if they are strong enough to form the span for lifting, and the halliard end shackled to a loop made where they join, roughly halfway along the dinghy's length. If a stiff breeze is blowing, the dinghy will present less windage when lifted up horizontal, and be much easier to manage on deck while being manoeuvred onto its deck chocks. If the securing points of the span are located just above half way up the stem and transom *on the outside*, then as the dinghy is swung in over the side deck it can be inverted with little effort, before being lowered onto its chocks. Fenders and the dinghy's cover can be hung down the topsides to avoid scratching them during the hauling-in process. If the dinghy cannot be turned the right way fore-and-aft before beginning the lift, it is usually quite easy to turn it round in mid-air before lowering onto the deck.

It is certainly a nuisance getting a tender on deck, but well worth while especially in bad weather. Towing even a small dinghy acts like a brake, particularly when going to windward in steep seas. Trying to claw off a lee shore hampered by a dinghy gradually filling with water can prove impossible. The modern technique of towing inflatables with the painter hauled very short so that the bow of the tender is right up on the aft pulpit does not totally eliminate the retarding effect; also the windage is serious, as proved by the way the inflatable will at times fly out to leeward. So whatever type of dinghy is used, it is best to find some method of stowing it aboard.

Some solid dinghies have the top part of the transom fitted with a watertight hinge, then the boat is carried upside down, stern aft, over the main hatch. By folding up the transom flap, access into the cabin is not much impeded and the tender keeps some water from getting through the main hatch.

Another trick is to have a tender with its fore end shaped like a catamaran, so that each part of the bow fits on one side of the mast. Such a dinghy may be on the foredeck with the two projections of the bow facing aft, or aft of the mast facing forward, or the twin bows can face aft and straddle the main hatch.

Some solid dinghies are in two halves, the smaller stowing inside the larger, each with its own ample buoyancy chambers. A better form of this technique is to have a dinghy with a short detachable bow or stern section in the form of a shaped watertight box which is quickly clipped onto the dinghy before or after launching.

Perhaps the most ingenious arrangement is to have a dinghy which forms the cockpit well. This keeps the weight low and eliminates windage. It does call for concessions of design so far as the shape of the cockpit and the dinghy are concerned. Self-bailing may be a problem though a system of bungs and possibly a dinghy centre-board slot can make sure that water flows back where it belongs fast enough.

=====27 *Stowing liferafts*=====

Anyone taking a boat well offshore should give serious thought to carrying a liferaft aboard. The best type and by far the most common for a yacht is inflatable, packed in a fibreglass canister made in two parts which separate when the 'rip-cord' or release line is pulled. The raft is inflated by an internal CO_2 cylinder. The canister varies in design according to type, and may be either cylindrical or box-shaped. The box-shaped ones are easier to stow aboard, and to man-handle through guard-rails. It is essential that the raft chosen is adequate for the number of crew aboard, and that all crew know how to operate it. If the raft is stowed below decks, crews should beware of pulling the rip-cord accidentally! It is important that the raft is returned to its manufacturer annually for servicing. On many races, a liferaft is a mandatory item of equipment.

If a liferaft is stowed well forward, there is a risk that the crew will not be able to reach it in the event of a serious fire amidships, when the engine or galley blows up. So it seems logical to stow the raft well aft, except that in the event of the boat being run down by a big ship, the stern is where the victim is likely to be hit, because the helmsman will naturally be steering away from the danger. The crew will rush forward out of danger at the last moment, so they will see the liferaft get damaged or disappear, very likely, at the moment of impact.

Putting the liferaft amidships must be the sensible place, we conclude, until we remember that there is seldom a low and protected location here. Besides, that explosion we have already worried about is going to take place just about under the raft!

As if this were not all very confusing, there is a second set of arguments about the stowage position. Should the raft be on deck or below? On deck there is the risk it will be swept overboard by a violent wave, or stolen, or become inoperative due to weathering. Just in case anyone thinks the last worry can be dismissed, the last time I inflated a raft it took the combined efforts of three of us to tug the valve release line free; we were hauling and swearing for untold minutes. A little salt water creates enough corrosion to make every sort of mechanism immovable.

Not that stowing a liferaft below solves more than a few of the outstanding problems. It is awkward and heavy to get up through a hatch and into the water. It usually takes up a lot of valuable cabin space. Though its weight is low and there is no windage, it must not be right down in the bilge, or near the engine, or far away from a hatch (which must be larger than the packaged-up raft).

In practice, the location is bound to be a compromise. On many fishing boats the raft is on top of the wheelhouse where no wave is likely to snatch it off, but it is almost unreachable especially in severe weather. It is to all intents out of sight, so no one ever notices external damage or the date, now ten years past, when it was last serviced! The theory is that as the boat sinks the raft floats off and the crew climb inside. This assumes they have not been washed away beforehand. Putting the inflatable up so high makes it very awkward for getting into before final disaster strikes, which at least has the desirable effect of discouraging the crew from abandoning ship as long as she stays afloat.

One of the best places to locate the raft is in the cockpit. Boats like the Weatherly 8.5 have a recessed locker in the bottom of the cockpit well where the weight of the raft is low; it is hidden from vandals and it is out of the weather, provided the space is drained and ventilated. Almost as good is a cockpit locker, but here it will usually be essential to have not only a lid over the locker which is appreciably larger than the packed raft, but also a fold-down or portable front to the locker so that quick launching is easy.

Where the raft is stowed in the cockpit, it must have something reliable to keep it in place when the boat turns over. The same applies to lockers and stowage containers in the cabin. A liferaft is a heavy object when it's not floating!

One way of securing a raft in a locker is to have a pair of Terylene or nylon webbing straps right round the raft with quick-release lashings secured to the tops of the locker sides or ends. These straps, if fitted with big handles, make it easy for several people to grip the raft and get it on deck swiftly. Even a small raft is a big load for a grandfather (riddled with arthritis) and his delicate grandchildren, who may be the people getting the raft into operation. On a racing machine, packed with gorillas, the crew are likely to be in a state of shock or fatigue or seasickness when the raft is needed and so two or three easily gripped ropes, at least ½ inch (12 mm) in diameter, at each end of the package, will be welcome when getting the lifeboat out of its stowage and up to the guardrails. These ropes or webbing straps have to be removed to let the raft inflate, so they must be fitted round the raft in such a way that they can be pulled off endways quickly. An alternative is to have a heavy gauge net under the raft and extending up the sides; when in dire trouble the crew seize hold of the top edges of the net instead of trying to grip the wet slippery bulbous surface of the canister.

If there is no special cockpit locker for the raft, there may be space under the tiller or on a framework bolted across the cockpit above the tiller, aft of the helmsman. Plenty of boats have cockpit wells which are too big for offshore work and it is good seamanship to reduce the internal space which will be filled with water when a wave comes aboard.

If the cockpit has no short length of deck between the forward end of the cockpit and the main hatch (an area usually called the bridge deck) it is easy to make one. There may be space beneath for a liferaft, even if it means widening or lowering the bottom of the cockpit well. Such a lower level will naturally collect water, so a pair of extra drains will have to be fitted and these will be beneficial, because less than one boat in a hundred has drains large enough to get rid of the water fast enough.

Liferafts on deck are best stowed right up against strong structures. Typical places are:

- Tight up against the forward coaming of the cabin top.
- At the aft end of a sunken foredeck.
- In a sunken foredeck locker.
- Close to the aft coaming of the cockpit, either forward or aft of the coaming.

The aim is to get the raft casing so close to a firm structure that breaking waves cannot get between the two. A wave which roars in against the exposed face of the canister just pushes it up against the coaming, but does not tear it free. In survival conditions, just when the raft is going to be needed, there are often repeated attempts by the sea to wrench the raft away, first by breaking over the deck with solid ferocity, then by turning the boat over, repeatedly.

Each of the two or three straps which hold the raft on deck have to be able to stand up to about a ton load, with a factor of safety of about 3. This also applies to the end clips, the eyeplates and their bolts, and quick-release lashings, and so on. The deck has to stand the load too!

The 2 inch (50 mm) webbing used for personal safety harnesses has the requisite strength, but the end-eyes must be sewn in, or made with a sail-maker's hydraulic press. A raft may be washed off by sliding endways from the hold of straps which have become slack through weathering and chafe over many months. To avoid this, there must be straps both athwartships and fore-and-aft.

Sometimes the raft is set in a strong wood or fibreglass cradle which is held down on the deck with at least six ⅜ inch (10 mm) bolts, well spread out. A good cradle has deep fiddles or upstanding sides and ends to keep the raft in place, as well as straps over. It may be incorporated in a halliard box round the mast, or ventilator boxes, or the aft cockpit coaming.

=28 *Fitting safety equipment*=

Safety gear, like insurance, is mostly a waste of money until suddenly it is needed. Then the best equipment, stowed in exactly the right place, becomes the most important thing in the world. If you've ever hauled a stricken boat off a lee shore in a roaring gale, you'll know the tremendous surge of relief when your carefully stowed towing warp runs out freely without snagging and comes taut as your boat creeps ahead into the plunging head seas, and slowly, Oh! so slowly, you get the other boat out of danger without your rope snapping or wrenching the cleat clean off the deck.

If you've been quietly cooking the evening meal when suddenly the dim cabin becomes all too bright with the eager flames of a well-established cabin fire, you'll appreciate a great big extinguisher. Odd is the man who can blithely go to sea with all sorts of inessential luxuries but only flimsy toy fire extinguishers.

If you go aboard a yacht owned by a member of the Ocean Cruising Club, people who have achieved membership only because they have made a major ocean passage, you will notice that all their safety gear is massive, chunky, of the best quality, and duplicated or triplicated.

Torches and flashlights

The most used piece of safety equipment is a portable light. Big, strong lights with long-life batteries are the only kind to have. Divers' torches which can stand up to a lot of moisture are ideal but expensive. Too many versions of the common rubber torch are unreliable and a better choice is an ordinary tubular plastic torch with a bicycle inner tube slipped over it and seized on to the torch at each end to keep out water. The glass needs bedding in Farocaulk or a similar waterproof compound to keep out water.

One torch is needed in the cockpit, one in the cabin entrance, one by the chart table and one forward, even on a small-to-medium size of boat. It is no bad rule to have one torch aboard for each member of the crew, and on the best organised craft the spare bulbs and batteries fit all the torches on board.

Torches need stowing on their own because if they share a locker with other gear, the glass gets broken and the torch may be switched on accidentally when the boat rolls. The one over the chart table is best secured with its glass downwards, so that if the main lights fail, the torch acts as an emergency chart table lamp. One way to achieve the necessary effect is to have a sailmaker stitch up a PVC or Terylene pouch which just fits the flashlight. The pouch, which is screwed to the bulkhead adjacent to the chart table, has most of the bottom cut away so that the light shines through. The same sort of stowage over the galley and in the engine compartment is worth having, especially in yachts with cheap electrical installations.

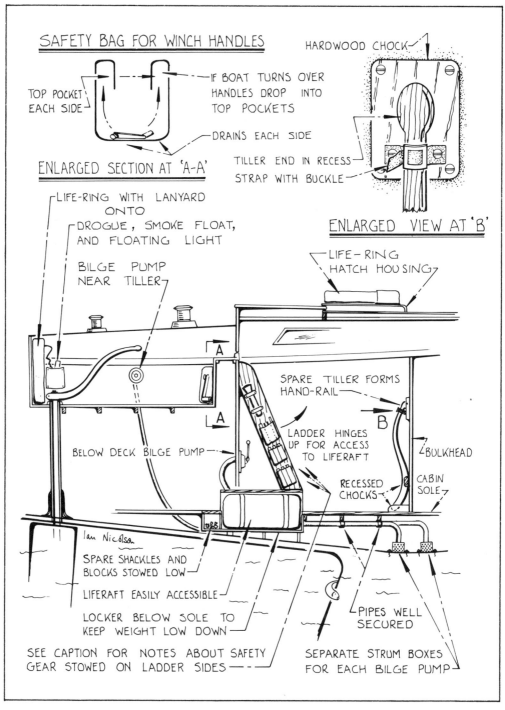

SAFETY BAG FOR WINCH HANDLES

HARDWOOD CHOCK

TOP POCKET EACH SIDE

IF BOAT TURNS OVER HANDLES DROP INTO TOP POCKETS

DRAINS EACH SIDE

ENLARGED SECTION AT 'A-A'

TILLER END IN RECESS

STRAP WITH BUCKLE

LIFE-RING WITH LANYARD ONTO

DROGUE, SMOKE FLOAT, AND FLOATING LIGHT

ENLARGED VIEW AT 'B'

BILGE PUMP NEAR TILLER

LIFE-RING HATCH HOUSING

A

A

SPARE TILLER FORMS HAND-RAIL

B

LADDER HINGES UP FOR ACCESS TO LIFERAFT

BELOW DECK BILGE PUMP

BULKHEAD

RECESSED CHOCKS

CABIN SOLE

Ian Nicolson

SPARE SHACKLES AND BLOCKS STOWED LOW

LIFERAFT EASILY ACCESSIBLE

LOCKER BELOW SOLE TO KEEP WEIGHT LOW DOWN

PIPES WELL SECURED

SEE CAPTION FOR NOTES ABOUT SAFETY GEAR STOWED ON LADDER SIDES

SEPARATE STRUM BOXES FOR EACH BILGE PUMP

Safety harnesses, or personal lifelines

These should be worn whenever the weather is even slightly angry. If someone falls overboard, but is still attached to the yacht, it is unlikely he will drown. If anyone has to have a lifebuoy thrown at him, it is an admission of failure and the chances of survival vary from moderate to minimal. Harnesses need their own separate stowage locker or pouches just inside the cabin, so that everyone going on deck can be clipped on before going outside into the danger. A row of hooks is quite good, as each harness can be seen and missing ones are promptly noticed. Also, harnesses dry out well if hanging up. But they tend to clang and rattle as the boat moves, so a row of pockets sewn onto a back cloth which is screwed up to a bulkhead or down the side of the companion ladder may be preferred.

Lifejackets

These are bulky and inconvenient to wear, especially if there is hectic work to be done on the foredeck. For this reason some crews prefer buoyancy aids and they find this gives a feeling of security combined with extra warmth in cold conditions. But a buoyancy aid is not satisfactory in the final emergency when a person may be in the water for a long time, perhaps less than fully conscious.

Buoyancy aids are only slightly less bulky than life jackets when it comes to finding stowage space and on plenty of boats there are not sufficient easily accessible lockers for this safety gear. In any case, if a lifejacket is stowed in a locker, it is not long before other gear is stuffed in and soon the jacket cannot be grabbed in a hurry. It is much better to keep jackets in the open, secured by a couple of lashings or quick-release straps, or lengths of shock-cord. This type of stowage ensures that everyone sees the jackets constantly and knows where they are; the jackets are ventilated and if parts start to corrode or wear, there is a good chance the trouble will be seen early.

The traditional place for lifejackets is by each bunk, and when a man is asleep there is usually plenty of space around him for a lifejacket flat folded,

---

◁   *Fig. 56   Steering safety gear*

Some items like life-rings must be available instantly and therefore have to be on deck near the helmsman and crew. It is a good idea not to stow both life-rings in the same place, so that whoever is closest to one can get it overboard instantly. Flashlights, knives, pliers, marlinspikes, white flares and red flares should be stowed near the companionway so that they are out of the weather but close at hand. These items are shown on the starboard side of the ladder and will be duplicated on the port side. This equipment can be in soft pouches or in wooden open-topped boxes.

Because the liferaft is heavy, it makes sense to stow it as low as possible, although it should not be right in the bilge where it may be wet for long periods. The casing shown in the sketch forms the bottom step of the ladder and each end of the casing is open for ventilation. It is reassuring for the crew to have the liferaft visible, too.

particularly above the foot of the berth. Other places worth considering are on the under side of the cabin table, up under the deck edge in way of a quarter berth, in nets under the side decks in the main cabin and secured to the under side of the cockpit locker lids.

Lifejackets are affected by sunlight and heat from exhaust pipes. Parts like the automatic inflation unit and light are likely to corrode if they are constantly wet, so areas to avoid are:

- Near hatchways.
- Low down in settee lockers which get invaded by bilge water.
- Below ventilators and opening ports.
- In cockpit lockers which are often opened in bad weather.

Lifebuoys and life-rings

On all but the smallest boats there should be two lifebuoys. The obvious place to stow them is within easy reach of the helmsman, but on boats with big crews constantly on deck, one of the buoys should be handy for the winchmen. It is usually rough when anyone goes overboard and under these conditions the helmsman may need both hands and much of his strength to control the boat, so he may be unable to throw a buoy, or throw it accurately.

Lifebuoys are often stowed in PVC or Terylene pouches which may be hung from the guardrails, or (to reduce windage) secured to the transom. At the end of a voyage it may be necessary to put them below to save them from vandalism and the effects of the sun. It is possible to buy standard racks made of thin stainless steel rod for the lifebuoys. These holders are available in chandlers and all the owner has to do is fix them direct to the guardrails or aft pulpit. However, the racks are not always fully reliable or strong enough and it may be necessary to add a stiffening batten or two, or secure the rack with extra hose clamps or lashings. Velcro is used on lots of boats to secure buoys, with one side of the tape glued or stitched to the buoy and the other to the boat. The idea is fine, but there are plenty of snags in practice. For a start, Velcro is expensive

---

Fig. 57 Handy stowage ▷

Just inside the main hatch is the ideal place to stow safety gear like flashlights, and navigational gear like the hand-bearing compass. To make a lot of stowage space cheaply, the racing boat trick of fitting side curtains port and starboard just inside the hatchway is hard to beat. The curtains can be extended well into the cabin and they help to keep the quarter berths and settees dry in rough conditions.

The curtains can be hung from hooks and so made portable provided the hooks are flat and do not catch on oilskins as anyone passes from cockpit to cabin. The bottom of the curtains may extend right to the cabin sole, or at least down to settee level, to form leeboards and spray deflectors. For extra stowage there may be extra pockets on the outboard sides of the curtains, and small pockets sewn on the inside and outside of the larger ones. There are a variety of materials which can be used for these curtains including waterproof canvas, PVC and other materials used for sail covers.

so there is a tendency to use too little, and in narrow strips. To be safe, a buoy needs about 25 square inches (0.016 sq. metres) of Velcro, even if stowed flat, such as on top of a hatch cover or on the cabin top.

If the old-style chocks are used to hold a buoy on a surface like the deck which is more or less horizontal, there has to be some extra restraint to prevent

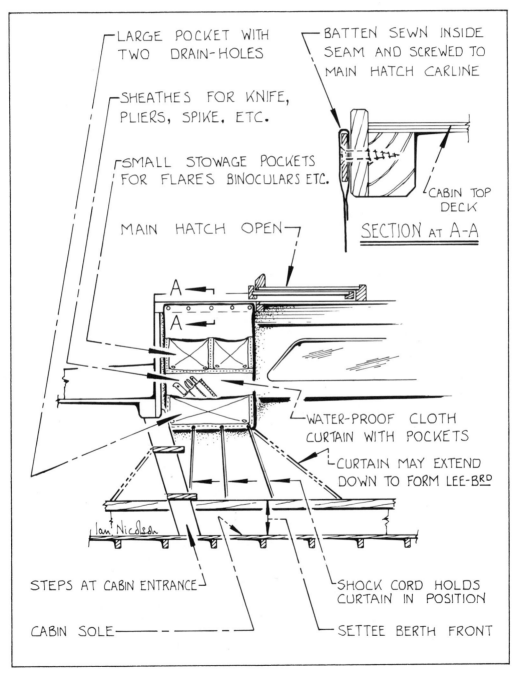

LARGE POCKET WITH
TWO DRAIN-HOLES

BATTEN SEWN INSIDE
SEAM AND SCREWED TO
MAIN HATCH CARLINE

SHEATHES FOR KNIFE,
PLIERS, SPIKE, ETC.

SMALL STOWAGE POCKETS
FOR FLARES BINOCULARS ETC.

CABIN TOP
DECK

MAIN HATCH OPEN

SECTION AT A-A

A

A

WATER-PROOF CLOTH
CURTAIN WITH POCKETS

CURTAIN MAY EXTEND
DOWN TO FORM LEE-BRD

Ian Nicolson

STEPS AT CABIN ENTRANCE

SHOCK CORD HOLDS
CURTAIN IN POSITION

CABIN SOLE

SETTEE BERTH FRONT

189

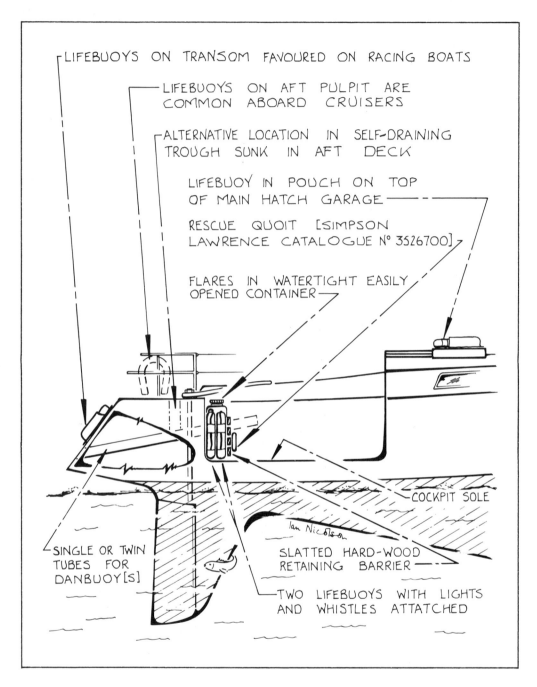

LIFEBUOYS ON TRANSOM FAVOURED ON RACING BOATS

LIFEBUOYS ON AFT PULPIT ARE COMMON ABOARD CRUISERS

ALTERNATIVE LOCATION IN SELF-DRAINING TROUGH SUNK IN AFT DECK

LIFEBUOY IN POUCH ON TOP OF MAIN HATCH GARAGE

RESCUE QUOIT [SIMPSON LAWRENCE CATALOGUE Nº 3526700]

FLARES IN WATERTIGHT EASILY OPENED CONTAINER

COCKPIT SOLE

SINGLE OR TWIN TUBES FOR DANBUOY[S]

SLATTED HARD-WOOD RETAINING BARRIER

TWO LIFEBUOYS WITH LIGHTS AND WHISTLES ATTATCHED

Fig. 58 Stowage for safety equipment

Lifebuoys are bulky, so they take up a lot of room. Also if they are high up, their windage is unacceptable on a racing boat and even on many cruisers. If the buoys are stowed on the transom they need some simple quick-release device such as throwing lines led to the cockpit, or pouches open at the bottom with a closure arrangement such as tapered wooden pegs which can be released from the cockpit. The aft end of the cockpit well is a good place to stow safety gear because the area is swept by the tiller and therefore not used by the crew when moving about in the cockpit.

190

the buoy from being washed or blown overboard in wild conditions. Some people use thin cotton line which is easily broken, but this is not reliable as it becomes weaker over the months due to exposure and rot. A better arrangement is a pair of Terylene ropes, about ¼ inch (5 mm) diameter, crossed over the top of the buoy, with an eye in the end of each line; one eye is pushed through the other and held in place by a wood wedge having a gentle taper. When the buoy has to be heaved over the side the wedge is snatched out and this releases the retaining lines with total certainty.

Probably the best stowage for lifebuoys is the special trough, recessed into the deck, located aft of the cockpit, or sometimes in the bridge deck, or by the cockpit seats. The trough must be fully drained and may be large enough to hold the liferaft. Because a puddle of water here will cause every sort of deterioration, the drain needs to be 1 inch (25 mm) diameter to ensure it does not become blocked with debris. Here, as elsewhere throughout the boat, the outlet for the drain should be above the static water line for safety reasons and it is quite usual to arrange this drain to discharge into the self-draining cockpit. On boats with no specially designed troughs it is sometimes possible to fit a simple bulkhead athwartships or fore and aft at the aft end of the cockpit, and drop the buoys in between the bulkhead and the cockpit well sides. The bulkheads stop 8 inches (200 mm) above the cockpit bottom so that water is never trapped around the buoys and there is a good circulation of drying air.

Bucket or bailer, or both

A famous surveyor, when asked what was the best bilge pump, replied: 'A frightened yachtsman with a big strong bucket.' There is so much truth in this remark, as anyone knows who has ever been in danger of sinking. A bucket does not break down, provided it is strong and not one of the cheap, flimsy household type. It has not got valves or pipes to clog up, it seldom wears out and however hard it is used, it is unlikely to disintegrate as some pumps do. Pumps also have a bad habit of coming adrift from the bulkhead, corroding at the valves and access hatch seatings. They also suffer from broken and lost handles, blocked suctions and kinked piping.

The best way to shift a lot of water out of the bilge is to use a swift scooping motion and for this reason a bailer can be more use than a bucket, provided the water level is not too far below the hatch coaming. But a bucket is better for fighting fires and it is also handy if the WC breaks down totally.

Some people use the ship's bucket as a gash bin in the galley. This means that the bucket is always in the same place, a known stowage position. On other boats the bucket is in the toilet compartment, in a bracket, and it is used for stowing sodden clothes. On a few boats it is wedged in the corner of a cockpit locker and used to hold the sail tiers. Whichever location is chosen, the bucket should always be in the same place, always visible and never under other gear. Like other safety gear, when it is needed there is likely to be a whiff of panic about and, under these conditions, no one should have to dig under a pile of sails, oars, ropes and gas cylinders.

A cockpit locker is not always the best stowage place for safety gear. In severe weather it can be unwise to open the lid because a lot of water may rush in.

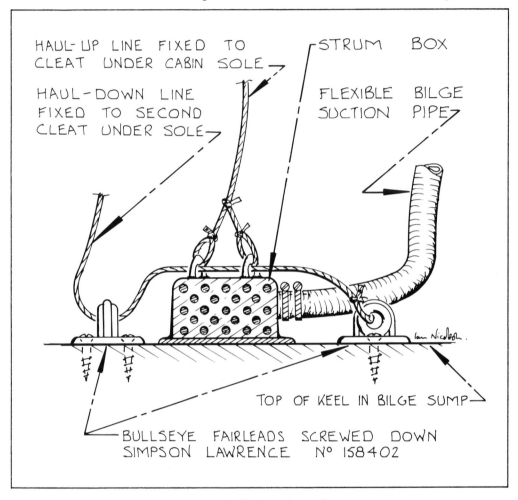

Fig. 59   Easily cleaned strum box

If the bilge is deep, it is often difficult and sometimes impossible to reach down and clean out the strum boxes. However, if they are not cleaned out they gradually become blocked up with muck and so the bilge pumps become less and less efficient. This could be disastrous in an emergency.

If the bottom of the suction pipe is made flexible and the top of the strum box has a line for hauling it up, this makes cleaning out quite easy. However, some strum boxes will not automatically drop right down into the bilge and this sketch shows a line designed to force the strum box back down onto the top of the keel. The haul-down line is permanently made fast to the eyeplate on the right, then it leads through the two metal eyes on top of the strum box, and on through the eyeplate on the left, then up to an accessible point just below the sole. This arrangement keeps down the amount of winter work which has to be done on the bilge pumping system.

However, a bucket is a fairly bulky thing to stow below, especially in a small yacht. This explains why some owners use the bucket as a container for the cleaning gear, or ship's tools, or bo's'un's stores, or small lengths of line. They may hang the bucket in the fore cabin or fo'c's'le with a strap or length of shock-cord around it to prevent it from swinging about at sea.

Radar Reflector

On any boat not used for racing, the only place to keep the radar reflector is permanently aloft. It should be as high as possible, not least because offshore in very bad conditions the wind may heel the boat a lot and lower the true height of the reflector, and it may then be blanketed off from ships' radar scanners by the height of the seas. The only reflector which should be considered is one of the high efficiency kind such as the Firdell. There should be a securing arrangement at top and bottom, each bracket being strong enough to withstand the rigours of life offshore. These include rolling non-stop for a fortnight, constant baths in corrosive salt spray and the occasional thump from the feet of a man working aloft.

When the reflector cannot be secured aloft permanently, it needs its own protected stowage where it will not be bumped or squashed by other gear. It should be near the cabin steps so that it can be hoisted without delay in the event of a sudden loss of visibility. It's surprising how quickly fog closes in; rain squalls are likely to be even more swift and are sometimes just as blinding.

A specially shaped shelf or locker by the chart table, or under the navigator's seat, in a fenced off section make good stowage spaces because those areas are close to the cabin access. However, it must be easy to grab the reflector without disturbing the navigator, since he will be plying his trade in a rush if there is an abrupt loss of visibility. Wherever the reflector is stowed, there must be no risk that it will be damaged in the event of a severe knock-down because the plates which form the reflector cease to be effective if they are distorted even slightly.

=29 *Marina requirements*=

If a boat is moored up in a marina with no special thought to her future life, she will suffer all sorts of sad ills. The most usual is 'marina chafe' which is found on the vast majority of marina-based craft. The most easily seen symptom is a roughness and lack of glossiness along the topsides, especially amidships and where the hull curves outwards. Sometimes there are scratches in random groups. In extreme cases there is not just a lack of gloss, but the chafe may even go right through the gel and expose glass fibres.

Where the warps touch the hull or deck or toerail, there will be chafe, sometimes deeply into the toerail or deck edge, or into fittings like aluminium fairleads. Marina chafe is cured by a full repaint so it is worth preventing.

Fenders

Plenty of fenders, big, chubby ones with stout lines, are needed. The careful owner realises that a plain fender can itself cause roughness of the topsides, though it will prevent serious scratching. To make fenders truly effective, they have to be in a soft cotton bag and every fortnight or so the bags have to be changed for newly laundered ones. In dusty, dry climates it may be necessary to change the cotton bags even more often if the boat does not lie quietly in her berth.

Because fenders get displaced in bad weather when the boat is heeling to strong blasts of wind and because fender ropes occasionally get chafed right through, it is advisable to have fenders spaced every 3 feet (1 metre), or even closer, regardless of the size of boat. With this close spacing, even if a fender stops working for some reason, the adjacent two will look after the boat. Very careful owners also screw to the dock side a set of those special fenders with recessed screw holes (See Fig. 60).

Warps, Cleats and Fairleads

Warps are just as vulnerable as fenders. It is a good idea to secure a boat so that if any two ropes wear through, or are cut by vandals, or get adrift accidentally, the boat is still safely tied up. Many marina-based craft are held by only four ropes, but six is a good minimum. Where possible there should be at least two ropes holding the yacht away from the sidewalk. This may be hard to arrange in summer, but in winter, when boats are not going out, it is often possible to have ropes led out from the 'offshore' side of the boat. These ropes can be led to

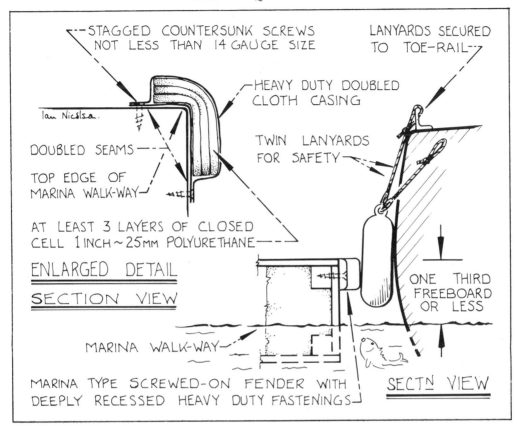

Fig. 60   Marina fenders

Even though a boat has plenty of her own fenders, wise owners make sure the the marina walkway also has continuous fendering at least in way of the middle length of the yacht. This is because yacht fenders get stolen, or puncture, or their lanyards chafe through; or in bad weather, when the boat is being heeled over by fierce gusts, they ride up and lie on top of the walkway.

The walkway should never be high otherwise in hurricane conditions the deck edge of the yacht may be pressed down below the walkway level and get caught under the top lip of the walkway decking. The sketch in the top left corner shows an ideal form of walkway fendering, made up by a local sailmaker. If the marina berth is very difficult to enter, this type of permanent fendering saves many a nasty scratch or dent.

cleats on the boat in the next berth, or to mooring bollards ahead and astern of her. Most people in a marina are happy to have an arrangement operating through the non-sailing months whereby boats lying afloat next to each other have warps led between them, so that each yacht helps to hold its neighbour off the walkway. This eliminates marina chafe and acts as extra security in hurricane conditions.

It is worth taking infinite trouble to ensure that the lead of all warps from the boat is as clear as possible, as even the most minute movement can over a period of time cause good warps to chafe through. Anti-chafe is desirable where warps cross over each other, as well as in way of fairleads and the edges of walkways. A direct line is always the best lead.

Incidentally, if there is even the slightest chance of Force 9 winds or worse roaring over the marina, boats should be moored up so that when they heel to the blasts, their masts do not tangle. This means that boats next to each other should not all be moored pointing the same way. In very severe conditions the windage of a mast is enough to heel some sailing yachts over beyond 45°, so before leaving a boat for the winter she should be studied from a position on the shore dead ahead or astern to see where the tilting mast will be after a frantic gust swipes it.

It is common to use old sheets for warps and springs. Worn sections are cut out and the parts where chafe is likely, such as at the fairleads and by the dock edge, are protected. A traditional form of chafe guard is made from rags wrapped round the rope and seized onto it at each end. This is not very effective unless inspected often. A modern equivalent is plastic piping threaded onto the rope and held in place by two lashings at each end. A single lashing seldom lasts half a year and once a lashing goes, the tubing slides along the rope and soon gets clear of the vulnerable part. These plastic tubes must be slipped onto the warps before the ends are spliced; it is not satisfactory to use plastic piping which has been slit open lengthwise because too often the warp gets forced out of its protective sheath.

Because even a new warp with a good tube protecting it can chafe right through in the course of one fierce gale, cautious owners use short lengths of chain in way of the fairleads and round the cleats on the dockside. Between these short lengths of chain there may be polypropylene rope because it is cheap and it floats, so there is little chance it will get foul around a propeller. The warps and springs are sometimes tied in a loose loop to rubber springs which take the snatch out of any snubbing as the boat pitches or rolls in a vicious sea. In fine weather this may seem a pessimistic precaution because the marina may appear to be a haven of perfectly sheltered water. In practice, almost every marina suffers an occasional vicious swipe from a malignant front which roars in from the very worst direction. It catches the marina short-staffed and, by devilish bad luck, the strongest blasts coincide with high tide. There is often some compounding misfortune; it may be that the breakwater or whatever protects the marina, is being mended or it has been eroded and no one has noticed, or it may have been designed without thought to that ultimate once-in-a-hundred-years gale. In these circumstances many of the boats in the marina will pitch and plunge like stallions gone wild. There have been cases of waves breaking solid over the decks of boats which are supposed to be snug in a safe marina. There are ample stories of rogue waves piling up, one on top of another, when big ships go past and leave a wash which doubles the height of an already fearsome sea. Under these circumstances warps with rubber shock absorbers may hold when others with no snubbers will snap or snatch the cleats out of the deck. For anyone who cannot find suitable specially made absorbers, ordinary tyres can be used. The tyre is placed about half-way along the warp or as convenient, and the warp made fast to each side of it, leaving a short 'by-pass' loop between. By having a continuous length of warp the boat is held secure even if the tyre tears apart.

A particularly ingenious way to reduce the chafing of warps is to fit cleats on the extreme edge of the deck, so that no fairleads are needed and the warps never touch any part of the yacht. Everything depends on the precise design of the hull and deck. Much the best place for these specially located cleats is on the bevelled deck edge or on cabin coamings which are almost as far outboard as the topsides. In theory, cleats could be mounted on the transom, especially if it has the now usual reverse rake with the top edge further forward than the bottom. However, it is usual to build transoms lightly, so unless the boat is of steel, or has been built for offshore cruising, it will almost certainly be necessary to stiffen up the transom before adding cleats to it. And it has to be admitted that the precise location, size and style of cleat will all be important if the good looks of the boat are not to be spoilt. A warp made fast to a transom cleat will have to lead aft; one made fast to a bevelled deck edge cleat can be led forward or aft, provided the warp extends diagonally away from the hull.

In passing, it is sad to look round any marina and see boats made fast by their stanchions in such a way that the stanchion bases are in time pulled out, though sometimes the warp chafes through on the toerail just before this destruction takes place.

Steps and Ladders

Boarding steps are not provided in plenty of marinas. Because modern yachts have high freeboard, there is a substantial distance to climb from the walkway or pier beside the boat up to the deck. For old people the distance can be awkward and at times, impossible. For a young and active crew the climb is nothing – they just grab hold of a stanchion and haul themselves up, causing the stanchion socket to become looser month by month. Inevitably one stanchion will almost always bear the burden, so this stanchion base flange will loosen and in time let rain and spray through the deck. Eventually the deck will be weakened and start to fracture. This is no exaggeration, as many surveys show. As there is a strong tendency to make yachts ever lighter, with thinner decks and smaller under-deck pads at stanchion bases, the trend is towards more frequent failures.

All this confirms that a boarding stairway fixed onto the walkway is a great advantage. If it is made in the form of a strong enclosed box with recessed steps up one side, the inside of the box may be used as a small store for paint, spare fuel cans, a reserve supply of fenders and all the things so essential but so annoying if they have to be carried in lockers on board or kept far away at home. Naturally the store door will be locked and valuable gear will seldom be stowed here unless the level of thievery in the area is negligible. If pilferers are a problem, the top step may be wired to a burglar alarm. It is essential, if a burglar alarm is fitted under the step, to have the whole walkway roped off at the inshore end, with a bold notice warning everyone to keep off. The people who go aboard the boats next to the burglar-proofed one, and the marina staff, have to be warned about the alarm.

On very big boats a set of steps is essential because the freeboard is so high. It is madness to have a side ladder belonging to the boat hanging permanently over the side, but if for some reason a side ladder simply must be used, it needs to be set so high that even when the marina is tortured by the fiercest tornado, the ladder never thumps the walkway or pier.

For a large yacht, the stairs may have a small derrick or there may be a pair of sockets to take the yacht's own cat davit so that heavy loads are conveniently lifted aboard. One reason for having steps for even quite small boats is that they make life safer and less crisis-laden when putting aboard heavy batteries, gas cylinders, dinghies and similar weighty stores.

If a bold notice on the offshore side of the stairs reads: Yacht 'GUESS-WHAT'. BACK TONIGHT. KEEP CLEAR, this should keep away visitors who are desperate for a berth in the marina. If you are the owner of such a well-labelled berth and you come back to find a visitor has 'borrowed' your marina slot, you are in a strong position to demand that he leaves at once and delivers aboard your craft a bottle of scotch for the temporary hire of your expensive piece of seascape.

30 *Drop rudders*

A rudder which can be lifted partly or fully out of the water suits:

1   Racing boats, since lifting the rudder reduces the wetted surface and so cuts down the resistance. Also adjusting the rudder may reduce the pressure on the helm thus further improving performance.
2   Boats which operate in shallow waters. To prevent grounding, or cut out the chance of damage when touching bottom accidentally, the rudder blade is pivoted so that it swings aft and up.

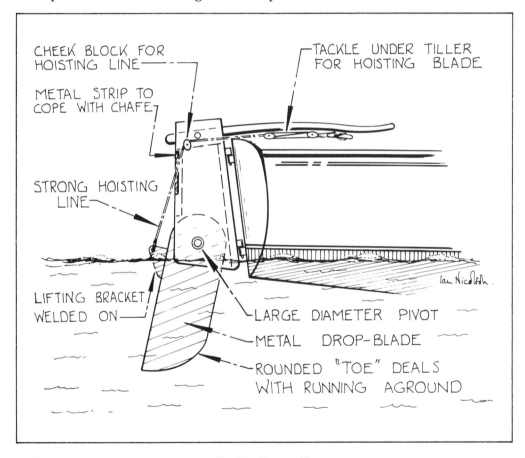

CHEEK BLOCK FOR HOISTING LINE

TACKLE UNDER TILLER FOR HOISTING BLADE

METAL STRIP TO COPE WITH CHAFE

STRONG HOISTING LINE

LIFTING BRACKET WELDED ON

LARGE DIAMETER PIVOT

METAL DROP-BLADE

ROUNDED "TOE" DEALS WITH RUNNING AGROUND

Fig. 61   Drop rudder

It is usual to make the blade of a drop rudder of metal so that it stands up to running aground. Even if a light metal like aluminium is used the blade will need a hoisting arrangement, so that the blade can to raised when the boat is in shallow waters, or is being hauled up. The power of the hoisting equipment gear depends on the size of the blade, but it is best to have over-powerful gear to deal with corrosion, mud on the pivot and other factors which will hamper raising the blade.

3   Boats which are trailed behind a car to the water and launched off a beach or concrete ramp. Without a lifting rudder it is often hard to get the boat afloat and easy to sustain damage when the water is not calm.

Vertical-drop type

The type of lifting rudder which has a pivoted blade is the easiest and cheapest to make, and is widely used. However for racing boats a rather rare version has a blade which slides vertically up and down. The blade is usually rectangular in profile, though the bottom may be rounded and it may be sloped back and down so that as it rises, it goes forward, having the forward and aft edges at perhaps 20° to the vertical. The fore and aft edges are parallel to ensure that the blade slides smoothly in the hollow box-shaped stock. This stock is hung on pintles and gudgeons on the transom in the usual way.

The blade has a hydrodynamic section, usually with rounded nose, a maximum thickness about one-third or two-fifths from the front and an aft end tapering away to a fine trailing edge. It is like the centre-board of a racing dinghy and they have much in common; for instance, it is expected to form a vital part of the resistance to leeway and by varying the amount of blade down in the water, the centre of lateral resistance is shifted forward or aft, to get just the right amount of pull on the tiller.

To raise the blade there will be a tackle, or winch, or hydraulic cylinder. Since the blade will be hollow and light, it is almost certainly going to be essential to have an arrangement to force the blade down as well as up. On both sides of the blade there are marks to show the crew just how far up the blade is. In due course, these marks will be entered into the same log book as that which records the settings of the sails for different wind strengths and directions. The board will be raised in light airs so that just enough remains immersed to give directional control, unless the main fin is so small that leeway is found to be excessive, in which case the rudder blade will be kept fully or partially down.

On a reach the blade will be raised at least a little, unless there is a shocking sea and the helmsman needs full blade immersion to keep control, or what he hopes is control! When the boat is hove-to, it is likely that the rudder will be one-third or one-half up, partly to reduce the risk of damage, partly to help the boat slither sideways when struck by a breaking sea. However, some boats need quite a large rudder blade area to keep them fore-reaching when hove-to in severe conditions.

Vertical-drop rudders need tuning and plenty of sea-time before the crew can get the best from them and in this they are like sails. One important aspect of this type of rudder is that the blade is so very vulnerable to grounding. On an ocean cruiser one would carry a spare blade and on any boat, the toe of the blade is generally rounded to try and minimise damage, as well as give a smooth water-flow.

Pivoting type

The much more common pivoting rudder usually has a simple flat steel plate blade. The profile of the blade will be well rounded at the toe, since it is expected that the rudder will rub along the sea bed often enough. The blade has to be thick enough to stand up to this treatment, so it will be about ½ inch (12 mm) thick on a 28 foot (8.5 metres) boat and around 1 inch (25 mm) thick on a 46 foot (14 metres) craft. The blade starts off galvanised (and ideally epoxy painted too) but chafe when 'smelling' the ground will cause rust to appear which will require annual maintenance. Anyone well supplied with cash will have a bronze blade and for lightness, there is aluminium alloy, which is cheaper than bronze but more costly than steel.

Every part of a drop rudder needs to be vulgarly over-size because there is so much wear, the effects of corrosion are so insidious and because the abrupt loss of the rudder takes the fun out of sailing. Typically, the blade pivot will be a bolt having a diameter about ¹⁄₂₀₀th the length of the boat, but above 35 feet (10.5 metres) overall length stresses are serious and the diameter of the pivot will be about ¹⁄₁₂₅th the boat's length. Bolts over ½ inch (12 mm) diameter are not easily found, so a length of round bar with a heavy split pin each end may be used. To save weight, thick wall tube may be used if the outside diameter is more than 1½ inches (35 mm).

Of course, these figures are rough guides and special circumstances will alter the scantlings. For rudders on boats over about 28 feet (8.5 metres) it makes good sense to thread each end of the pivot and have a flange screwed on. The flanges are screwed tight and locked in place so that the sides of the stock are prevented from splaying outwards when the blade exerts a sideways force.

About one-third of the blade area must remain housed between the sides of the stock at all times to give lateral support, otherwise there is a risk that the blade will bend or break or jam. To ensure that the blade swings up and down easily, washers are fitted each side at the pivot and a waterproof grease is applied copiously when fitting out and at intervals thereafter. Clearances should be measured by sea-going, not engineering, standards, to cope with such contingencies as the growth of weed on the blade.

To make up a drop rudder it is important to have a detailed drawing, especially when the blade is to be made by one of those specialist firms which cuts out curvaceous shapes from large metal plates. Here, as always, the clever designer finds out what material is available locally before doing the drawing. In section, the leading edge should be rounded and the trailing edge left square cut. If it is to be galvanised (and only the hot dip type is any good at sea) the holes for the pivot and lifting tackle are drilled first. There may also be a hole for a downhaul tackle.

The stock is often made of hardwood with the grain running vertically. It will be in the form of a flat thin box with no bottom; both the front and back sides are partially omitted to give space for the blade to swing up and down. Above the blade a spacer piece of the same sort of wood is fitted. It is slightly thicker than the blade plus its two pivot washers. The sides and spacer piece are secured together with glue and through-bolts, or perhaps on a small boat by glue and screws driven in from both sides.

On very small boats the whole drop rudder may be bought as a standard unit from a chandler who supplies racing dinghy gear. Even if the rudder blade cannot be bought, the stock, tiller and pivot unit may be obtainable and a suitable blade made to suit the size and type of boat. If the stock looks about right but is perhaps a bit light, maybe it can be strengthened, or just copied with all the parts thicker.

Dinghy stocks are made from steel or aluminium tube of a rectangular section and they can be copied with increased scantlings for bigger boat sizes. For many people, working in wood is cheaper and in many ways a stock made of wood looks better, especially if kept brightly varnished. If the stock is of wood, the spacer piece should extend quite half the distance down from the top and there may be metal stiffeners, or the side straps of the pintles and gudgeons can be used for reinforcing the stock. There should be three sets of pintles and gudgeons, unless the boat is little more than a big dinghy and over about 43 feet (13 metres) four sets are needed for peace of mind offshore.

Every part must be over-strong, because drop rudders have one characteristic which persists over the generations and it is their tendency to break. Accidents happen in bad weather, or when the parts have become weakened and are suddenly asked to work extra hard – for instance when dodging through crowded moorings. A rudder failure at this time results in an expensive crunch and much bad temper ensues.

The tiller is fitted in the normal way and it may be fixed or lifting. However, it must be stronger than usual because at times the helm may be forced over when the rudder blade is dragging through glutinous mud. Other parts which need to be stouter than usual are the fixings of the gudgeons and pintles. Six bolts in each part is not excessive. The arrangement for lifting the blade should pre-suppose that there is weed wrapped round it and intense side pressure because the boat is hard on the wind. A sheet winch which can take either the downhaul or the up-haul may be neater and even cheaper than tackles for lifting and lowering. Alternatively, a reel winch which winds on a flexible wire and stores the wire on the drum may be best. The winch will be mounted on top of the tiller, or on the aft deck, with the rope or wire led through a lead block almost in line with the pintles.

Where lightness, floatability and low cost are needed, a metal blade may not be acceptable. A wooden one can be built up using a sheet of marine ply with hardwood glued on each side. The side cladding should be rift sawn and the grain 'reversed' to cut down the risk of warping. 'Reversing' involves having the grain in the starboard side angled the opposite way to the port side. This form of construction makes it easy to have a blade which is hydrodynamically elegant. If the blade is moderately damaged due to grounding, it is not hard or tedious to fair the blade anew.

Whatever form a lifting rudder takes, there should be an arrangement to prevent the whole unit from lifting off its pintles by accident. Once made, it should be taken out on trials. Hang over the stern and watch it critically while someone else steers. If it flexes, strengthen it. If any part looks less than rudely over-strength, take it home and make it stouter. If this seems excessively cautious, try getting back to port without using the rudder.

31 Fitting seacocks

For every hundred boats that sink or start filling with water at least thirty and probably fifty suffer from seacock troubles. Seacocks leak, break, get trodden on, are left open when everyone thought they were closed, are closed but not completely . . . the problems are numerous and nasty. Yet there are few bad seacocks; it is mainly poor installation which causes the chaos.

Selecting the precise location for a seacock is seldom easy because each one should be out of the way yet reachable without effort. The lowest cocks should not be more than 18 inches (550 mm) from the cabin sole down to the centre of the cock handle. This is to ensure that anyone with a very short reach can turn the cock off in an emergency. Where a seacock has to be deep down out of reach it should have an extended handle. This may take the form of a universal joint secured to the axle of the cock with a rod extending upwards and a handle on top of the rod. Alternatively the handle on the cock may be given a pair of light ropes led upwards through cheek blocks secured to the hull, then the crew pull on one rope to shut the cock and the other to open it. With this type of remote control it is important to use the type of cock which has stops to limit the travel of the handle at the fully open and fully closed position. If these chocks or stops are not fitted on the seacock, they should be put on the hull.

Seacocks which let in water, such as engine cooling units and toilet water inlets need to be low, then even when the boat is heeled or rolling there is little chance that air will get into the pipe. For discharges like sink outlets it is best to have the cock high, perhaps even above the waterline. With a hole well up on the hull there is a good chance that if anything goes wrong a plug can be pushed in from outboard. If the cock is clear above the waterline but at the boot-top and if the paint line is dark, the outlet will not easily be seen and it will not leak when the boat is on moorings unless there is a sea running. This is one of the simplest yet best safety precautions any boat can have: on some ocean cruising craft the designers contrive to have all the outlets just above the static waterline and keep the inlets down to one or two extremely reliable points, each serving several purposes.

Where possible a seacock should be on a flat part of the hull so that the flange fits neatly. If the hull is heavily curved, a doubler pad is fitted with its outer face tight on to the round of the hull and its inner face perfectly flat. The doubler pad is often made of hardwood or marine ply and it should have its inboard edges bevelled; its area should be eight or twelve times that of the seacock flange; and its top should be designed to avoid trapping water. The doubler pad helps to reinforce the hull which will be weakened when a hole is cut for the inlet. Even when no pad is needed to give a flat face, there should be some

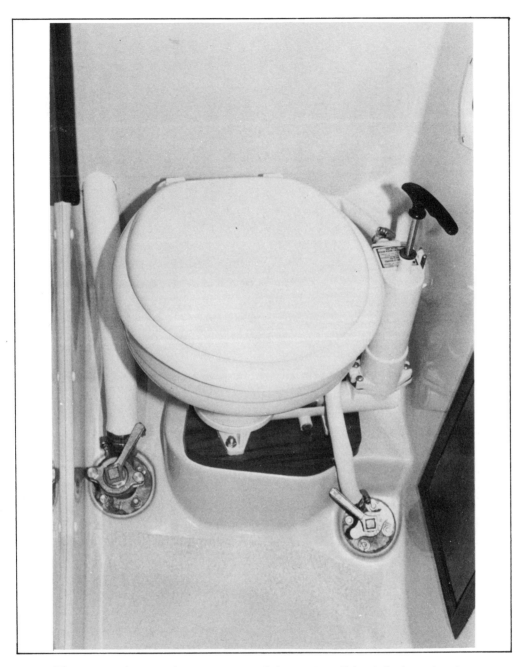

These two toilet seacocks are easy to reach for turning off, but in bad weather they are vulnerable and may be kicked or trodden on. The hose clamps on the plastic pipes have not yet been fitted. To prevent recirculation through the toilet, the inlet cock is forward of the outlet one, but ideally it would also be much lower.

form of local doubling-up of the hull shell, not least to take the heads of the countersunk bolts which hold the seacock flange to the boat.

Where the hull is almost flat, the builder may add a few layers of extra fibreglass to give back the strength he is going to cut away and he then grinds the flange of the seacock just enough to make sure it lies intimately on the hull shell. Sloppy builders rely on the bedding compound to take up the difference between the curvature of the hull shell and the flat flange of the seacock. Sometimes they tighten up the flange bolts so much that they cause the hull to bend locally, or strip the bolt threads, but then there is no limit to the butchery a bad builder will perform.

When selecting the site of a seacock it is best to keep clear of bulkheads, partly because there will be local glassing-in which gives an uneven hull surface, partly because the seacock handles have to swing through 90° and this needs space. Other structures like engine bearers should be avoided for the same reasons. It is best to fit the seacocks before the cabin sole is laid. But the positions of the sole bearers should be pencilled in first, then the seacocks are sited so that they can be reached without contortions. Whenever possible the cocks should be kept clear of heavily treading feet. Builders carrying awkward loads down into the hull will step directly on to an obtrusive seacock and bend it, perhaps causing a hidden fracture. Crews lurching about in a gale-driven boat will scarcely notice if a booted foot comes down accidentally on top of a seacock located up the hull side and half hidden by a toilet. Often the best place for a seacock is inside a little cave-fronted locker on its own. If the seacock is in a big locker, some idiot will put an anchor on top of it.

When it comes to buying seacocks, only the best will do. For racing boats the type that shuts down flush outside, so as to leave no hole showing on the outboard is needed, as this minimises the burbling of the water along the boat. For less fanatical racing owners and for those who cannot pour money into their boats but want to enjoy club racing there are lightweight seacocks made, for instance, by Simpson-Lawrence of aluminium bronze to BS 1400 AB1-C. Alternatively there are various plastic cocks, which are admittedly light and free from corrosion but are sometimes unable to stand up to the rough and tumble of life afloat. A sensible builder will apply that famous crude test, which consists of treading heavily and repeatedly on the part to see if it will take abuse.

When in doubt, go for a heavy duty pattern, like the Simpson-Lawrence version made of gunmetal. It has three bolts holding the body in, each with a shake-proof nut, in contrast to the light-weight version which has only two bolts. For small inlets there is a simpler type of skin fitting which consists of a length of threaded pipe which passes through the hull. On the outside is a flange with a back nut on the pipe forming the inside flange and a gate valve screwed on to the inboard end of the pipe to serve as a seacock.

One disadvantage of this type of cock is that the valve is not clearly seen to be open or shut according to the position of the handle, as on the normal seacock where the handle turns through only 90°. In a moment of fatigue or panic it is easy to forget which way to turn a gate valve (which is like a tap with a wheel shaped handle) to shut it off. All seacocks need to be marked with OPEN and SHUT notices whose meaning is unmistakable to the most panic-struck or idiotic crew. These should be made with paint or glassed-over, permanent signboards. Alternatives like self-adhesive tape or pencilled notices do not stand up to moisture and wear afloat.

When fitting a seacock the main inlet hole is cut first, using a hole-cutter. This is a tool which fits in an electric drill and has a length of saw blade bent to a circle. Most hole-cutters have a selection of differently sized blades and the one to choose is the one that will make a hole slightly too small. If it appears that one particular blade will produce a hole just the right size, it is likely that the 'chatter' as the cutter works through the hull will produce an oversized hole. When the hole has been cut out, it is enlarged little by little using a grinding tool or file until the seacock's spigot fits neatly.

Sometimes, due to lack of space inside the hull, the original hole cannot be cut from inboard. A little pilot hole is drilled outwards through the hull and the main hole made from the outside to get over this difficulty. If access is terrible, for instance down inside a thin fin keel for instance, it may be necessary to lower a light bulb down inside the hull until it lies right where the seacock is to be. From outboard the light will show through and the centre of the seacock can be marked with a pencil. The light has to be moved before drilling begins, otherwise the bulb may be shattered when the drill penetrates the hull shell.

If the bolts for the flange are bought from the same source as the seacock, they should match in size and in the formula of the metal so that corrosion is less likely. The connecting pipe and its hose clamps are bought at the same time to ensure that they all fit.

The seacock is put in place and rotated until the pipe stub is facing the right way. In confined spaces it will be worth taking trouble to fit the plastic tube on to the cock and lead this tube to its destination to make certain that there is space. Sometimes the builder has to turn the cock in an unexpected direction and lead the plastic tube in a subtle way round obstructions for a clear path. Pipes should be clipped to bulkheads or to stringers or to the hidden side of furniture or along sole bearers and not led across open gaps.

With the skin fitting in position, the bolt holes are drilled through the hull using the holes in the flange as guides. Countersinking is done slowly with repeated checks to avoid sinking the bolt heads too deeply especially where the hull thickness is slight. Waterproof bedding compound is put on all round the flange and smoothed level so that the whole flange is covered by about ⅛ inch (3 mm) of this sealant. As the fitting is tightened down, the bedding should ooze out evenly all round. The same bedding material is put on the bolt necks as they are pushed home and more is put under the washers. First the nuts are put on hand tight, then they are tightened up a little at a time with a spanner, top and bottom, left and right, never in series 'round the clock'.

Self-locking nuts may be used, or locking nuts may be put on over ordinary nuts, or one of the special fluids, which secure nuts against shaking loose, can be used.

Under one nut there will be the connection which joins the seacock electrically to the sacrificial plate and to the other fittings below the waterline to minimise corrosion. On cheap boats and racing boats built down to a minimum weight this corrosion protection is omitted.

=32 *Reducing corrosion*=

Boats hidden away under the parched dry earth in tombs in hot dusty Egypt, have lasted unchanged for several thousand years. Apart from the people resting in these graves, everyone else has a lot of trouble trying to preserve their boats. The lesson from Egypt is simple: keep everything totally dry all the time.

In practice, it is hard to keep a boat dry when in use, so the clever owner only puts his boat in the water when he wants to use it. When it is ashore he keeps it in a dry, drip-free shed (if such a thing exists in any boatyard). Once it is in the shed, he dries it inside and out and keeps condensation away by gently warming the boat all through. He smears grease over anything metallic which might get damp and empties all cavities and containers, mopping out and drying the last drips. At this stage we are all roaring with laughter because it is so often impossible to get the inside of a boat even moderately dry. For instance the bottom of water tanks are usually inaccessible and it is often difficult to remove the mucky mixture of fuel, rain water and mud which has settled in the lowest part of fuel tanks. Even with a long arm on some boats no one can reach into the far corners of the bilge and behind the cabin lining where moisture lurks on the tops of stringers, soaks into the bottom of the wood bulkheads and even into the fibreglass where the resin has not been applied thickly enough.

If things cannot be protected from moisture in the winter when ashore, how much more difficult it is when the boat is afloat. In theory, all one has to do is to coat everything, especially metal parts, with a skin of some material which is impenetrable by water. This is surprisingly difficult, partly because so many coatings are only semi-waterproof and in time water creeps through the skin and in under its edges. Other protective skins cannot stand up to knocks, even gentle bashes, so that water finds its way in once the fitting is the victim of normal tough life afloat. Paint, especially on exposed edges, is very vulnerable to bumps and galvanising does not stand up to scratches. Nylon sheathing goes at the edges and weathers. All protective skins fail when abraded by a rope running out over them or when the boat runs aground. Most ordinary fibreglass gelcoats are porous in a subtle way and even those wonderful epoxy resins are not perfect, since they are so hard they are brittle and liable to chipping at the drop of a spanner.

In spite of all this bad news, plenty of people are determined not to be beaten and they resort to various stratagems. One is the multi-coat technique which is based on the thought that if some coatings are porous and some are fragile, and some are soft but waterproof, then the clever thing to do is to have two or more different coatings on top of each other.

A favourite batch, used by people who are hard up but like to go long-range cruising, is hot-dip galvanising followed by de-greasing and then a build-up of paint coats, starting with undercoating (one, two or three layers), then an enamel coat. The paint in time needs renewing but with luck, the galvanising survives for decades.

A variation on this theme is galvanising followed by layers of fibreglass cloth and epoxy resin. This is more costly but it is easier to get a tough overcoat which can be ¼ inch (6 mm) or more thick, since it is only necessary to go on applying layer after layer of glass chopped strand mat, or woven cloth, or better still alternate layers of these. For gauging the number of thicknesses needed to achieve a given thickness and similar information, consult *Boat Data Book*.

The fastening holes in a fitting which is to be galvanised have to be oversize because the zinc metal deposit partly fills each hole. A common allowance which fits most working situations is ⅛ inch (3 mm) extra diameter. This extra is added regardless of the bolt diameter and it is often necessary to reamer out each hole very gently before fitting the bolts. If fibreglass is to be added, then a further allowance has to be made. This will depend on the amount of glass to be built up, but it is best to fit the bolts onto a fairly thin layering of glass, then build up the glass over the bolt heads.

It is good practice to lay two layers of glass all over the fitting, but only one in way of the holes, then after the fitting has been bolted in place two more layers are put over the exposed surfaces, including over the bolt ends. And of course, the fitting is bedded down in the usual way to exclude water on the faying surfaces.

Bolts should not be hove down tight direct onto fibreglass, so semi-hard washers are needed under the bolt heads and under the washers which go under the nuts. All this is elaborate and it is small wonder that few boatyards and not many amateur builders go to this trouble. Which explains why there is so much corrosion about on so many boats.

So far we've been thinking about preventing corrosion above and below the waterline by stopping all water from getting at components. However, metal fittings like skin fittings, also propellers and their shafts, cannot easily be totally enclosed in watertight skins. These things live permanently below the waterline. Metal fittings are made from different materials and, being immersed in salt water, they act like an electric battery. This phenomenon is called electrolysis, or galvanic action. The less noble metal is eaten away and in time it may completely disappear. Sometimes the disappearance is dramatic because the part erodes until it no longer has the strength to do its job. Propellers fall off, seacocks break and allow a sudden inrush of water.

To make life more complex, it is not necessary to have two different metals together under water. If a piece of metal is in an area where the water flowing past it is bubbling and aerated while another part is in the smooth uninterrupted flow of water, the chances are that galvanic action will begin and parts will be eaten away. Sometimes this process seems at first glance so like the bore-holes made by woodworm, that it looks as if there are metal-eating worms about.

Then again, if a piece of metal has uneven or different paint coatings (and few paint films are fully watertight) this can result in erosion. Or if a metal part is subject to a high stress while a nearby part of the same fitting has no great stress, electric currents will flow and the stressed part is liable to corrode.

Another situation which can cause this galvanic corrosion is when nuts and bolts are not precisely the same material. As nuts are not always made by the same firm which makes the bolts and a third firm will very likely make the washers, there is little chance that all three will use just exactly the same grade of metal. When one thinks of the great variety of stainless steels and the big range of bronzes, it is small wonder that fastenings are subject to galvanic corrosion. Skin fittings, too, have an inner and outer part, both of which can be of a different material from the bolts, nuts and washers which hold the fitting.

There is more bad news. Corrosion can also be caused if an electric current from the ship's supply leaks through a fitting immersed in the sea. Because the inside of any small craft is damp most of the time and saturated the rest of the time, stray electric currents are escaping all the time. The top of the battery in any boat is often dewy with condensed water or leaks or splashes up from the bilge. So even if there is a battery isolation switch and even if the crew remember to turn it off whenever the battery is out of use, there is still a good chance that there will be at least a little seepage of current from the battery. In passing, this trouble is one reason why on some well-kept boats there are isolation switches right on both battery terminals. This is more effective than a single isolator and far better than those switches which are located in an accessible and convenient position some distance from the battery.

All this might seem just cause for despair, but there is help at hand. What the clever boatbuilder does is to reduce the chances of galvanic action by using metals which are close together in electrical potential. This is one reason why it is good practice to have all fittings and their fastenings below the waterline made of bronze. At least this should keep down the amount of erosion which takes place, especially if trouble is taken to find out the exact formulation of the materials used. Because there are so many stainless steels and because they have such a reputation for being treacherous under water, some knowledgeable builders will not use them at all below the waterline.

There is a second line of defence which is called cathodic protection. This normally involves the use of zinc plates which are fixed to the hull and metal parts below the waterline and are designed to be eaten away. They are often called 'sacrificial plates' and this name exactly describes their purpose in life. In the normal way they do not need renewing every year on yachts, though sometimes they erode so fast that a new set must be fixed in place annually. If a boat is hauled up and 30% or more of a plate has disappeared, it is time to fit a new one.

On fibreglass and wood hulls, the anodes (as the sacrificial plates are called) are bolted on the outside close by the parts liable to corrode. Inside the hull there are electric cables from one bolt holding each anode to a bolt on each part liable to corrosion. The cable should be at least ⁵⁄₃₂ inch (4 mm) diameter and, if the length is over 6 feet (2 metres), it should be at least ¼ inch (6 mm) diameter. Insulated cable with a PVC sheathing is used. Each end of the cable has a welded-on solid metal tab, one of which goes on an anode bolt, the other on a fitting bolt, to give an excellent metal-to-metal bond.

Inside a fibreglass or wood hull there is a wood chock in way of the anode. Sometimes the internal wood block gets badly affected by the current flow and becomes soft. This is why hardwood rather than softwood is used and it is protected by paint or fibreglass. It is good sense to make the chocks easily renewable. If part of the hull structure is used as the backing block, it may be necessary in time to renew this, and that is always more expensive than changing a simple chock.

On steel vessels, the anodes are bolted or welded to the hull shell. Welding is preferred because bolts have been known to become loose, for instance when the anode has eroded right away and ceased to give protection. Leaking at an anode bolt can also result if the boat rubs up against a quay wall or a lifting out sling gets caught on the anode.

However, some yachts have hull surface finishes which are spoiled by welding: furthermore in remote regions it is not easy to get old anodes stripped off and new ones welded on. If this work has to be done on the beach between tides, bolting is often much simpler than welding.

On aluminium hulls, anodes are bolted on. For alloy hulls there is also a clever technique using anodes which hang over the side of the vessel as she lies in port, so that when she is under way there are no protruding lumps on the hull to slow her down. On a fibreglass or wood boat with a steel rudder or skeg or similar fitting, the anodes are secured directly onto the fitting, just like on a steel hull.

A whirling propeller cannot have an anode attached to it, so the anode is fitted to the hull and wired up to the engine or gearbox or, if in doubt, to both. There may be a flexible coupling on the propeller shaft and this will act as an insulator because it will have a rubber or plastic insert separating the two flanges of the coupling. This insulation is by-passed by a piece of cable with welded terminals, secured to the bolts holding the flanges. In addition or alternatively, there may be an anode in the form of a collar round the propeller shaft.

Anyone who has had experience with the disconcerting way electricity behaves in and around small craft will want to know the answers to a dozen questions such as: How many anodes should be fitted? Just where should they be located? How big should they be? Should there be one on each side of the boat? How long will they last? And so on and on.

The answers to these questions depend a lot on experience. There are so many variables and alternatives that it is best to get specialist advice for any

212

craft unless there is a similar boat with a successful collection of anodes which can be copied. Even here, care is needed because erosion varies in different geographical regions and with different electrical gear on board. For good advice there is one firm which has a worldwide reputation as a result of its work in this specialised business. It deals with all types of craft in every country bordered by the sea. It pioneered the design and use of anodes and other techniques for combating erosion and it is used by naval architects, owners, builders – in fact everyone concerned with the problem. The address is:

M. G. Duff Cathodic Protection Division, Chichester Yacht Basin, Birdham, Chichester, PO20 7EW, England.

This firm will answer all the questions relating to a particular boat provided they are given enough information. This includes: type of ship, waterline length, beam and mean loaded draft, hull material, number and diameter of propellers, material and size of hull fittings such as shaft support brackets (P-brackets), skin fittings or seacocks, also type of service for which boat is used. It makes a lot of sense to send them drawings of the boat with information about all underwater metal parts.

Anodes will often last several years, but sometimes they get eaten away in a single season, perhaps because there is an unexpected factor like a mains electric leak into the water in the marina near the boat. Anyone planning a long voyage is well advised to renew the anodes before starting, and to take a spare set. Some owners who haul up their boats every year always buy two sets of anodes at once, just as they always keep a spare stock of shackles and engine gaskets. Because anodes work by allowing their surfaces to be eroded, it is important that they are never painted over. However, their steel securing plates and bolts should be well painted.

On racing boats and high speed motor boats, the usual type of protruding anode is not satisfactory. Typical anode sizes are 3 inches × 1½ inches (75 mm × 40 mm) in section, and are annoying to a man trying to get his boat to hustle along fast. One way to eliminate water drag is to recess the anodes into the hull; but of course as soon as there is any significant erosion of the sacrificial plate, there is then an indent on the hull surface and this is almost as bad as a protuberance, so frequent anode renewal is necessary.

Another trick is to put the anodes in 'dead' water, such as on the aft face of an immersed transom. Alternatively there are anodes which fit snugly round propeller shafts like collars and if these are put between the P-bracket and the propeller boss, they may slightly reduce water resistance. Flat strip anodes may be fitted aft of P-bracket palms, perhaps with some fibreglass fairing over the ends, or the anode may be tucked up behind a keel or skeg.

All the foregoing may be disconcerting to anyone who only wants some basic advice on the best sort of anode to fit on a common type of boat. So, with the proviso that it is always worth getting specialist advice if in doubt, or if the boat or her service is unusual, here are some broad principles for small fibreglass and wood craft:

One anode is needed for each propeller. It should be located fairly close to the screw and on a direct 'sight line' with it, but not so as to disturb the flow of water to and from the propeller.

On the inside of the hull the bolt ends must be accessible and the linking cables should be kept as short as possible. This often results in the anode being located roughly on a line between the P- or A-bracket and the gearbox and a good deal nearer the former.

For a boat with each propeller less than 29 inches (740 mm) diameter, each anode should be about $7 \times 3\frac{1}{4} \times 1\frac{1}{2}$ inches ($180 \times 80 \times 40$ mm). This assumes that there is not much area of exposed stern shaft or tube and no P- or A-bracket. If there is a lot of metalware below the waterline, then the same size of anode will suit propellers up to about 20 inches (500 mm) diameter.

The anodes should be $12 \times 3 \times 1\frac{1}{2}$ inches ($300 \times 75 \times 40$ mm) for each propeller of the order of 36 inches (900 mm) diameter, but again, if there are long lengths of stern shaft or tube and a shaft support bracket, this size of anode suits propellers up to about 30 inches (750 mm). For a propeller up to about 60 inches (1.5 metres) diameter and again with a stubby tube and shaft outside the hull, the anode size to match each propeller will be typically $18 \times 4 \times 2\frac{1}{2}$ inches ($450 \times 100 \times 60$ mm) but with long exposed shaft and the necessary bracket, the propeller size limit for this anode will be about 50 inches (1.27 metres).

══ 33 *Ladders and staging* ══

Every day when a boat is being repaired or built, the ladder up her side will be used 20 times. On some of these occasions the person climbing up or down will be heavily laden. By the end of the day he will be tired, maybe distracted by some crisis or difficulty, he may be in a hurry to get home for a stiff drink. Under these circumstances a ladder which is not wide, strong, solid and safe is likely to cause a crash.

The same applies to staging alongside a boat. It will at times be used by several people; two of them may be energetically rubbing down the hull or working with heavy tools. Sometimes the crew on the staging will be man-handling an engine or hefty anchor winch up onto the deck.

Though boatbuilding accidents are rare, a substantial proportion of them come from ladders and staging. It is easy and wise to have the best of this equipment because it does not cost much more than shoddy stuff. Good ladders will last decades, even when used and abused daily. Good staging feels safe and forms a rigid platform which in turn results in careful work. Even if an amateur is building just one boat and does not expect to use these aids again after the boat has been launched, it still pays to buy quality and ruggedness. If the boat is kept, then each winter she will need some work, so the ladders and staging come in useful year after year. If they are bought to suit a variety of sizes of craft, they can either continue to be used by the owner when he changes boat, or sold off to someone else building or repairing a similar boat.

All items of staging, ladders, planks and so on should have the boat's or owner's name painted several times on them to discourage borrowers and thieves. A stencil with the boat's name is useful for marking lifebuoys, boat-hooks and items which may fall overboard or need labelling. This same stencil is ideal for identifying ladders and staging quickly and neatly. Ordinary paint, especially the slightly thickened residue in the bottom of a paint tin, applied with a short-haired brush is used to put on the name using a stencil. A stencil can be made by cutting the letters out of thin cardboard, or a metal one can be bought through a builder's merchant or engineers' tool supplier.

Whilst a name by itself may not stop determined people from borrowing or stealing gear, a padlock and thick chain should do so. Each trestle plank needs a hole through, near one end, for the chain. An old length of stout rigging wire with an eye each end can be used instead of chain. Whatever is used, it must be long enough to loop through all the ladders, staging, trestles and similar equipment, before going round the boat's cradle or the trailer she lies on.

It is important that the chain or wire is not looped round boat props, because these can be knocked out to release the staging and ladders if the thief is ruthless. The fact that with one prop out the boat may fall over is either not realised, or does not worry some of these sub-humans.

Ladders

These may be of wood or aluminium and should have solid serrated rubber feet to stop them slipping. The top needs a lashing onto the boat's toerail or some similar strong point and, if the ladder is to be set up for a long period, a lashing each side is recommended.

Where the ladder touches the hull there must be some form of padding. Rags should not be tied round the ladder for protection because when the ladder is taken down they will touch the dusty ground and pick up grit. Next time the ladder is put up against the hull the rags will grind away the gelcoat or painted topsides and may do more harm than an unpadded ladder. A better method of protecting the hull and deck edge is to hang a piece of carpet over the topsides just where the ladder will go, using a lashing at each top corner of the carpet. More carpet may be laid on the deck and cockpit seats to stop grit from being ground into the surfaces during the months when the boat is being built or repaired. Each piece of carpet should be fairly new, clean and secured down so that it cannot slip.

Ladders must not be rested against guardrails because the wires will never be rigid enough and the vibration as anyone climbs the ladder will tend to fatigue the wire. Because the ladder top should rest on the deck edge, a new ladder may have to be cut down to the correct length. During its life a boat will not always be laid up with its deck exactly the same distance above the ground, one year the keel blocks may be thicker than previously. So when making a new ladder or cutting an existing one to fit a particular boat, a surplus length of about 10 inches (250 mm) should be left above the deck edge.

The best place to secure the ladder is by the aft pulpit, but on one side of the boat – not up the stern. Anyone going up or down the ladder then has the pulpit to hold onto during the awkward stage when getting off the ladder and onto the boat's deck. It therefore pays to secure the aft pulpit to the deck at an early stage when building a boat. When refitting it may make sense to release the guardrails aft for easier access, provided no one is going to rely on them when moving about on deck.

An ordinary ladder is far from ideal for working on a boat a lot. It is too steep and narrow and needs two hands to traverse. A set of steps is much easier to use, as these rest on four or more feet, are inclined less steeply, and have wider treads. Even so, there must be padding between the side of the steps and the hull, as well as a stout lashing holding the steps right against the hull. Better still are the modern type which are made of metal and look like semi-portable stairs or safety steps. These are ideal for the professional boatbuilder as they form staging as well as steps. They are often mounted on wheels with brakes to hold the steps when not being moved and there are banisters up one or both sides. Each tread is wide and often has a non-skid surface. Where standard staging is required, one end of the plank can be supported by this type of steps and the other end by a normal trestle. Though these super-steps cost about

3 times as much as ordinary steps and about 5 times the cost of a good ladder of the same height, they are recommended by factory safety inspectors and such bodies as the Royal Society for the Prevention of Accidents. They last almost forever and, with a little adapting, can be used as a platform for swinging the champagne against a new boat's bow at launching time.

Whatever type of ladder or steps is used, at the bottom and top there should be a mat so that everyone going aboard wipes his feet. If this precaution is not taken dirt accumulates on the deck and in the cabin but, much more serious, the deck and cabin sole will get scratched and disfigured. When a boat is lying out in the open the carpet will get wet so a coconut mat or one of the modern plastic equivalents should be used. These can stand up to rain and weathering and work well even when saturated.

Staging

For working on the topsides of a boat or working from outboard on a narrow side deck, for painting and polishing or repairing a hull, staging is needed. Some people take risks and use a couple of 40 gallon drums set on end with a plank laid on top. Others stand on an old chest of drawers and incidentally keep tools in the drawers. The trouble with this idea is that the drawers are so heavy when full of tools they have to be taken out every time the chest is moved and the furniture itself may not be rugged enough to stand up to a heavy tread. An old table is also a popular form of primitive staging, especially as it is so much wider and therefore safer than the normal staging plank, which is typically only about 10 inches (250 mm) wide.

The usual type of staging, however, consists of two trestles with a plank laid on top. The trestles may be like sawing horses, but for most jobs these are too low. A more popular type is made like a set of steps with treads spaced about 18 inches (500 mm) apart so that the plank can be set at the most convenient height. In practice when working on staging for some jobs it is best to stand up and for others sitting gives a better stance, resulting in a steadier hand.

It is a bad idea to have two adjacent planks on the same level because when the load is on one, the other will not bend, so there is a step between the planks which causes accidents. Where the staging seems unsafe, it is better to rig up a safety rope between the trestles at waist height, rather than have two planks to increase the width of the walking area. When two planks are used side by side, they need strapping together with wood bars above and below, tightly lashed so that as a worker walks on one plank, the adjacent one bends the same amount.

A safety rope, even if it is not tight, gives confidence out of proportion to the extra security it provides because anyone walking along the plank can grasp it and steady himself. Better than a rope is a wood or tubing handrail lashed to the staging at each end. If a rope is used, it should be as tight as possible, but if anyone presses down on it, there will be a tendency for the trestles to be pulled together. This is counteracted by tying the trestles to the boat's toerail or to stanchion bases or other strong points. Even when no safety rope is rigged, lashings are needed to secure the trestles, especially when energetic work is being done. Lashings tend to pull the trestles in against the hull and as with ladders there must be clean soft padding to prevent scratching and chafe. Anyone rubbing down the topsides or just polishing them will cause the whole staging to wiggle and wriggle. Where any part of the staging touches the hull a series of fine scratches will appear unless there is good padding keeping the temporary structure away from the boat.

Because they have four legs, trestles often rock when they are set down on an uneven surface. Driving a wedge under the leg which stands clear of the ground is a bad idea; the wedge does not give a flat surface and it will tend to work its way out even when nailed in place. It is better to have a piece of flat wood secured upwards into the short leg with at least two fastenings.

For the professional boatbuilder or the wealthy amateur there are some lovely devices for supporting planks. Some of these support devices are in the form of adjustable towers built of piping complete with platforms at the top. Some have wheels at the bottom, some have adjustable legs, the most expensive even have motors to move them about – and cost accordingly.

To get a set of special trestles may require some searching. The first place to try is the local builder's merchant where there may be some second-hand units for sale. Other sources are contractors' magazines and industrial equipment catalogues which are found in good public libraries. Anyone who wants to use staging for a short period can hire it from a Do-It-Yourself firm or from a builder's merchants. Perhaps the quickest cheapest way to get staging is to make it up. For this, wood is the cheapest but aluminium the best for long life and the minimum weight. To make the staging planks light, they should be built up of a light thin plank with flanges on the bottom so that the finished product looks like a flattened inverted U section. The vertical parts are never nailed in place, always screwed or bolted. They should be glued too because this makes a most remarkable difference to the stiffness of the planks. They should be test-loaded and over-loaded before being used.

34 *Templates*

A template is a full size model of a finished part. In practice it is usually a simple two-dimensional outline shape, though it may be three-dimensional. Made of paper or wood or metal, the crudely shaped template, deliberately too big is first roughly shaped to fit the place where the final product will go, then offered up to the intended position and the edge marked accurately. It is trimmed so that it now fits precisely. To check that it does so it is laid in place and examined all round. It is taken out of the boat and laid on the material which is to form the final product, which may be a bulkhead or a galley side, a foam plastic cushion or a cabin sole board. The template is held down firmly while a pencil is drawn round its edge, or a sharp scribing tool used to make the outline. The finished product can be cut out with confidence knowing that its size is exactly right.

There are a dozen reasons for using templates. They save carrying heavy pieces of material in and out of a boat for marking and shaping. They reduce the risk of damaging fine wood or veneer or finish of any sort by too much handling. They save time if a single template can be made for port and starboard components which are identical but opposite handed. If there are several items which are alike, such as the locker lids for berth tops, they save measuring out each one individually and eliminate the risk that one may be marked out wrongly. They are of enormous advantage to a professional builder who is making a series of identical boats because once he has made a set of templates he can use them again and again on boat after boat. Some builders have templates which they use even on different sizes of boats. For instance, they may like to embellish their craft with pin-rails; to reduce the time it takes to make these fittings they will have a complete set of templates for all the parts.

For amateur or professional, templates can be expected to save time, money and material. Anyone fitting out a standard hull may be able to hire from another builder (or from the hull moulder) templates for such parts as the bulkheads, windows, furniture ends where they have to fit the curvature of the hull, perhaps the curved tiller and so on. A template for a part like a shaped tiller is a great asset because it can be taken to a woodyard and laid on various rough cut planks until one is found with the grain running the same way as the tiller curves.

If no templates are available, or only a limited set, anyone building a sistership of an existing boat can lift templates from the completed boat. It is best to get the owner's permission first. This job needs care, otherwise the furniture will be damaged if the templates are being made from wood. But it takes only a few minutes to lay a sheet of smooth, stiff paper over a bulkhead, tear out a few small holes in the middle and Sellotape across the holes to hold the paper in place, then crease the paper all round the edge to get the shape of the bulkhead. Due care and allowance has to be made for the edge glassing of the bulkhead. And if the bulkhead edge is bevelled, the paper should be laid on the aft side of a forward bulkhead and the forward side of an aft one as these are the largest faces.

Other parts which can be templated off an existing boat include the floors, cabin soles, the rudder blade if it is to be of wood or metal, furniture fronts, weather-boards, engine bearers, tanks – in short, anything which has to be cut out to a specific shape.

Another use of templates is in the planning and styling of any part, but especially a deckhouse or furniture part. If the owner or designer is not sure that the final product will look right, or suit the boat's crew, or give enough room, a set of templates can be made up and put in place temporarily. This technique is strongly recommended if the deckhouse of a boat is hard to style. The template will show what the final job will look like. Not only the shape but also the colour, the windows, the location and type of fittings like sidelights and lifebuoys can be studied from all angles. They can be changed, put back as they were, altered slightly or boldly and all at small cost. It is a great way to achieve a fine appearance and is well recommended historically. Those beautiful canoe sterns which Fife designed were first worked out on the drawing board with the rest of the boat's shape. The building work was then begun, with the whole hull delineated by the moulds which were clad with temporary stringers or ribbands. This showed the designer what the final hull would look like before any of the real building work was begun, apart from the backbone consisting of the stem, keel and outreach. At this stage the real drama of the design came in. Fife would work at the difficult problem of the stern shape until he was satisfied that it was as sweet and curvaceous as it could be. The moulds, which are a form of template, were faired off here and filled out there, adjusting the shape little by little, until it was perfect from every angle.

On one occasion this artistry took a whole week, but the result was entirely worthwhile.

It is this sort of thing which makes yachts so very much more beautiful than any mere sculpture or painting and it is about time that the world realised that good boat designers and builders are better artists than the rest of the so-called art world. After all, boats have to stand up to conditions at sea as well as look beautiful. If some sculptors used templates, they would soon see that the final product was better left unproduced.

The simplest material for templates is stiff paper. There is one type sold by house builders' merchants in long rolls about 6 feet (2 metres) wide, which is good because it stands up to rough treatment, within reason. From artists' shops it is possible to buy less expensive papers of various sorts in a variety of widths and thicknesses. As ever in boatbuilding, it pays to buy the toughest even if it is the most expensive. The trouble with artists' shops is that they tend to sell papers in limited widths and joining edges with tape or staples is a chore, besides introducing a possible source of error due to change of shape.

Shops which sell drawing office materials stock various papers of which heavy cartridge paper is often the best. It comes in widths up to about 4 feet 6 inches (1.5 metres) and being white, it is easy to mark clearly. It is useful for doing full-size drawings of fittings, for making extra copies of the profile of the yacht when deciding on the best colour scheme. After painting one drawing with white topsides and a red boot-top, and another pale green with a dark green boot-top, and so on, the drawings are pinned up at eye-level and studied for a few days. The best colour-scheme will soon be obvious.

Ordinary brown parcel paper can be used for templates but it tends to be too thin and it needs a wide bold marker, not a common ballpoint or pencil, to show the instructions clearly. Like all papers, it is easy to use. A sharp pair of large scissors to cut around the carefully penned-in outline, or the creased line is all that is required. There will be times when the shipwright will be tempted to tear the paper along a well-folded line – avoid the temptation as the end product must have a sharply defined, neatly cut line for accuracy.

Professionals tend to use wood more than paper for templates, not least because they often want to keep the pattern for years and papers change shape with moisture. Wood expands when damp, but seldom enough to affect the value of the template. The disadvantages of wood are its tendency to split (because it is used in thin laths) and the need to cut, shape and join it up, because it is not available in wide pieces. In practice, ply is often used instead of solid wood; but even the cheapest ply is far more costly than paper. Also ply only comes in widths of 4 feet so to make up a wide bulkhead template it is necessary to have at least one join.

Between wood and paper there is cardboard. It is popular because it is so quickly shaped with scissors and it is used for parts like floors where the template must have some stiffness.

Plywood templates can be made from any available off-cuts or the cheapest ⅛ inch (3 mm) material. Being smooth both sides, it is easy to mark clearly and the very thin types of ply can be shaped with shears or a sharp knife.

Solid wood for templates is often made up from local low-cost soft wood about 4 inches (100 mm) wide. Solid wood templates are typically about ¼ inch (6 mm) thick, or maybe this thickness 'off-saw' planed on one side only. Some shipwrights work with unplaned wood, but it does not take marks easily. There is nothing so useless as a template which cannot be precisely identified or which is clearly labelled '&)(@' but no one can decide whether this is 'Port' or 'Stb'd', so no one knows which side it goes. If it is to make up a bulkhead shape, one piece is laid against the topsides and a pencil scribed parallel to the inside of the hull. This shape is sawn out, often with a band saw or jig saw. A second piece is held with its top where the first piece stopped and the next part of the hull curve is scribed and cut. These two shaped parts are joined by a doubling piece which typically will lap about 12 or 18 inches (300 or

450 mm) each side of the join, with at least 3 nails each side of the butt. The nails go right through and are hammered over in a firm clench. Alternatively a joining piece, which is perhaps 1 inch (25 mm) thick, will be used and screws put through the thin laths into the joining piece. It is handy to use two pairs of clamps or mole grips to hold the laths to the joining piece prior to putting in the fastenings.

Any template is difficult to make unless there are two pairs of hands. Certainly if any dimension exceeds 2 feet (600 mm) two people will do the job in a quarter of the time one person will struggle through it. For anyone who has to work alone there is a lot of help to be gained from plasticine, Sellotape of the widest strongest kind, mole grips, clamps, sometimes wood wedges and so on; but really it is an extra pair of hands which is needed. Properly organised amateur shipwrights have children well trained for this sort of job; mine started at the age of four.

Engineers, who always do things differently from shipwrights, use metal sheet and bent wire for templates. In particular they bend lengths of wire to show the shape needed for piping, exhausts and so on. Often the wire springs back and is unreliable as a template unless it is very stiff, in which case it is hard to bend. For exhausts and many piping jobs I prefer joined-up lengths of wood having the same width as the pipe's diameter; then there is no doubt that there will be space for the pipe. Also the run of the pipe is obvious and if there is a risk that a hot exhaust will pass near anything vulnerable, the wood template will show the danger.

It takes a lot of time to cut out a metal template but the end result is stronger and more reliable than a wood shape. It is ideal for marking out a large number of identical parts so it is used on production lines, especially if the parts are to be cut out with a router. The guide of this machine is run along the firm, smooth edge of the template and as a result the part cut has a neat, clean edge which often needs no further finishing. Instead of thin metal sheet, thicker sheets of plastic such as ½ inch (12 mm) Tufnol is sometimes used because it gives a better guide to the router; with 1 or even 3 mm metal sheet, the guide may slip over the edge. Also materials like Tufnol are lighter and more pleasant to handle than sheet metal. However, there is no excuse for using new Tufnol (which is expensive) unless a great many identical parts are being cut out or cheap, scrap off-cuts are available for the templates.

As soon as a template has been cut out and before it is trimmed, faired or cleaned up, it should be marked. Go to town on this! Put the boat's name or type, describe the part in detail and say which way up and on which side it goes. Don't worry about duplication of information because one omission here can cause endless delays and waste time, materials and temper.

When marking the 'TOP' put the word near the top and have an arrow pointing to the top. The same with 'PORT' or 'STB'D.' and 'OUTBOARD'. Quite recently I designed a new deckhouse for a 60 footer and it was wonderfully wrought in teak, with elegant carved corner posts and superb finishings inside. It took a top yard a whole winter to build and cost untold thousands. When it was finished it was in every detail just what the owner wanted and he was delighted, except for one item – the aft windows. When they arrived from the glass-makers they were exactly the right shape except that one corner was cropped off in a mysterious way. To get over the problem the builders filled the missing corner with wood for the summer and fitted new windows next winter. The whole trouble was caused because the shipwright making the templates had added a little piece at the vital corner where his material was not quite large enough. The templates were sent by lorry to the glass-makers and on the journey the critical corner piece broke off.

The moral of this story is: Make templates strong enough to stand all the journeying they have to make. Also, make sure that where there are joins it is obvious, so that if these break, everyone concerned will be aware of the fact. If that shipwright had labelled his windows 'FOUR SIDED' or 'THREE SIDED' the glass-makers would have realised that the corner was not supposed to be cropped off. Better still, he might have supplied a simple sketch with each window shown in rough outline. This is a good idea anyway, because where there are, say, seven windows each side, they will be numbered or lettered in sequence. But some idiot is bound to start fitting them the wrong way round, so the sketch will show that No. 1 is the forward one.

Incidentally, when making templates it should not be assumed that the port and starboard sides are identical. By all means make just one template for both sides, but then take a lot of trouble to ensure that the template *WILL FIT* both sides. Even windows which look identical port and starboard are sometimes different in a subtle way which makes it essential to have a set of templates for each side. When making window templates, the instructions written on them should include notes about the opening. Plenty of builders jig-saw round the shape of the windows and send the cut-outs to the window-maker. This is fine provided it is made very obvious that the templates are not the size of the glass, but the size of the glass plus that part of the frame which goes through the cut-away opening. If the glass is made the same size as the cut-out the shipwright will have to enlarge the apertures by a small amount all round to fit the windows – a real waste of time, especially as the amount to be cut away will be so small that it will be hard to mark and to cut with a jig-saw.

One thing a template-maker should never do is add instructions about altering the outside shape. A note painted on a template, even in letters a foot high, which says something like 'ADD ¼ INCH HERE FOR WHOLE OF TOP EDGE' is asking for mistakes. The only ways to deal with this shortage of size are either to add exactly the right amount of material to the template edge and secure the addition strongly; or to make a new template the correct size. The latter is much the better way.

The only instructions which *are* permissible relate to bevelling of edges. The template should always be made to the largest size so that no allowance has to be added when making the final product; the bevel can then be shaved off later. For example, if the template is for a bulkhead which is fitted right forward where the boat has a lot of shape, the template will be made for the *aft* face of the bulkhead. When the template is complete it is laid on the marine ply which is to form the finished bulkhead and a pencil line drawn all round. The saw is taken round the pencil line, leaving the line just showing. The bulkhead is offered up to make sure it fits – but because the template was carefully made and trimmed, we know this is just a small sacrifice to those twin gods of boatbuilders, Precision-Fit and Double-Check. The bulkhead is taken down and the bevel is taken off the edge all round. The bevel angle will vary going down the hull from sheer to keel, so the bevel angles are marked round the edges of the template.

Templates are an art form. In the mould lofts of big shipyards, men used to spend their lifetime making templates and developed all sorts of tricks. For instance, a bulkhead amidships is slightly larger than one just forward or aft of it. So a template can be made for the biggest bulkhead, then trimmed down progressively for the next bulkhead. After the biggest one has been marked off on the bulkhead material the template is taken back into the hull and trimmed to suit the shape where the next bulkhead will lie. Once that bulkhead outline has been transferred to the ply which will form the actual bulkhead, the template can be used yet again, and so on.

When a tank has to be fitted into an awkward place, a full size three-dimensional template is needed to make sure that the tank is as large as the space will take and yet shaped so that it will get through the access hatches.

There is one final thing to remember about templates. If they are well made, they may have value when no longer needed – there is always that other man who is just about to start building a sister ship and maybe he can be coaxed to buy your set of templates.

35 *Employing a naval architect*

Among the treasures of the National Maritime Museum at Greenwich, London (UK), is a modest bit of paper which is the oldest known design drawing of a ship. It is 300 years old, naturally a little primitive, a bit short on detail, perhaps the scale is slightly suspect, but it is useful and my goodness, how much better than no drawing at all.

There are people who like to work to standards which date back more than 300 years, but it is short-sighted, likely to waste money, time and materials and it often results in unexpected snags holding up or spoiling the job. Drawings are worth having even when just changing a few bits of furniture or improving a deck layout. For completing a fibreglass hull or doing any major job, the cost of the drawings is saved a dozen times over.

The cost of getting drawings varies vastly. Some people work on the principle that the way to get the best is to employ the world's most celebrated and expensive design talent. Others go to the opposite extreme and find a young, half-trained draughtsman who is prepared to work in the evenings (often on a kitchen table instead of a proper drawing board) for almost enough money to keep him in beer for a few weeks. Both approaches are fraught with problems and both may give unexpected levels of success, or failure.

The top naval architect may be so busy that he hands the job over to a junior in the design office who is not properly supervised. The struggling young draughtsman may have a touch of genius and may be prepared to work far into the night to make his first commission a rampaging triumph. On the other hand, the top designers tend to have a lot of experience and so avoid most of the established mistakes, whereas the youngster may never have been told of the horrors of an over-balanced rudder; he may never have seen an ultra-light mast whip like a dancing snake; he may honestly think that stainless steel is safe below the waterline. Just to confuse the issue, some senior naval architects still use stainless steel below the waterline, when they should know better.

At least part of the dilemma which arises when a naval architect or draughtsman is employed is easily solved – go for the man who has indemnity insurance. This means that if he does make a mistake which is serious, at least the cost of putting it right will be borne either by the designer himself or, if it is too costly for him, he can fall back on his insurance company. These insurances cost a lot, so only full-time professional designers have this protection. They can only get it if they are good, because no insurance company wants to cover someone whose boats keep sinking or turning upside down, or blowing up.

In Britain, it is easy to find out which designers have insurance because they are members of the Yacht Brokers, Designers and Surveyors Association (YBDSA). It is a condition of joining this organisation that all members must be fully insured. The address is 'Wheelhouse', 5 Station Road, Liphook, Hants GU30 7DW, England. As the members spend a lot of time flying all over the world, an owner who lives outside Britain can still make use of the services of these well established naval architects. Some of us are in America or the Caribbean at the beginning of the month, in France or Sweden in the middle, and in Greece or Saudi Arabia at the end because we are in an international business; normally the insurance protection extends world-wide.

For anyone who wants a designer in UK or elsewhere, the local boating and technical magazines have advertisements naming the established designers. It is often good policy to employ someone local so that he is available at short notice for consultations. For any builder, amateur or professional, the job is speeded up and costs kept down with a local designer available to discuss the next stage of construction, or to get a special drawing to simplify a difficult part, or to get a sketch for a sub-contractor. Things like pulpits, tanks, mast steps, winch bases and boarding ladders, are always easier to make, and cheaper, neater and more professional, if they are built to a scaled drawing and not a crude squiggle on the back of an envelope.

Just as important, the designer to select is one who is familiar with the boat type. There is such a big difference between racing and cruising craft, between inshore and offshore boats, between power and sailing vessels, between fibreglass and wood, between steel and aluminium.

The designer chosen should be someone who is friendly with the builder and his type of boat. For a young man, there is a lot of sense in going to a youthful designer who will sail the boat with the same eagerness and intensity as the owner, once the boat is afloat and especially during trials. An old arthritic designer who is too stiff-limbed to go aloft in a bo's'un's chair, or too crusty and complaining to crawl into awkward corners of the bilge, may suit an old owner who sympathises with the hastening ills of advancing age, provided such a designer has accumulated the experience of many hard-working years.

Having selected a designer, it is essential to tell him the style of boat or improvement which is wanted. The best way to do this is to put down the requirements in three lists: the first shows all the essentials; the second includes items which are favoured but not vital; the third details unimportant items which should be worked in if they can be included without making concessions to the first two lists. This applies to building a completely new boat or to finishing off a hull, or to modifications to an existing boat.

Among the essential data will be the available money for the job, the standard of finish (which may vary from super-luxury down to 'adequate commercial') and the purpose for which the boat is to be used. There will be a statement about the numbers and experience of the crew, also the place where the boat is to be kept in case there is a ferocious tide or a shortage of water depth or a lack of maintenance facilities.

The second list will include such features as the preferred engine, toilet, compass, radio and so on. In practice, the item chosen may be too big or need too much power (in the case of electric and hydraulic equipment) or not be available, so second choices are listed.

The third list includes minor items of trim and furniture, little luxuries and gadgetry to be added if cash is available at the end of the project.

This listing is advisable whether the boat is an entirely new project or just a modification. When I worked for a famous designer many years ago, we were approached (rather furtively) by a fellow who wanted us to build a boat which must:

1 Have a range of 3500 miles.
2 Survive hurricane conditions.
3 Have a top speed of 35 knots.

We looked at this list for a long time and could see no way of fulfilling it without enormous expenditure. We said that he could have any two of the conditions without too much difficulty and he settled for the seaworthiness and the range. He asked for a small hold to be built into the boat and we later learned that he used his vessel to smuggle nylon stockings into a country where these garments were highly taxed!

It is very much part of a designer's job to state that certain requirements either cannot be met, or not without an unacceptable risk. In the life of every long-toothed designer there has been at least one occasion when he has sent a letter to a client saying, 'I will not put in that particular feature into your vessel unless you insist I do so and your insistence must be in writing and exonerate me from all blame if unpleasant consequences ensue'. This letter is sent off by registered post. Anyone who gets such a letter knows he has a good designer because it takes courage and deep experience to write it. Such a letter should be heeded.

One reason for employing a naval architect or ship's draughtsman is to ensure that the finished job looks right, is right and attracts favourable comment so that when the boat is to be sold, she fetches a good price. An experienced buyer can tell after a few minutes wandering around any boat whether she has been built by an amateur or a professional, unless the amateur is exceptionally skilled and works to good drawings. Most amateur-completed craft and those made or modified by non-professionals are not so very different from boats which have had only professionals aboard. The differences lie in the way bulkhead edges are finished, in the way the cabin sole is laid, the rounding of wood and metal edges, the placing and fastening of the deck fittings, and so on. Since these details are easy enough to learn with the right drawings and guidance, it is logical and cheap to have them. In practice it is likely that a naval architect will save 2 or 3 or even 7 times his fee on any job which involves changing a rig or cabin plan or some bigger alteration. For smaller jobs it may be a question of negotiation, but often naval architects have scales of fees for individual drawings and sketches.

It is usual to ask a naval architect how much he will charge before he starts a job. His fee scale will depend on:

(a) How fashionable he is – a famous architect who gets plenty of mentions in the yachting magazines is in a position to charge high fees; he sometimes makes hay while the sun shines because fashion is fickle.

(b) How well established he is. An old firm with a solid office and drawers full of designs has a reservoir of experience built up over the years. This sort of firm tends to be good because it is knowledgeable, so it can turn away doubtful jobs and charge a full or even a high fee for its work. It usually gives better value than other types of design offices.

(c) A lot depends on how big the job is. It is the construction plan which takes the biggest percentage of the time, so the more complex this is, the higher the total fee. Engine plans, electric and electronic plans, spaghetti-like hydraulic layouts, are costly in drawing time, so far as the designer is concerned. Supervision is also time-consuming and so adds a lot to the fees.

(d) If a set of stock plans is being bought, they will be cheap but they are seldom a bargain. Often they are outdated, sometimes they are sold by a naval architect who gives no back-up, or alternatively he may charge for every phone conversation once the plans have been bought. So in the end a builder pays a lot or does without critical advice. Sometimes the plans are the product of a designer who has a low level of skill and in a desperate attempt to get into the market, he sells his plans at a very low cost.

(e) Semi-stock plans are almost always better than stock designs. These are plans which are available in several forms. On the basic lines and construction plan the designer will draw up a special rig, engine lay-out or cabin accommodation which suits the owner. Here we often have a bargain, especially if the naval architect is skilled and can draw out a product which is right up to date.

However costly or cheap the drawing work is, whether it is a complete set of drawings for a 100 footer (30 metres) or a simple sketch of a new bilge pumping system, it is good practice to pay something in advance. If the designer does not ask for some cash up front, it may be that he is already so mentally immersed in the job that boring matters like money are forgotten. Seize the opportunity and pay him at least a quarter of his fees – however big or small they are. The goodwill this gesture generates is worth a thousand times the financial cost and more effective than any number of convivial drinks together.

Once work is making substantial progress, the clever owner makes regular payments whether or not he gets bills. While it is true that there can be fewer jobs more pleasant than designing small craft, even naval architects need money to support their families. A hungry man, or one with a grouse, never does his best work. The owner who commissions even a modest drawing of a small cabin alteration is in the position of the great patrons of the Arts. The generous owners get the best treatment in any design office – naturally.

The cost of drawings for a new boat or for alterations to an existing one vary greatly. It is common practice to base the naval architect's fees on a percentage of the cost of the work done in the boatyard. Where the work is being done by an amateur, the man doing the drawings will say something like: 'If this alteration to the main saloon (or rig, or plumbing, or whatever it is) were done in a good yacht yard it would cost X. My fees for this type of work are 10%, so my bill is X over 10 plus local taxes'.

In practice, the design fee will vary between about 20% and 2% of the cost of the shipwright and other trades work. For a very small alteration on a little yacht, the drawing may take almost as long as the work in the yard, and the overhead expenses of a design office are now sometimes as high as those of a small boatyard. At the other end of the scale, a very big yacht can be designed in little more time than a middle-sized one, so the hours spent leaning over the drawing board are not many more. But a super terrific ultra stupendous yacht will cost 30 times as much as a plain middle-of-the-road millionaire's yacht. So the very top yacht will have a design fee down to perhaps 2%.

It is usual to add some expenses onto the design fees. The most common is the expense of visiting the vessel during the building or alteration. Travelling expenses include the cost of a night in a hotel if the boat is far from the naval architect's home, also his meals, the taxi to the airport, and so on.

Anyone contemplating alteration work on a boat will soon realise that the drawings, inspection work, and the expenses relating to visiting a boat which is distant from the naval architect's office can add up to a substantial sum. They can amount to a third or more of the cost of the work done by shipwrights, engineers, electricians and so on. But in practice these professionals' fees are well worthwhile. Almost always a naval architect saves the owner many times the fees paid out.

On one occasion, after I had *finished* my work on the boat, I saved the owner several hundred pounds.

It was evening, and we'd worked on the boat all day. The owner, yard manager, and two of the yard foremen were in deep conversation because an electrician had made a mistake. I was some way from the boat, and was peeling off my overalls, and getting ready to drive home. My mind was on that long strong whisky waiting for me when I reached my own fireside. Vaguely I was aware that the group talking were getting more and more morose. Something was wrong. I walked over to them and asked what the problem was. They told me that a main electrical cable had been omitted, and to run it through the boat would mean tearing out furniture, lining, flooring and carpeting. The whole job would take days, then all the parts and fittings would have to be put back again. More days, and more money.

After a minute's thought, I said:

'The boat is steel, with a hollow steel rub rail, so run the cable inside the rub rail'. There was an electrified silence (excuse the pun) then the owner said: 'Thank you, Ian. I owe you a damn good dinner, with a bottle of port at the end of it.'

It is in that sort of situation that experienced professional advice pays so handsomely.

Amateur and professional shipwrights soon find out that the cheapest source of drawings and advice is seldom the best.

=36 *The owner's handbook*=

An owner's handbook is a collection of technical information about a boat. It is more than the builder's specification, because it includes all sorts of data which the owner gathers year by year, and the best handbooks are often compiled by the oldest and most careful owners. As these fellows change boats they get better at collecting and tabulating the information and they learn about more and more sources and types of gear, fastenings, paint, glues and all the many things which make up a boat.

There are boatbuilders who provide booklets or multi-page brochures, and they label them 'Owner's Handbooks' but they fall short of the bulging notebooks which individual owners compile. These builders' publications omit some information because there is the worry that it could be useful to rival firms. Other information is left out because it does not apply to every boat in the class, or because the current production run is different from the first one when the booklet was first brought out.

Anyone who has compared a motorcar manufacturer's 'Owner's Handbook' which is written for the car buyer, and the 'Repair Manual' which is for the car mechanic, will know that owners come off far worse than technical staff. What a boat owner wants is a totally comprehensive book of technical information and he can have a lot of enjoyment making up this 'technical log', just like a cruising log.

Of course, every one-off boat designed in a reputable drawing office will have a comprehensive specification and this may form the basis of a good owner's handbook. But even here, the owner will want to add a lot of information, especially after the boat is a few years old and has been equipped with new or additional electronic equipment, sails and rigging. So if there is a specification available, it should certainly be the basis of the handbook, but it will need additions and modifications. Such diverse information as

> The mast-maker's local agent's address,
> The best supplier of epoxy resins for repairs,
> The phone number of the compass adjuster,
> The amount of paint needed to antifoul the bottom,

are all unlikely to be included in any designer's specification. However, on one or two occasions our design office has gone to just such lengths to look after an owner and his boat. We sometimes surmise that this is perhaps the reason why our boat design office is the oldest in the world.

Experienced owners keep a copy of the owner's handbook even after they have sold the boat so that they have a marvellous reference book for future craft. If there is doubt about what size of winch to buy for a boat, it is so handy to say to the crew:-

'You remember the main halliard winch we had on the old *Spray-Swallower,* it always seemed to me to be a bit too small. You took 3.53 minutes to get the reef out on the beat home the year we were second in the Lipton Cup. Now if we'd

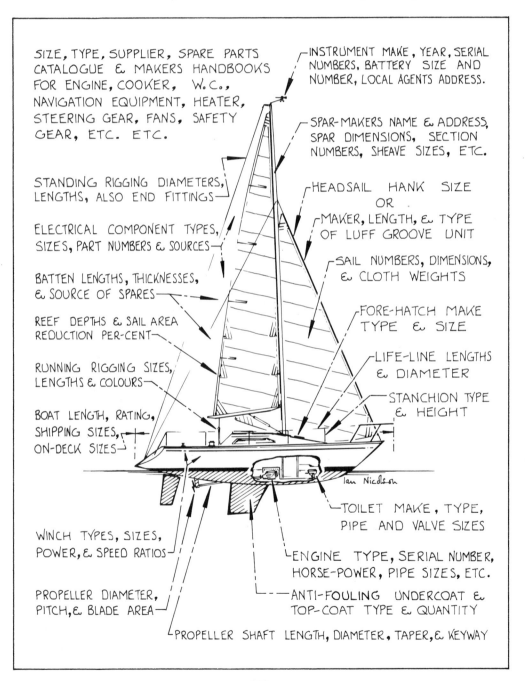

SIZE, TYPE, SUPPLIER, SPARE PARTS CATALOGUE & MAKERS HANDBOOKS FOR ENGINE, COOKER, W.C., NAVIGATION EQUIPMENT, HEATER, STEERING GEAR, FANS, SAFETY GEAR, ETC. ETC.

INSTRUMENT MAKE, YEAR, SERIAL NUMBERS, BATTERY SIZE AND NUMBER, LOCAL AGENTS ADDRESS.

SPAR-MAKERS NAME & ADDRESS, SPAR DIMENSIONS, SECTION NUMBERS, SHEAVE SIZES, ETC.

STANDING RIGGING DIAMETERS, LENGTHS, ALSO END FITTINGS

HEADSAIL HANK SIZE OR MAKER, LENGTH, & TYPE OF LUFF GROOVE UNIT

ELECTRICAL COMPONENT TYPES, SIZES, PART NUMBERS & SOURCES

SAIL NUMBERS, DIMENSIONS, & CLOTH WEIGHTS

BATTEN LENGTHS, THICKNESSES, & SOURCE OF SPARES

FORE-HATCH MAKE TYPE & SIZE

REEF DEPTHS & SAIL AREA REDUCTION PER-CENT

LIFE-LINE LENGTHS & DIAMETER

RUNNING RIGGING SIZES, LENGTHS & COLOURS

STANCHION TYPE & HEIGHT

BOAT LENGTH, RATING, SHIPPING SIZES, ON-DECK SIZES

Ian Nicolson

TOILET MAKE, TYPE, PIPE AND VALVE SIZES

WINCH TYPES, SIZES, POWER, & SPEED RATIOS

ENGINE TYPE, SERIAL NUMBER, HORSE-POWER, PIPE SIZES, ETC.

PROPELLER DIAMETER, PITCH, & BLADE AREA

ANTI-FOULING UNDERCOAT & TOP-COAT TYPE & QUANTITY

PROPELLER SHAFT LENGTH, DIAMETER, TAPER, & KEYWAY

had a more powerful halliard winch I reckon you could have cut the time to under 3 minutes and that would have given us the Cup. Am I right?'. And the crew will grumble and mumble something about any b*****d can sit back at the helm and criticise but yes, that winch was too small and the next one should be two sizes bigger.

Also once an owner's handbook has been compiled, it tends to be so useful that one wants to be able to make each successive one even better and having previous editions is a help.

Format

My own view is that a handbook is so valuable that I prefer not to use any old notebook, but buy a special large one with a tough hard cover and a resilient spine. The type of book which opens out flat is best because so often it is useful to be able to photostat a page. In practice the best handbooks are loose-leaf ones, so that makers' leaflets can be inserted in the correct chapters. A loose-leaf folder is convenient when it comes to photostating because the appropriate page can be taken right out. Also loose-leaf files have lots of capacity, but when they are too full it is easy to start Volume 2.

It is handy to be able to tear advertisements out of magazines and include these in the handbook and here again, a loose-leaf folder is what is wanted. If the advertisement is small, it has to be stapled onto a large piece of paper which is then put into the folder. Some people like to tape small pieces of paper onto full size pages, but after two or three years tape loses its grip and the information may be lost.

It is best to have a contents list right from the start and to group things together, so that the section on Spars is followed by the one on Sails and then one on Rigging and then another on Rigging Spares (which details such things as reserve shackles, blocks and rope carried on board and kept at home). It also makes sense to write on alternate lines to start with, so that extra notes can be added later. In the same way, I always start off by only using the right hand side of each pair of pages, then as further information comes in it can be added on the opposite page.

A loose-leaf format helps with the index which is as useful as the list of

---

◁   *Fig. 62 Owner's Handbook*

When making up a handbook, every scrap of technical information should be included. After all, if a new electrical part is bought and it is the wrong voltage, or a new rigging piece is ordered and it arrives just too large to fit into the other components, a cruise may be spoiled or a race lost.

During fitting out, materials often have to be bought during the week for use at the weekend. If insufficient antifouling is taken to the boat, repainting cannot be completed; and if too much is bought, it is a waste of money because this material should not be stored for a year.

This drawing is just a guide to the compilation of a handbook. Some people will want to include the weight of each item so that when ordering new equipment an attempt can be made to reduce the total weight of the boat.

content sections. As firms move, get taken over, go bankrupt or change their products, the index will need modifying and if it is in a fixed-page book, this will be awkward or impossible.

Whatever the format, it is worth having two copies of the handbook, one on board and one at home. The one on board can be filled in when storm-bound in harbour, or when all the novels on board have been read and so the crew are short of mental stimulus, or when a bright idea flashes into someone's mind concerning the inadequacy of the boom downhaul, or the poor lighting in the fo'c's'le. It only takes a few minutes to write down the specification of the offending parts and during the following week, when ashore and far from the boat, it is easy enough to get improved equipment if there are full details.

Contents

Anything to do with the design, construction, outfitting, maintenance and repairs, cruising and racing, buying and selling of a boat can be included in the handbook. It will, like the logbook, be very much an expression of the owner's temperament, experience, skills and prejudices, and those of his wife, and his crew.

There will be whole chapters of addresses – the designer, builder, cushion-maker, window-maker, the timber yards who stock marine quality plywood and hardwood, and so on.

There will be one or more chapters on the engine, bearing in mind that this machine likes to break down when far from home. So we need the names and addresses of mechanics living near distant harbours, and stockists of spares all round the coast. Though engine-makers' handbooks are useful, they always lack such information as the size of the cooling water connection and the inside diameter of the dip-stick tube down which we have to thrust the oil suction pipe when we want to change the sump oil.

Another chapter will be about safety gear. It will have the dates when the lifebuoy float lights were bought, as these have a limited life. Other notes will come from the annual autumn jaunt well inland after dark when old flares are let off, far from the coast. On these occasions some types of flare are found to be less use than a seasick glow-worm and so they are not bought in future.

Also in this section will be the date the liferaft was bought, its serial number in case it is stolen, its size in case we decided to take it with us when we change boats, and a warning when we will have to start saving to buy a new one because after 10 years these things start to die.

A chart list is worth having, not least because it will include the date each one was bought. This will act as a warning when it is getting out of date. Owners with children will have a sub-chapter of charts they would like, or indeed any other small items which the boat needs, and as Christmas or birthdays approach children should be encouraged to scan these pages. Better than dreary ties or handkerchiefs any day. . . .

There is almost no limit to the extent of the contents. When I'm building or altering a boat I use the handbook as a work list, writing each job on the left page and the material used opposite on the right. This means that in future years I know exactly the type, size and amount of everything which goes into each part of the boat. If anything breaks, I have the sizes of the part so it is easy to specify the replacement just that much thicker and stronger. If it comes adrift, the fastenings must be thicker or more numerous. If it never lets us down, even when racing to windward in a screeching half-hurricane, we know it is tough enough and we can use the same scantlings in future.

Selling

Yacht brokers have a difficult time selling many boats because they cannot get enough information about them. If the boat is near the broker and he is not too busy, and is conscientious, he will visit the boat and take down pages of notes about her. But if the boat is a small one so that the broker's commission is meagre, or if the boat is tired and unloved, so that she will be hard to sell, no broker is going to take much trouble over her.

On the other hand, if anyone breezes into a broker's office and hands over pages and pages of photostats detailing every last bit of gear on board, the broker is going to think:

1 This is a meticulous owner, so he must have kept his boat well.
2 This boat is going to be easy to sell because all the answers to questions a buyer will ask are listed here, and it will be easy to sound convincing when trying to reach an agreement.
3 Even if the survey of the boat shows up defects, it should not be too hard to get the trouble put right with such a copious supply of technical information.
4 This owner has done so much of the preparation work for the sale it is only fair to make sure that this broker's office does as well.

In passing, if a broker does not react enthusiastically when presented with all these pages of photostats about the boat, it must be obvious that he is not the broker to employ – he's too tired or cynical, or ignorant, and there is bound to be a better one in the next seaport. However, no broker should be trusted with the original owner's handbook or specification as he will most certainly lose it, or lend it to a potential buyer who will lose it. Alternatively, one of these people will so covet the handbook that he will somehow accidentally retain it (no yachtsman would actually stoop to stealing, naturally) because it will be so useful for the yacht's sisterships, even if it does need extensive modifications.

Any experienced buyer, on being presented with reams of paper detailing every aspect of a boat is bound to be impressed. He will realise that a lot of trouble will be saved during the familiarisation period. A lot of phone calls, money and time will be saved when getting new equipment or parts for existing gear and the chances of a successful first racing season, or a comfortable succession of cruises, will be much increased.

If the buyer is going to take the boat to a sailing ground remote from her former home, or if the craft is a slightly unusual one, the value of the owner's handbook is further enhanced.

Buying Another Boat

It is a dramatic business, buying a boat. Apart from getting a house, a boat is the most expensive thing we buy, so there is inevitably a good deal of tension and emotion about. This distracts from the important job of selecting exactly the right craft. It is so easy to be led astray by fancy carpets and elegant cabin lining, not to mention the seller's copious liquor.

Anyone armed with an owner's handbook which he has made up himself for a previous boat will have a guide when buying another boat. He will know the size of sheet-winch he needs for a given size of headsail, and how big the fuel tank should be for his type of cruising. It may tell him how long a cooking gas cylinder lasts when his girlfriend is involved in her favourite pastime of baking fruit cakes. This means the size of the gas bottle locker can be scrutinised with expertise. The handbook will include a list of members of the Association of British (or American) Sailmakers, so the maker's name on the sails can be inspected, to ensure that the products come from a reliable source. And so on.

A handbook which is kept up to date will have notes about gear failures. When looking over a new craft it is so effective to be able to turn to the broker or seller and say. 'We gave up using that type of halliard winch after two broke in the '79 Fastnet,' and later 'Our experience over 25 years is that those particular inflatable rafts have a life expectancy of only 7 years.' Both buyer and seller then know that a price concession is expected, on good grounds.

After An Accident

Anyone who has ever been involved in the mending of a boat after even a slight accident, will know that there is one source of delay above all others. This is the searching for and ordering of the materials and parts necessary to put the boat right. I've seen massive holes in boats patched over and neatly renewed in a matter of days. But in contrast I've known boats trapped ashore in a boatyard because a couple of stanchions to match the undamaged ones cannot be found in any of the chandlers for a thousand miles around. Ask any boatbuilder about repair work and he will tell you that once he has got a good team of men around him, and provided the insurance assessor does not delay, quite substantial repairs can be completed in a week or two. What holds things up, time after time, is obtaining some small part.

Any yard which has the use of a comprehensive owner's handbook will therefore be delighted. Though all yards have numerous sources of supply, there are now so many parts on every boat it is hard to keep track of every manufacturer and wholesaler. Besides, when a firm stops manufacturing an item or goes bankrupt its stock is often taken over by another organisation. Keeping track of this regular shift of stocks is hard for a boatyard, which is another reason why the owner's handbook which is totally comprehensive and updated is such an asset.

There is another aspect of an accident which throws up a further use of the handbook. When an insurance assessor inspects a damaged boat he cannot help noticing if she is well kept. If she is, he will conclude he is dealing with a careful owner. If the owner produces a detailed list of the parts damaged, together with the names and addresses of the replacement suppliers, the assessor is going to be impressed. He will feel that he is dealing with someone who deserves every backing. If in time there is a disagreement between the owner and the insurance company, or between owner and boatyard, or between the owner and the skipper of another boat involved in the same accident, the fellow who has his paper-work in perfect order starts out with the useful advantage that the assessor knows he is dealing with a conscientious owner.

Index